# ARE WE LEARNING FROM ACCIDENTS?

A quandary, a question,
and a way forward

## NIPPIN ANAND

# ARE WE LEARNING FROM ACCIDENTS?

To my mother, who passed away on the day
I finished writing this book. I love you mum.

Om Shanti.

# Contents

# Contents

# Preface

Can we really learn from accidents? For a very long time I believed that when we humans are confronted by suffering on a mass scale, learning is difficult, almost impossible. I could have written an entire book to argue that there is little learning from accidents.

Since I embarked on this research I have experienced a shift in my perspective. Beyond safety science, engineering and human factors, as I researched more widely across disciplines – theology, religion, mythology, social psychology, analytical psychology, anthropology, linguistics, neuroscience and biology – I have arrived at a viewpoint radically different from where my journey started. As my perspective about learning from accidents shifted, so did my focus of enquiry. Beyond accidents, I became interested in understanding how we humans make meaning of misfortune. And, more specifically: when we are faced with misfortune, how can we really learn?

As I look back in time, I am coming to realise that my views about learning from accidents were far too

Preface

focused on the external world – the policymakers who approve of tenuous regulations, the ship owners who invest in poorly designed ships, the ship managers who operate those ships at any cost, the meek seafarers in desperate need of a job, the paper-safe oil companies who play by the rules to manage their reputation, and the cargo owners who search for the cheapest rust buckets in the market to carry their goods. I had matured enough to understand the point that in a competitive world with questionable regulatory standards it is not 'human error' that is to blame for accidents. That much is expected of a student of philosophy and sociology who has been a mariner for more than a decade.

As I delved deeper to question my inner world, I found that my imagination was still anchored in the same place: not the seafarer but the ship owner to be questioned; not the standard operating process but the design to be made fail-safe; not the ship captain but the cargo owner to be held to account. But I have now realised that I was busy reallocating blame from one part of the system to another. When I look back, what kept me going in this unconscious mode for many years was a sense of righteousness that I was not part of this corporate, profit-driven machinery. I was more drawn to, and sympathetic to, the worker.

My worldview was, however, naïve. It took me a while to realise that I was sitting in a castle built in the air, reshuffling blame like a financier transacting currencies from one part of the world to another to maximise profits. The uncomfortable truth for me was that beyond this feeling of moral superiority nothing had really changed in my inner world. It has been a journey, and when I look back, much of my learning has come from stepping outside my comfort zone to arrive at a new point of view.

So many of us are wedded to our imagination, and we blame things wrong in life on bad luck. Jung summarised it so eloquently in saying, 'If you do not make the unconscious conscious, it will direct your life and you will call it fate.' For how long are we going to hold fate responsible for recurring problems in our lives? At some stage we must learn to conquer inner fears and question the fantasyland within. Why does this happen to me? What am I missing? What can I do about it? These questions will remain unanswered forever unless we are willing to take a critical perspective of our beliefs and myths.

Learning from accidents – what does learning even mean? When I think of learning, I often question my role as a parent. What do we do when despite our best efforts our children refuse to grow, cause us too much pain and consistently point at others for their failures? For all the marvels of positive psychology and the happy-ending lullabies that our society has so uncritically embraced as an 'innovative' approach to parenting and schooling, children must learn to endure pain – hopefully, though, inflicted by others, not their parents and family. The suffering that comes from painful experiences is integral to learning and flourishing. Learning does not come from the comfort of the familiar but from the painful realisation that our worldview is so limited in this vast universe.

A large part of this book is devoted to learning from a specific accident narrative. I had the rare privilege of meeting face to face at length with the captain of the cruise ship *Costa Concordia*, to hear his perspective of the accident. But my focus in this book is less on the captain's narrative and more about my own meaning and learning. Through personal stories, reflections, confessions, trials, risks and experiments, this book is a documented account of my own assumptions, biases, fantasies, myths, and beliefs coming to the surface. You will find many glimpses of my life woven into this book – a master mariner with a history of working at sea; a PhD in social sciences with a master's degree in economics and social psychology; a safety inspector; an existentialist; a brown-skin man living in the West; a non-practising Hindu; a parent of two beautiful children; a responsible son; an annoying, but loving, husband to a very caring wife; and an imperfect person.

It is not my goal to assert the accuracy of my work in this book. I find solace in making my biases and assumptions known to myself and to you.

We are creatures of story. When we tell stories we create space for doubt and questions, but when we distribute facts and evidence we get busy filling those gaps. I have deliberately chosen to tell a subjective story in this book to help you learn to doubt your worldview and question mine. I would like to see you being critical and mindful as you read through this book; my overall aim is one of helping you mindfully tackle risks.

That is the objective of this book and in my view, the future of skills in an uncertain world. I hope that through this book you will experience the joy of learning and living by unleashing your imagination, unlocking your potential and recognising the bedrock assumptions in your thinking. I hope this book will liberate you from dogma, live without fear, and help you to show compassion, love, kindness and flourishing, and to practise listening. I hope that you will begin to question your beliefs at the deepest level, the level where most of us have simply accepted our life and matter as is.

# Author's Note

Graphics and semiotics marked with an asterisk (*) are copyright to Social Psychology of Risk (SPoR) and Dr Robert Long. This intellectual property cannot be replicated without permission.

Any typos or mistakes are the result of my own fallibility. I have come to realise that fallibility is an inevitable human condition, and one which, when it comes to learning, we must embrace.

# Acknowledgements

Everyone needs a mentor, but few are fortunate enough to find a good one. Thank you, Dr Robert Long, for walking alongside, sharing your wisdom, and for being a true friend.

Dr Steve Shorrock, thank you for being a friend and a light in moments of loneliness and darkness.

Dr Pedro Ferreira, a huge thanks for being a thinking partner and a critical friend.

Oessur Hilduberg, thank you for planting the seeds of inspiration within me for this lifelong journey.

Professor Helen Sampson, thank you for seeing in me a scholar at a time when even I did not.

Caroline, thank you for being so diligent and thorough with editing my work. You came in late into this research but made a big difference.

Niamh, you are one of a kind who can take my vague ideas and turn them into such beautiful illustrations. A big thank you for being so consistent and responsive.

# Acknowledgements

Nakeeta and Nihaal, thank you for turning my assumptions upside down by asking so many innocent questions. I love you beyond words.

Irma, from you I am learning the power of critiquing with compassion to those who we truly care about. Our love is eternal.

# The Book Cover

## The front

Everything is significant. Nothing never happens!

The background colour grey represents ambiguity. The title colour, orange, depicts the connection between the physical and the spiritual world. We embark on a learning journey by submitting wholeheartedly to the unknowable and making a commitment to seeking wisdom.

The image of a lion and a mouse represents how we should think about learning. The emphasis is not on the mouse speaking *up* or the lion making the effort to listen. The image symbolises the power of relationship in learning. In this relationship, the mouse has the courage because it dares to come out of its burrow to meet with the lion. The lion has the power; it can choose to remain arrogant. But the lion is humble as well; it stays calm, and listens with patience.

In learning, what is needed is a meeting between the lion and the mouse. This book is an invitation for one fallible person to meet another with an open heart and mind. One cannot deny fallibility, for that is the essence of all existence.

At the heart of the book is the idea of 'embracing fallibility'.

## The back

The Dutch philosopher Baruch Spinoza once said, 'Not to lament, not to laugh, not to curse but to understand.'

On the back cover there are four monkeys. Their gestures follow Spinoza's wise words symbolising our reactions when things go wrong – finger pointing (cursing); mocking; apologising (lamenting); and seeing life as a puzzle to be solved. Such is the delusion of control and the denial of fallibility that give human beings a sense of moral superiority over others, but neither is helpful for learning.

# How to read this book

In my workshops, I begin by saying, 'Don't believe a word of what I say.' This book is written as a subjective, biased and open-ended enquiry into an accident. It is not to be read literally, but with feelings and emotions and by keeping subjectivity in mind. I do not wish my reflections and arguments to persuade you. In fact, the very idea of persuasion would mean an attempt to prove something that goes against the message of this book. It is not my purpose to win you over to my viewpoint.

That said, I have taken almost seven years to write this book. All these years I have striven for accuracy. But in the end, my accuracy is only as good as the limits of my imagination. Is it not paradoxical that I call something mine (my book, my writing, my opinion, my understanding) and then claim objectivity about what belongs to me? How can my truth be universal? That would be a denial of Self. Do not believe a word of what you read in this book; instead search for your own truth.

I would suggest reading the book in small chunks and taking the time to relax, meditate, go for walks, sleep over ideas, dream, think and reflect. There are several models, figures and personal stories included in the book to stimulate your reading experience.

But don't just read it. Do something with what you learn. Ruffle some feathers, blow a horn, make new friends, sing a song, dance in the rain, bake some bread, write a poem, visit a graveyard or just upset your boss (but not too much). Take a chance. There is no learning if we don't complement reflection with action. There is no learning without risk.

# Foreword 1

In industry, there is often talk about 'organisational learning'. After accidents, the refrain 'lessons have been learned' nearly always crops up from organisational representatives. But organisations do not learn. People do. Equally, organisations do not care. People do. This might seem pedantic in that, of course, organisations comprise people. But organisations also comprise technologies, rules and procedures, infrastructure and assets, within a legal entity serving particular purposes. Even the people in organisations come and go. Many of us have experienced how much things can change – and how many 'lessons' are unlearned – when senior leaders come and go, as they do every few years. And there are many people, each with their own values, attitudes, assumptions, beliefs, practices, and histories. They all learn different things, in different ways, for different reasons, in different places, over different times.

The point is that we often like to anthropomorphise organisations as if each were a person. At the same time, we like to bureaucratise learning, caring and change. It is as if we can strip away that which cannot be controlled by process. This includes trust, faith, hope, and doubt. It includes compassion, empathy and humour. And it includes symbolic thinking, ethics, diversity of thought, complex and nuanced language, and cultural transmission. Most of these qualities or characteristics are uniquely human. We even talk about 'changing culture', and the need for this, as if this were an engineering project. We keep talking about this, over and over again, after and between every major unwanted event. I have sometimes performed a thought experiment about this as changing the values, attitudes, assumptions, beliefs, practices, and histories of one person ... then multiplying this by hundreds or thousands of people and their relationships.

For as long as I can remember, people have been my 'special interest'. I remember studying human beings consciously as a small child, and from my early teenage years I bought and read books on people and relationships, and the curious things that we believe and do, from mundane rituals to adopting extreme beliefs and joining cults. As far as I could tell, few or none of my friends took such an interest. I felt like a stranger in a strange land, looking at something truly extraordinary: human behaviour.

I found a friend when I met Nippin Anand in 2018 at a workshop in Cardiff, Wales, on 'Safety-II'. Safety-II was then an emerging theory about safety, organisations, work and people, proposed by the eminent safety scientist Erik Hollnagel. Five years or so after its birth as a concept, Safety-II was being put into practice by a relatively small bunch of confused but curious practitioners. At the workshop, Nippin talked about a tragic marine accident in a way that I had never heard before. He had talked in person to

Captain Francesco Schettino, the main protagonist of the story, to try to understand his perspective. Nippin did this as a safety scientist, anthropologist and, importantly, as a former Master Mariner himself. He also did this as a *person*, displaying some of the characteristics that I mentioned earlier.

The method and style of this human encounter was very different from an accident investigation interview. The story and insights that emerged were very different from what one could find in the accident report, or any accident report, where such testimony is neglected, approached very differently, or else distorted to such an extent that it can become meaningless or misleading. This typifies epistemic injustice.

Nippin started to question assumptions and explore uncomfortable truths about not only shipping but the safety profession itself, and its myths and rituals. Since then, I have heard Nippin present on *Costa Concordia* several times. Not everyone would agree with the perspectives, insights or conclusions. That is not the point. Or rather, it is *exactly* the point: there are always multiple perspectives. Some are more convenient than others. Some are hard to accept, perhaps because they challenge deeply held assumptions and cherished beliefs.

In the years that followed, Nippin and I discussed psychology, anthropology, mythology, philosophy, and religion, in the context of safety, work and life. We often approached each of these from different schools of thought, and with different lived experience. But we seemed to think in a complementary way, valuing similar things, such as interdisciplinarity (or transdisciplinarity), multiple perspectives, thick descriptions, synthesis, and ethics.

I have been especially curious about how Nippin has taken a wider angle on religion, and how this affects our thinking about organisations and safety. The religious origination that I have most identified with throughout my adult life has been Quakerism. It has affected how I've thought about many aspects of organisational life, such as hierarchy, leadership, followership, fellowship, group processes, and conflict management. It has influenced how I think about language, semiotics, learning, symbolism, simplicity, rituals. It has also affected my attitudes toward equality, diversity and inclusion.

Nippin's religious heritage in Hinduism could – on the surface – hardly be more different, in terms of history, liturgies, rituals and sacraments. But beneath this, there are similarities that may affect how we view people. Quakerism emphasises the concept of the 'Inner Light', the belief that every person has access to the presence of the divine within them. Hinduism teaches the concept of the 'Atman', the individual soul or inner self, which is considered a spark of the divine. Quakers have historically been involved in movements for peace and social justice. Hinduism's teachings include principles of *ahimsa* (nonviolence) and the importance of treating all beings with respect and compassion. Quaker worship – especially in the UK – often involves silent contemplation, with individuals waiting quietly. Hinduism includes practices such as meditation (*dhyana*) and contemplation, where practitioners seek to connect with the divine through silence and stillness. Both traditions encourage individuals to seek truth and spiritual understanding through personal experience and direct revelation, rather than relying solely on external authority or scripture. Two religious traditions, one well over 3,000 years old, and one around 370 years old. One born into, and one chosen as an adult. How can this be separated from ourselves, or our work?

I don't think it can. Our religious heritages and orientations infuse into our way of being. And then there is our broader cultural background and life experience. I grew up in a working-class family, in a small northern English former mining and textiles town, in a small family business, as a white-skinned, intellectually- and artistically-curious boy. I have carried this around with me throughout my life, moving around in the UK, then Australia and France. Nippin has his own very different story, but he too has moved around the world, carrying his culture and seeing those of others.

But what has any of this got to do with learning from accidents? Surely, religion and culture – with their values, beliefs, myths, symbols, rituals, means of transmission, and institutions – couldn't be further apart from accident investigation! Beneath the specifics, we carry our religious heritages around with us into our work, whether in safety or other professions. These heritages affect how we view truth, ethics, purpose, wealth, success, and relationships. It's a fascinating thing to think about. And yet, we largely ignore how our history and religious and cultural backgrounds, even those of our parents and grandparents, encoded as they are into our upbringing, affect how we approach life now. This is especially true for activities that we have deemed scientific, objective, methodical, and institutional, like safety management, including accident investigation and learning from accidents.

Whatever your story, it affects how you see the world, how you interact, and how you learn. No amount of bureaucratising can bleach this from your approach to work and life. The problem is that more often than not we cannot see our external (or internal) cultures. In his book, *The Invisible Language*, Edward Hall, an American anthropologist, wrote in 1973, 'Culture hides much more than it reveals, and strangely enough what it hides, it hides most effectively from its own inhabitants'. Sometimes, it takes a non-inhabitant to 'make the strange familiar and make the familiar strange', as Nippin likes to say. I moved from the UK to Australia and there were differences, but they were not profound. I then moved to France, a metaphorical stone's throw from England, and the differences *were* profound. The shock of contrast and difference exposes to 'us' what is normal to 'them'. But sometimes, it might just take a different approach to seeing, thinking, feeling, relating, communicating, and learning. This means going beyond non-thinking and non-feeling, with their sentry slogans, myths and rituals.

That is what this book is about. It is unlike any other book that I am aware of about learning from accidents, and it shows why we – in our organisations – often don't. It goes beyond analysis, beyond theory, beyond disciplines, and beyond profession. You are likely to be surprised, challenged, and perhaps irritated. And if so, it is worth your time.

Dr Steven Shorrock

# Foreword 2

The first contact I had from Nippin was many years ago when he ordered a book. It was just a book order; how could I know that this would lead to the most invigorating experience in my life?

Let's jump forward to April 2023, and my plane lands in Chennai, India. Here I am to work with this man Nippin who I have only met on Zoom and by email. Yet, strangely I am nervous in this strange land, like nothing I have seen before. I had read *A Passage to India* by E. M Forster, completed a unit in the History of India as an undergraduate and have many Indian friends in Australia – but nothing had prepared me for this.

The purpose of my visit was to work with Nippin and his team undertaking the MiProfile Survey and to do work on leadership with executives from the second largest shipping company in the world.

When we exited the plane and the terminal, the first thing that hit me was the heat, the humidity and the poverty. The walkway was crowded with people, with many wanting to get my fare. I must have had a neon light above my head saying, 'Here's a sucker Aussie'. Our driver was not there to meet us; there had been some confusion in arrangement, but confusion is normal in this country and no one gets stressed about it.

After battling through the traffic madness, I finally arrived at the motel and meeting Nippin was like meeting my brother I had not seen in some time. We instantly resonated and were abuzz with so much to share and discuss. Luckily, we had time for several semiotic walks together and I felt at home in this place. The richness of myth, ritual, faith and love in this place knocked me over.

Then as we worked together with this company, I realised Nippin understood the Social Psychology of Risk like few others. This is helped by Nippin's voracious appetite to read and with no fear to read across the disciplines. His comprehension of life/being, phenomenology, existential philosophy and myth/ritual is extraordinary.

So, what can I say about this book? If you are a safety person looking for an endorsement of a comforting worldview, this book is not for you. If you are open to being challenged in thinking, prepared to embrace transdisciplinary thought and semiotics, and fascinated by the enactments of fallible humans, then this is your book.

Nippin's insightful discussion of the *Costa Concordia* disaster and his reflections on Captain Francesco Schettino are alone a good reason to read this book.

What can we learn from such an accident? What is our disposition towards accidents, incidents, harm and suffering? Where do we go for challenges in learning? Do we even know what learning is? What are our taboos, places we do not go in mind and spirit? Can we cope with dissonance and discomfort in learning? These are some of the questions this book will stir in you if you are one to read it. So, I commend this book to you. May you find it enlivens you to a better understanding of fallible humans and therefore better know yourself.

Dr Rob Long

Grandad, Guitarist, Journeyman and Friend

# Introduction: Failure was Never an Option

An unexamined life is not worth living.
Socrates

It was 2 April 1995. At age eighteen, shortly after passing out from high school, I was going to join my first ship, as a deck cadet. At the time, my Singapore-based employer expected his Indian cadets to bear the travel expenses to join their first ship – a practice now considered a breach of maritime labour rights. Apart from the stress of organising the finances to fly me from Mumbai to Singapore (roughly US$400), my working-class parents were worried about their elder son going away from home for an eighteen-month tenure. The rumour went around that life at sea was harsh. Most cadets would quit and return home in the first few months. Few stayed on board and survived until the end of their contract. As I was packing my bags on the night before leaving, my mother came to my room and said, '*Beta* (Son), I hope you will not return home like others and bring shame to our family.' As the elder son in the family, I felt an immense burden on my shoulders. I knew in that moment that failure was not an option. And so I survived a job for eleven long years – a job that I hated from the very first day until failure came knocking at my door with a force that outweighed my resilience.

It was during the winter season of the year 2002. I was on a container liner service trading between Japan and West Coast United States. I was in the middle of my night watch, the ship approaching Irago Bay Pilot Station, and bound for Nagoya in Japan, ETA (estimated time of arrival) 0345 hours. As a seafarer you learn the metaphorical meaning of ETA and how it varies across geographies, cultures, trade sectors, from country to country, and from port to port. In Japan there were no written rules, but for a container ship the term 'ETA' meant 'PTA' (precise time of arrival); no allowance for flexibility in the timing. In Japanese shipping companies a popular myth floated around. Imagine two ships sailing from Seattle bound for Japan, and both are caught in a storm; one arrives late but intact, and the other arrives on time but has lost one of its anchors in the weather. The company fires the captain of the former and retains the captain of the latter. In my circumstance, no one said that safety was not a priority – but we all knew what missing the ETA would mean.

That night there were moderate headwinds, a swell of about 3 metres and visibility down to about 3 miles. On the bridge I had with me Melvin, an able-bodied seaman. We were about 20 miles from the pilot boarding grounds, and on a course parallel to ours, each about a mile way, were two vessels – a car carrier on our port bow and a Taiwanese container vessel on our starboard quarter. We were all going at approximately 20 knots, and bound for the same destination.

That was my mental model – which was soon to be destroyed. Without warning, Ship A (in the diagram) on our port bow turned to starboard in an apparent attempt to cross our bows. For us, turning to port was not an option due to the shallows on that side. With the ETA ever-present in the deepest recesses of my mind, slowing down or stopping the engines never occurred to me, despite the bright luminous sign 'safety first' on the front panel, full-engine controls on the bridge and a friendly chief engineer standing right behind the bridge panel. Without hesitating, I rang the captain, saying, 'I need you on the bridge *now*.' He arrived in less than a minute. Still in his pyjamas, he ran into the chart room to check the ship's position, came back to the radar screen, apparently took less than five seconds to adjust to night vision, and ordered Melvin to turn the wheel hard a-starboard.

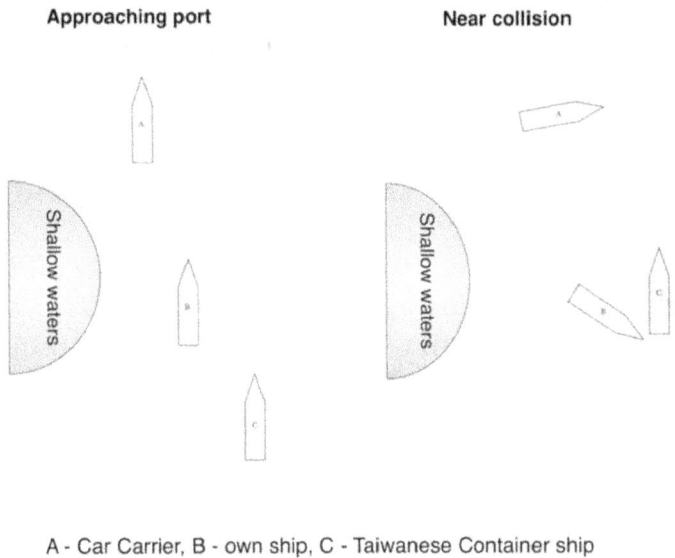

**Approaching port**          **Near collision**

A - Car Carrier, B - own ship, C - Taiwanese Container ship

Figure I 1: A near collision

I switched to manual steering, and Melvin started executing the turn. As we were swinging to the right, the Taiwanese vessel (C) on our starboard quarter maintained its speed and course, apparently completely indifferent to the situation. It took about 45 seconds for our bow to swing down the length of that ship. Those were the longest 45 seconds of my life! I have no idea how close we came to collision, but to put things in perspective a bottle of water thrown from our ship could have easily landed on that vessel. I would have no difficulty calling it a near hit.

The next morning when I woke up at 10 am, nothing seemed normal. By this time, Melvin had leaked the news to all crew members. Everyone I met on the way to the bridge was smirking. I could sense in their eyes how badly I must have screwed up the night before. The chief engineer, a good friend who I enjoyed socialising with almost every evening, caught me in the alleyway. He was curious to know why I had not crash-stopped the vessel: 'After all, this is exactly why these devices are designed, Nippin,' he said in an uplifting tone. I felt apologetic and ashamed, and replied: 'I'm sorry, Chief, but I have *no idea* why I didn't.' As I arrived on the bridge to lay down the passage plan for the next port, the captain was standing at the front window, having a coffee. I said, 'Good morning, sir,' but his body language was reserved. He was not giving out the same friendly vibes I had felt in the past.

For context, I will say a few words about my past rapport. Arriving on time in port or negotiating heavy traffic had never been a problem for me. I was in my third year as an independent watch officer. I had never missed one ETA nor shown hesitation in a difficult situation. But from here on, things changed. When I was on the bridge, the 'call captain' mark on the chart – the position at which the captain arrives on the bridge before arrival in port – shifted further down on the chart at every port arrival. And navigating high-traffic areas suddenly became a big deal, with doubled watches, increased presence of the captain on the bridge and detailed night orders. I started to lose my confidence. In every manoeuvre I performed, my watchman could sense my anxiety no matter how hard I tried to maintain calm. At the end of my time on the ship, I knew that the feedback from the captain wouldn't be good. But after sailing with that captain for almost four months, I never expected just a dry goodbye. His metamessage was clear: 'I hope I never get to sail with you again.'

Almost a decade passed, and the nightmare scenario kept recurring in my dreams. I felt ashamed, guilty and wholly responsible for the near-accident. I should have never allowed my own vessel to become sandwiched between the two other vessels. I should have slowed the vessel or crash-stopped it. What was the big deal in delaying the vessel? At the most we would have arrived a few minutes late. Why so much hesitation? And why had I not called the master much sooner? Questions of this sort kept haunting me, and I went into a negative spiral. I continued sailing for another year, but never really came out of the experience.

The motivation for writing this book started off with me questioning and journaling my inner world of guilt, shame, and trauma that followed from this near-accident. Over the years, these reflections and confessions have served to restore my self-esteem, health, sleep and more. Beyond healing, as I turned towards researching theories and stories of human fallibility I discovered that in most cases the purpose of learning is implicitly understood as controlling errors, preventing people from being harmed or enabling safe conditions at work.

But much of the literature is silent on articulating what learning even means. Where do we go for the cues and indications of learning? How do we recognise our assumptions and biases in investigating and sharing narratives of accidents to create better learning outcomes? What questions do we ask, and which do we avoid (even without knowing)? How can we better engage with people involved in accidents and learn from them? How can we truly and practically learn from accidents?

My thoughts on the matter have resulted in an attempt to provide a range of practical methods and intuitive tools embedded in a *coherent* philosophy to create opportunities for learning from accidents. It is my humble view that one cannot learn from accidents (and, for that matter, from life) without an ethic, a philosophy and a method of enquiry to understand fallible humans.

## The outline of the book

This book is intended to be a subjective, biased and open-ended view of one of the most famous accidents in the maritime history: the capsize of the *Costa Concordia*. It is the story of a master mariner, the captain of that ill-fated ship, who through his actions and inactions became known as the infamous cause of the accident. The story is told by another master mariner, one who met with a near-accident. Subjective reflection is therefore inevitable and intertwined in this story, but such subjectivity is an advantage in knowing and feeling the story of another. This is precisely the starting point for discussing an appreciation of learning. I am less concerned about what went wrong on the day of the accident. I am far more interested in bringing to the surface what is hidden in my own unconscious, Captain Francesco Schettino's unconscious, and the shared beliefs of our society. Both the maritime industry and society at large are convinced of the culpability and stupidity of a captain who navigated the ship into a rock and then irresponsibly ran away from the scene. This book stands up in contrast to a society that would rather scapegoat the captain and hold him single-handedly responsible for the accident.

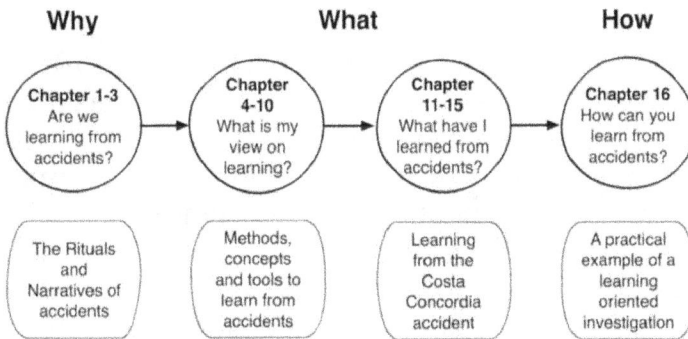

| Why | What | How |
|---|---|---|
| Chapter 1-3 Are we learning from accidents? | Chapter 4-10 What is my view on learning? | Chapter 11-15 What have I learned from accidents? |
| | | Chapter 16 How can you learn from accidents? |
| The Rituals and Narratives of accidents | Methods, concepts and tools to learn from accidents | Learning from the Costa Concordia accident |
| | | A practical example of a learning oriented investigation |

Figure I 2: The outline of the book.

Before I tell the captain's story, my intention is to articulate the current state of 'learning from accidents'. Chapter 1 explains the transdisciplinary approach to my work. I dedicate Chapters 2 and 3 to the rituals and narratives of accident investigations, to comment on the current state of affairs in learning from accidents. In Chapter 2 my aim is to help you appreciate that the human need to find meaning in misfortune has not changed very much in many centuries. To realise this, we need to understand the power and meaning in rituals and learn to question our existing approach to accident investigations through the lenses of ritual performance.

In Chapter 3 the focus is on how we create narratives of accidents. The assumptions and biases in our accident narratives illustrate how we relate to and learn from failures. In this chapter, I examine the two famous accident narratives – the Capsize of the *Costa Concordia*, and the Miracle of the Hudson River. I try to bring to the surface the hidden myths, power and meaning in accident narratives.

Much of the literature on learning from accidents is silent on a basic question: What do we mean by 'learning'? And so, my aim in Chapters 4 to 10 is to question some basic assumptions and beliefs about learning from accidents with a specific focus on how human beings learn. I deploy a transdisciplinary framework[1] to articulate the importance of learning, unlearning and decision making in accident models, methods and investigation processes. Through these seven chapters, I have drawn a contrast between the Cartesian model of education and training against

---

[1] Using religion, mythology, theology, anthropology, social psychology, cognitive sciences, linguistics, evolutionary sciences and neuroscience.

a holistic view[2] on learning. I have deliberately kept away from definitions and hypothetical testing of propositions, and have instead used stories and visuals to relate my experience of learning.

It is against the background of holistic learning that I turn to the next section of this book, Chapters 11 to 15. Chapter 11 provides a brief description of the Costa Concordia accident to set the background.

What did I learn from Captain Francesco Schettino during our meetings? What do I find worth sharing? Chapter 12 is dedicated to understanding the famous sail-past. In this chapter, I articulate my views on the culture of cruise shipping and how it had led to the normalisation of cruise ships 'kissing the shore'.

Once we have framed a problem, the rest of our life goes into reacting to our framed realities. Chapter 13 is an attempt to reframe a prevalent myth in our society – speak up, own your mistakes and raise your concerns if you want to be heard. By examining the team dynamics on the bridge of *Costa Concordia* shortly before the accident, Chapter 13 provides some critical perspectives about 'error management' and 'psychological safety' prevalent in the risk and safety industry.

Captain Francesco Schettino was formally accused and charged for taking a considerable time in deciding when to abandon the ship. His 'late' abandonment was considered by the formal investigation report as one of the main reasons for the rise in death toll

---

[2] Relational, intuitive, unconscious, semiotic, experiential and embodied.

when the ship capsized. In Chapter 14, my aim is to shed light on the assumptions within the emergency and contingency protocols about how professionals make decisions, and to compare those assumptions with the captain's lived experience in the handling of the crisis. This comparison is made within Karl Weick's framework of social sensemaking (Weick, 1979). The aim of this chapter is to understand how fallible humans manage the unexpected, as against how we think emergencies are managed, on paper.

Not a day goes by that we don't see people being shamed and blamed and held to account for their mistakes in populist press, social media and news. Within the risk and safety industry, there are even warning slogans against blaming others for their errors when an accident happens. Yet, as a society we humans have an inclination to scapegoat, and have done so for millennia. The *Costa Concordia* accident is a telling example of holding one person – the captain of the ship – to account for his decisions, and framing him as the main cause of the accident. Chapter 15 sets out to ask some foundational questions about the human tendency to find a scapegoat in an accident.

Can we find a balance between analysing failures and fixing problems in the outer world, and acknowledging and understanding the mysteries of our inner, unconscious being? How can we start to observe our subjective selves and our unconscious assumptions in our own accident investigations? How can we turn failures into opportunities for learning and self-reflection? The final chapter provides an ethical framework for how we can learn from an accident rather than be simply 'schooled' by accident investigation training and its associated mythology. In that chapter, I use the iCue method based on the Social Psychology of Risk framework to demonstrate a learning-focused investigation in practice.

Learning and change come with patience. One person at a time. One conversation at a time. There is no such thing as organisational learning. Organisations do not learn: people do.

I hope this book will inspire you to craft your own learning journey and realise your infinite potential.

# 1

# A Transdisciplinary Approach

This book takes a transdisciplinary approach i.e. it draws upon a range of disciplines to address the question of learning from accidents. I came to transdisciplinary thinking with a natural predisposition towards it. An ardent student of mathematics from early years at school, I graduated with a diploma in nautical science. Thereafter, I worked at sea for 11 years to obtain a Master Mariner's Licence, studied neoliberal economics as a postgraduate, acquired a PhD in social sciences and anthropology, worked in regulation and certification of ships for six years, and have recently obtained a master's degree in social psychology. I am now devoting time to studying mythology, neuroscience and consciousness.

Part of the reason why I chose to self-publish the book was the transdisciplinary nature of my research which, in my view, the traditional publishing sector is not fully prepared to embrace at least at this stage. One publisher I approached read through the first few pages and responded: 'Fundamentally, I'm getting safety – the absence/reduction of harm – and human factors from this outline.' I wondered how he made such a fundamental connection with the introductory text of the book until I noticed from his email signature that his specialisms were law, transport, and health & safety. We humans are unique in that we create rigid disciplines, then bend the world around us to serve those disciplines. But what good is the rigidity of a discipline when it keeps us from engaging with the message of this book?

A transdisciplinary approach acknowledges that no one discipline has the ability to comprehend human nature in its entirety. Traditionally, academia has always found it a challenge to support transdisciplinary thinking; the historical/political landscape of our educational institutions does not sit peacefully with this approach. The divisions between university buildings, departments, disciplines and faculties emerge from monodisciplinary theoretical and methodological choices, and in turn constrain them. The politics of campuses, territories, competition, possession, research grants, power and professionalisation work against Transdisciplinarity, only adding more obstacles and tribal wars.

In a Faculty of Social Sciences, when speaking about risk and safety it can be difficult to include research in religion and mythology (Midgley, 2003) (Douglas, 1992). Similarly, I find it interesting that when you are researching human behaviour you cannot talk about the neurosciences (including the study of consciousness) but are restricted to psychology. Such are the limitations of advancing monodisciplinary knowledge that it can sometimes become the pursuit of knowledge for its own sake. When I discovered the Social Psychology of Risk (SPoR) and its ability to hold different disciplines together in tension, I felt freedom, and all the strands came together so gracefully.

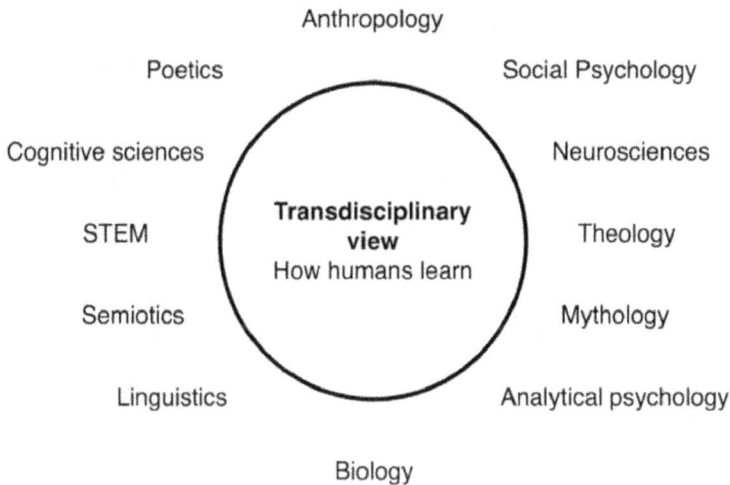

Anthropology

Poetics          Social Psychology

Cognitive sciences      Neurosciences

STEM      **Transdisciplinary view** How humans learn      Theology

Semiotics      Mythology

Linguistics      Analytical psychology

Biology

Figure 1.1: Transdisciplinary thinking.

# A transdisciplinary view on learning

Often, our expectation from learning is to arrive at a particular truth. In accident investigations there is an implicit belief in arriving at a 'root cause', and then addressing the cause with 'corrective actions' as the learning outcome. This mindset has emerged from the foundations of safety as an engineering discipline.

In this book I take a different view on learning; not as a quest for certainty, but with the humility to accept that despite our best efforts, we shall at best arrive at a temporal, unstable truth. Learning will always be a journey, never a destination. While Hegel's standpoint is that learning arrives at synthesis, according to Ellul learning always remains in dialectic. Learning is not discovered in stasis, but in the constant ebb and flow between competing ideas, through dialogue and conversation. Learning is the unending movement in search for truth that holds true to the context. This applies to all scientific discoveries; they are true up to the point that new theories and concepts emerge and challenge the prevalent state of affairs. In learning, our understanding of truth always remains incomplete.

A transdisciplinary view on learning also coincides with the ancient wisdom. The Indian word for myth is *mithya*, meaning partial truth, whereas *satya* means absolute truth. Similarly, the ancient Greeks in their search for truth acknowledged the balance between *mythos* (beliefs) and *logos* (concepts). Perhaps, the primitive humans were aware that their truth was always incomplete and with this mindset, they might have been more open to listen to another person's partial truth instead of imposing their own view on the others.

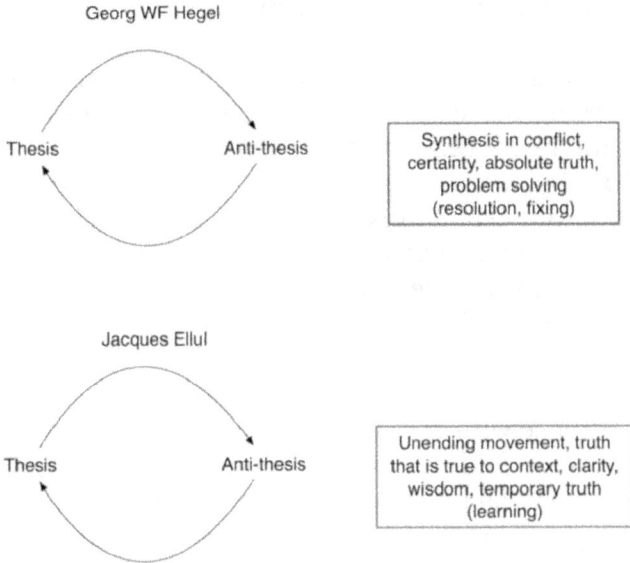

Figure 1.2: Comparing Hegel's idea of truth with that of Jacques Ellul.

Figure 1.3: The mandalas.

**Learning from mandala symbolism**

In May 2023 we were in the city of Chennai, India, working on diagnosing the culture of a shipping company. Every evening in our hotel the staff would gather to create mandalas with flowers, grain flour and clay lamps. One evening we decided to participate in the ritual. We participated in the ceremony and decorated the mandala along with the hotel staff. In the morning, the mandala would be wiped out.

For those who are unfamiliar with a mandala, it is one of the oldest symbols of Indian subcontinent. But mandala-like symbolisms have existed in every culture across geographies and time. The word 'mandala' originates from the Sanskrit word *mandal*, a circle. The outer circle of the mandala symbolises the universe while the inner circle represents the Self. The inner circle placed at the centre of the outer circle symbolises Self in peace with the outer world. The mandala also consists of diametrically opposite ends illustrating the need for balancing the tensions between competing values in life. For instance, the need to earn money should be balanced with family time. The need to seek power should be balanced with humility and similarly, learning should be balanced with unlearning.

Learning is akin to a mandala – balancing competing values, experiencing the tension between the opposites in life and being comfortable with the impermanent nature of life and truth.

Podcast on Mandala Symbolism:
https://www.youtube.com/watch?v=Utwh8_3ytOI

Another way to think about learning from a transdisciplinary perspective is through the metaphors of mysteries and puzzles. In puzzles there are problems to be solved, and eventually the answer brings an end to our puzzlement. In mysteries, we realise that neither is the outcome of our actions knowable, nor can the issue we are trying to understand be defined at the start (Kay & King, 2020). With both mysteries and mandalas, we remain mindful and open to what may come next.

And so I hope that the image of a mandala and the thought of mysteries will inspire you to remain humble, open-minded and curious in learning from accidents (and life).

# 2

# The Ritual of Accident Investigations

———————⟡⟡⟡———————

This chapter is an enquiry into the rituals of accident investigations. We will begin with an understanding of rituals and a framework to understand the hidden power and meaning in rituals. This framework will then be applied to the rituals of risk and safety, with a specific focus on accident investigations to question if we are really learning from accidents.

*Can accident investigations be seen as rituals of learning?* This will be the guiding question of this chapter.

> - Understanding rituals
> - Frameworks for understanding the meaning and power in rituals.
> - Questioning the meaning and purpose in the rituals of accident investigations.
> - Can accident investigations be considered rituals of learning?

Figure 2.1: A general outline of the chapter.

# A community ritual

Figure 2.2: A makeshift ritual in Hamburg, Germany; this white bike, surrounded by white roses, lilies, black ribbons, snowdrops and personal items, caught my attention. The text on the placard by the top of the bike, translated into English, went:

On 30.01.2023, our daughter died here on this crossing. She was on her way to the KITA to pick up her son. She was run over by a truck. She died at the scene of the accident. On that day, our grandson waited in vain for his mum. For us, the world has stood still since then. We miss her very much, we will never hear her voice, her laughter again and miss our conversations together. We will no longer be able to hug her and feel her warmth. It is so infinitely difficult to continue living without them.

We would like to thank from the bottom of our hearts all the first responders who were on site at the accident site and supported our daughter!

We miss you very much, in gratitude your mum and dad!

An old German lady approached me to check if I knew what I was photographing. She explained, pointing me towards the placard, what the bicycle and flowers meant to the community. She then turned towards a passing truck to explain what had gone wrong: 'These are long trucks with a blind spot, and sometimes the drivers can't see what's happening behind them when they take a sharp turn. The government has passed a law so new trucks will be fitted with a special device to prevent such accidents in the future, but we still have a lot of these old trucks around and we can't do much about it.'

The first rule of anthropology is that everything is significant. What was the significance of this ritual to the community? How well did the ritual fulfil its purpose? Let us begin with addressing this question starting with an understanding of rituals. Once we understand how to question the meaning and purpose in a ritual, our next step is to find out if and how the rituals of accident investigations serve their purpose.

## Rituals

A ritual is the enactment of a culture. In other words, a ritual is how culture is *performed*. The first image of a Ritual (with big R) that usually comes to mind is of birth ceremonies, funerals, birthdays, marriages, graduation days, baby showers and Christmas gatherings, or the distant Rituals of the indigenous tribes of Australia or the American Great Plains, or the Maoris of New Zealand. But even listening to a podcast in the train, washing the car at the weekend, going to the gym or out for a morning walk and putting kids to bed are examples of rituals (with small r) in our everyday lives.

You may think that these are chores and routines of everyday life. Why should we call them rituals? For this, we must draw a distinction between a routine and a ritual. Our daily lives are full of routines, from how we get out of the bed to how we shower, put on our clothes, comb our hair, prepare breakfast, leave home for the office, return home, share a meal with our family, and go back to bed. How do we know which of these routines qualify as a ritual?

Routines are a cluster of habits that can be organised in a sequence; and they lighten our cognitive load. Habits are bodily actions which through repeated performance become automatic (Shore, 2023). How we reach out for a comb, which part of our hair we select to comb first, how much pressure we apply to the comb, and how many strokes until we consider our hair done are a cluster of *habits* that form the *routine* of combing. Unless something unusual happens, nature has given us the capacity to accomplish almost all routines through our habits in a pre-programmed mode.

Rituals give a cultural meaning to our routines. Let's take an example. Some years ago, I would observe my neighbour next door washing his car almost every weekend. I was surprised why someone would spend hours outside in freezing temperatures washing, shampooing and cleaning their car (which already appeared spick and span) until I realised the hidden meaning in this routine. My neighbour was washing his car with his garage door left open. The garage was well organised, with a set of DIY tools on display. That's when the cultural meaning of this routine struck me. It was his way of demonstrating to the neighbourhood (1) his masculinity within the household and (2) his organised life. It is not common, at least in my experience, to observe women washing their car on their day off. That's when I started to pay more attention to the hidden meaning and power in routines. Even a routine as simple as cleaning teeth can be turned into a ritual if it extends beyond just personal hygiene to include looking and smelling good. The marketing and advertising agencies know so well how to turn routines into rituals: elevate your life when you drink coffee with your wife, or bring a smile to your face with a certain brand of toothpaste. Whereas a routine serves a function or a practical need, a ritual extends to give symbolic meaning to the routine. A ritual is a routine with soul and spirit. More on this as we discuss symbols in the following section.

Let us return to the example of the deceased cyclist in Hamburg and observe the ritual in this accident. The sudden death of a young cyclist is a tragedy for the family. A ritual is evoked, and the girl's bicycle is erected in the spot where she died. Around the bicycle are the white flowers, bouquets, personal items, sleeping angels, and the personal message from the family with a Christian symbol. At the time I took the photo, it was almost eleven months since the accident and the bicycle was still secured to the fence. A dedicated spot for a memorial on a public pavement means that the local authorities would have granted permission for the bike to remain there for that long. The decision to create a makeshift memorial in a public space with a personalised message means that beyond the family of the deceased, the wider community, the general public and public bodies participated in the ritual.

The ritual sought to share the family's pain and grief with passers-by. On the family's message there were no details about how the girl was killed except that she was hit by a truck. Even though a passer-by told me that a policy had been mandated to prevent future accidents, it was clearly not considered necessary to include this news in the message on the bicycle. Rather, the ritual was about grieving, and expressing gratitude to the community for their support.

When misfortune hits us, and the world comes to a standstill, rituals become a source of inner resilience. They are not intended as a way of dealing with the outer world.

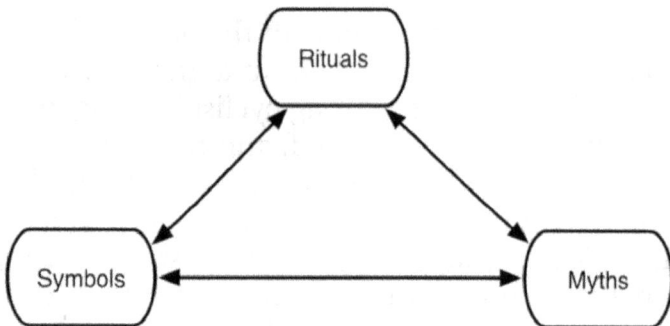

Figure 2.3: The triarchic relationship between rituals, myths and symbols.

As we discuss the meaning of rituals, it is important to appreciate the meaning of myths and symbols as well. The triarchic relationship between rituals, symbols and myths is central to understanding the meaning and purpose of rituals.

## Symbols

Symbols extend beyond the obvious and the literal in what an image (text, letters, words, phrases, signs, and narratives) signifies to a group (or culture). When we study 'science' (i.e. STEM subjects) in a search for absolute and objective truth, symbols are reduced to their literal meaning.

We may be surprised, even annoyed, when people see things differently from us. While a road sign may display a speed limit of 30 mph, what does this mean to a road user? A novice driver may strictly obey the limit, taxi drivers may apply their local knowledge and exceed it, and someone new to the country may struggle to understand what the speed limit even means. Word meanings and sign-systems are rarely literal. The real meaning of a word, a sign or a story comes from understanding what feelings and emotions the word (or a sign) generates for us, and what *significance* it holds for a culture.

The bicycle of the deceased in Hamburg symbolises a material culture. In a material culture, artefacts and physical objects are used to communicate a message. Because life is treated as matter at the bodily level, flowers and personal items were kept near the bicycle to *actualise* the loss of life. In many Mediterranean countries wayside shrines are erected, signifying deaths from road accidents.

In non-material cultures, however, such as Hindu and Buddhist faiths, it is ideas, beliefs, ethics, rules, dress codes, manners, etiquette, laws and penalties that take precedence over material objects. The symbolism associated with the loss of life does not involve memorials or personal items; instead, the dead are cremated, and their ashes are poured into a river to initiate the final separation of the soul from the body.

Figure 2.4: A sign on a country road in the UK warning drivers that in 200 yards they will need to slow down to 30 mph. The two bars below the speed limit represent the 200 yards.

The colour white symbolises purity and salvation almost universally, and in Hamburg the offering of flowers represents community support for those who have lost their loved ones. The collective presence of the flowers, the bicycle, the personal items (in white), the black ribbon and the Latin cross intensifies the message. You only need to replace a black ribbon with a pink one, however, or place a gadget alongside, to see how the symbolic meaning of the ritual shifts significantly. Symbols operate as a sign-system to indicate a meaning.

The bike painted white and placed in a conspicuous public space will symbolise different things to different groups. It emotionally draws tourists close to the scene, as in my case. It also reminds cyclists of their vulnerability on the road, and it may even draw the attention of drivers of trucks and large vehicles to the dangers they can create on the road. The understanding of symbols and the symbolic meanings hidden within a ritual makes us aware of the limitations of our own worldview, and may also help us appreciate other forms of life.

## Myth

A myth is a story believed to be true by a group of people (though that group is unlikely to call it a myth). Because these stories operate at the unconscious level, people do not always know why they believe in them. Unlike the objective, undisputed truth which would be considered universal to all, or a fantasy that may be your own truth alone, a myth is the truth of a specific culture. Every culture has its own myths, and people of every culture live by their own myths. We protect and defend our myths against those who belong to another culture.

Science views myth as the opposite of truth. A search for absolute, objective and microscopic truth has led modern science on the path towards debunking stories that people have believed to be true in the past. It is assumed that unpacking and questioning the assumptions in our beliefs, layer by layer, will help us come closer to an objective truth which will give us more certainty in our lives. But this understanding of myth, as I will consistently illustrate in this book, is relatively new to humankind, and is rather misleading.

Myth does not need falsification or debunking. All life is lived in myth. If what we know today may change tomorrow, then Science – i.e. any attempt to establish objective truth – also has its own myths. For instance, how do we know with certainty that green tea is good for health? How do we know for sure that antibiotics are best suited to kill infections? What could be the long-term implications of consuming antibiotics? What could be the trade-offs and the hidden unknowns? What if new solutions create new problems? These are not easy concepts to digest when we are seduced by the myth of certainty, perfection, stability and a search for objective truth.

In the bicycle accident, what is the underlying myth (or belief) in the ritual? What can we learn about the beliefs of this culture by observing their ritual? The origin of this myth goes back to the tradition of erecting makeshift memorials, a custom whose origins are lost in the mists of time.

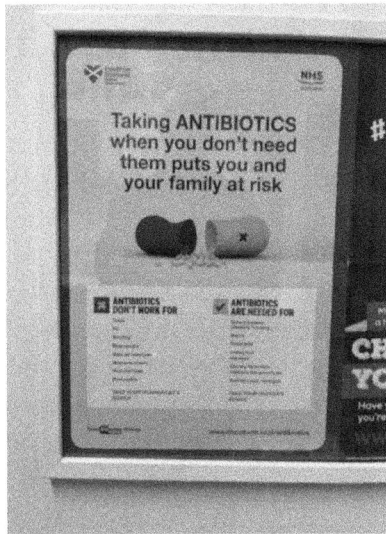

Figure 2.5: A poster by the National Health Service, UK, warning people against the inappropriate use of antibiotics. Consumption of antibiotics to cure symptoms of flu and colds, and regular dosing of farm animals with them, means that some antibiotics have become less effective. We are now entering an era of 'super antibiotics' – but who knows when this new technology will meet the same fate as antibiotics?

When death is natural – in old age, for instance, or as a result of prolonged illness – the death ceremony usually follows the customs of the culture. But when death is unnatural, as in an accident, a makeshift memorial serves as an interim solution to cope with the sudden loss before the body can be permanently disposed of. Another myth is that the place where the life ended, in this case where the accident happened, is considered more important than the place where the body of the deceased is buried. It is because people in this culture feel more connected with the place where the person was last seen alive than where the body was eventually buried. The myth in this story goes that life matters from where it physically begins to where it eventually ends.

## Does the makeshift ritual fulfil its purpose?

As the name suggest, the makeshift ritual serves the purpose of mediating transitions. It gives us predictability and order when we confront radical uncertainty (Kay & King, 2020). Between the sudden death of a family member and the performance of their death ceremony, the makeshift ritual provides both separating and integrating two dimensions of human experience to come to terms with the misfortune. One sees every day examples of how rituals can successfully mediate transitions ranging from rites of passage marking significant transitions in life (birthdays, weddings, baptism etc.) to the use of familiar greetings to overcome the anxiety of facing a stranger ('how are you'; 'hello'; and 'nice to meet you') or familiarisation and induction rituals (programs) used for welcoming new employees in the company. If makeshift rituals are intended to mediate transitions, we can see how well the ritual is aligned with its intended purpose.

Every culture creates its own rituals to give meaning to the mysteries of the universe: nature becomes Mother Nature, sky is where heaven belongs, a deadly disease is the spell of an evil being, a goat carries with it the sins of entire society, a bicycle gives us the strength to move forward, gargoyles and griffins become symbols of protection – and identifying the 'root cause' brings closure to an investigation. We seek moral reasoning in random phenomena, we feel a sense of control when we can name a problem, and we find solace in putting a face to the faceless. We humans find it easier to deal with the mysteries of the universe by turning towards rituals.

## Ritual components

The table below provides the components of the rituals. As we proceed into accident investigations, each of these components will help us to observe the visual and audible performance of the ritual. Put simply, each component below will allow us to improve our listening and observation skills.

| Ritual | Description |
|---|---|
| Dissent | Is there questioning in the ritual performance? |
| Repetition | What is repetitive in the ritual? (Words, phrases, metaphors, gestures, etc.) |
| Code | "What is the coded message (jargon, technical terms, etc.) in the ritual? Think of a coded message as language that is peculiar to a group." |
| Place | Where is the ritual being performed? |
| Metaphors | What is the discourse of the ritual? |
| Authority | Who has the authority and power in the ritual? |
| Sequence | What is the sequence in the ritual? |
| Mimesis | What is being imitated in the ritual? |
| Efficacy | What creates efficacy in the ritual (time saving)? |
| Habit | What is communicated unconsciously and habitually in the ritual? |
| Gestures | What are the bodily gestures in the ritual? |
| Myth | How did the ritual originate? What is the shared story? |
| Symbol | What is the symbolic enactment in the ritual? |
| Apparel | What is the attire and clothing in the ritual? |

Figure 2.6: Ritual components based
on the Social Psychology of Risk.

## A ritual of 'lessons learned from accidents'

I present the example of a maritime investigation agency performing the ritual of 'lessons learned' following an accident. The purpose of this exercise is to observe the ritual and find out if we are learning from accidents. The accident involves the capsize of the PCTC (car carrier) *Hoegh Osaka* when the ship was departing from Southampton on 3 January 2015. The official investigation report, published on 17 March 2017 by the Maritime Accident Investigation Branch (MAIB) of the UK, highlighted a combination of human and organisational factors that led to the accident.

I invite you to view the video link published by the investigation branch as we work our way through this ritual http://bit.ly/41YOXxk.

We begin by observing how the MAIB shares the lessons following the accident investigation. The chief inspector of the MAIB is formally dressed. He begins by thanking all the stakeholders involved in the accident investigation for their cooperation and assistance. He states:

> it has required the branch to draw upon a broad range of expertise to establish what happened, why it happened and identify lessons for future safety.

The video shows an aerial view of the *Hoegh Osaka* being salvaged during the night, with the chief inspector's voice in the background explaining the sequence of events shortly before the accident. The rescue of the crew and the successful salvage of the ship is perceived as a fortunate outcome. It is also

acknowledged by the chief inspector that in a slightly different situation, the outcome of the accident
would have been far worse.

The video then changes from night to daytime,
with the capsized ship in focus. The chief inspector
is heard in the background explaining that once the
ship had settled into a stable condition, the MAIB
inspectors boarded it to collect evidence, including
the ship's loading computer. A team of inspectors
can be seen boarding the ship via a rope ladder. The
video then shows investigators gathering evidence
from the ship, but this time there is no audio. A team
of investigators can be seen holding torches and
pulling ropes to guide them through unlit machinery
spaces to access the logbooks and electronic logs
situated at the bottom of the ship's engine room.
Another investigation team can be seen walking
on the main deck of the heeled ship to access the
bridge. Inside the bridge, a lot of equipment, files,
furniture, tools and rubbish is scattered on the floor.
After unscrewing the data logger, the investigator is
seen extracting the evidence from it, placing it in an
'evidence bag', sealing the bag and writing the ship's
details on its label.

In the next section of the video, the chief inspector
presents the main causal factors of the accident:

- The stability conditions did not meet the international stability requirements for ships proceeding to sea
- The calculations also demonstrated that while
  the ship was able to safely execute a similar turn
  at Calshot at a minimum speed of 10 knots about
  seven minutes before the accident, it had insuf-

ficient residual stability to survive the Bramble Bank turn when proceeding at 12 knots (accompanied by the visuals of a nautical map)

- *Hoegh Osaka*'s cargo loading plan had not been adjusted to account for the ship's usual European port rotation, which resulted in the ship leaving the port of Southampton with a higher centre of gravity than normal
- The number of vehicles which were designated to be loaded in the pre-stowage plan was significantly different from the final cargo tally, and the tally's estimated weight of the many items of cargo was less than the actual weight (accompanied by pictures of cargo holds)
- A key causal factor in the accident was the routine practice onboard of adjusting the ballast tank quantities entered into the ship's loading computer so that its output reflected the observed draft readings taken at the end of loading
- Additionally, the ship's automatic ballast gauging systems had been largely inoperative for some time, and the ship's staff were not keeping a proper log of the distribution of ballast
- The actual distribution of ballast onboard when *Hoegh Osaka* commenced its voyage had a near-adverse impact on the vessel's stability, and had no resemblance to the distribution of ballast used by the crew to calculate the ship's departure condition
- Had the ship's staff adhered to a more robust regime of ballast control so that the actual distribution of the ballast had been entered into the ship's loading computer, *Hoegh Osaka*'s inadequate stability could have been identified, and it would have been entirely possible to resolve the situation by taking on additional ballast.

While the chief inspector presents the learnings from the accident, the visuals of the damaged and toppled cars can be seen on deck. In one photograph, a steel plate with a measuring tape can be seen.

In the concluding section of the video, the focus is back to the chief inspector. Standing outside his office, he ends with the following message:

> the Master is ultimately responsible for ensuring that his or her ship has the adequate stability for its intended voyage on the completion of cargo operations and before it sails. A loading computer can be an effective tool for that purpose but only if accurate information is entered into it. It is therefore imperative that the working practices adopted by the PCTC ashore and afloat ensure that there is always a sufficient time and accurate cargo data provided on completion of cargo operation to enable the stability of PCTC vessels to be properly calculated before departure. There is a collective responsibility for all decision makers in the PCTC industry to support the masters of these vessels in ensuring that the commercial pressures do not result in an erosion of the basic operational safety standards. The *Hoegh Osaka* accident is a stark reminder of what can happen when short cuts are taken in the interests of expediency, and I would urge you all to carefully read the MAIB accident investigation report and take onboard the important lessons that it contains. Thank you.

At the end of the video, the front cover of the accident report can be seen, with a photo of the ship aground. Then there's a brief message of thanks to the National Police Air Service for providing the aerial footage of the accident.

## Observing the ritual components in practice

Let us observe what we hear and see in the video within the framework of ritual:

1. Place: The video appears as a formal event in a public office. It is not clear who else is participating in this event, but since this is a public video (on YouTube), it would be a fair assumption that the video is meant to communicate the 'lessons' to a wide audience.
2. Code: The use of maritime jargon means that the video is specifically produced for the maritime community.
3. Apparel: The attire of the chief inspector is formal, and the message is conveyed in a formal manner.
4. Metaphor: The expression 'stakeholders' at the beginning of the video is an indication of the extent to which business language has gained penetration in public discourse; in this case in a formal accident investigation report. The report ends with the reminder that 'commercial pressures do not result in an erosion of the basic operational safety standards'. But the language of the investigation in itself is influenced by commercial metaphors. If you think I am being overanalytical or pedantic, consider the use of the term 'community' instead of 'stakeholders', and observe the difference. Words matter, and when we choose our words consciously, it influences our decisions and actions (Lakoff, 2014) (Long, 2012).
5. Discourse: Without setting out the context of the situation, the chief inspector begins by saying, 'What happened, why it happened and identify lessons for future safety.' Shortly afterwards, he can be heard saying, 'In a slightly different

situation, the outcome of the accident would have been far worse'. Is it possible to imagine a slightly different situation without knowing the actual context of the accident?

6. Discourse: The rescue effort and salvage are perceived as the fortunate outcome of the accident. The term 'fortunate' means that the rescue effort must have been seen as a matter of chance. The desire to understand 'what went right' and how the ship was refloated does not form part of the discussion. There is no mention of co-ordination, communication, heuristics, skills, situated experience and resilience of the rescue personnel in the successful handling and co-ordination of an emergency operation in the middle of the night. In a BBC News post shortly after the accident, the captain and the pilot were commended for their decision to deliberately ground the ship on the sandbank to avoid more serious consequences, but this decision was never revisited in the accident report (BBC News, 2015).

7. Symbols: The visual representation of a team of inspectors gathering evidence in the dark and carefully preserving the evidence in a plastic bag is meant to show that truth is objective, and that accurate truth can be established so long as the data is not contaminated by human bias.

8. Repetition: In the backdrop of point 7 above, the report reflects the subjectivities, biases and political constraints of a government agency. Within the 83-page investigation report, the term 'chief officer' appears 132 times, and 'Master' 89 times. By contrast, the organisation responsible for the safety management system appears in the report on only 60 occasions. Of the 24 conclusions drawn from the report, 16 are centred on

the vessel and the behaviour of the ship's crew. (MAIB, 2016)

9. Discourse: The causal factors of the accident are presented in a prescriptive manner by establishing breaches of rule compliance. A descriptive view of why those breaches would have occurred is not presented in the accident report.

10. Metaphor: The metaphor of 'ultimate responsibility' of the ship master is situated in obedience and conformance with rules and procedures, leaving aside the empowerment and autonomy essential to exercising the authority of a ship captain.

11. Repetition: The use of the terms 'normal', 'practice', 'routine practice', 'working practices', 'adjusted' and 'short cuts' can be observed on several occasions both in the video and as part of the formal investigation report. There is no attempt to engage with what is considered normal and routine practice from the crew's perspective.

12. Discourse: The narrative is framed as a mechanistic problem. The representation of mechanistic problems can be observed in several visuals such as computers, control panels, stability calculations, the cargo loading manual and the measurement of steel plates.

13. Metaphors: The chief investigator acknowledges the problem with the design of equipment and systems. At the same time, the expectation is that the operator should have done more to avoid the accident. The term 'adjusted' means that the operators are expected to adjust their behaviour to accommodate the expectations of the organisation, and the physical and social context.

14. Symbols: At 2.10s, a 'Safety First' sign can be observed in the video. What emotions and feelings would such a signage trigger to those watching a capsized ship because of the 'commercial pressure'?
15. Symbols: The video shows various photos of machinery breakdown and damage to cars in cargo holds, symbolising destruction and chaos.
16. Dissent: Since the YouTube comment feature is turned off, there is no opportunity for community engagement. But this could also be a feature of technology.
17. Sequence: The video begins by thanking all the 'stakeholders', and ends with thanking 'the National Police Air Service for providing the aerial footage' of the accident. No gratitude is expressed to the emergency response team, the pilot or to the seafarers.
18. Discourse: Neither the report nor the presentation brings to the surface the seafarers perspective. There is no recognition of the fallible humans in an accident.

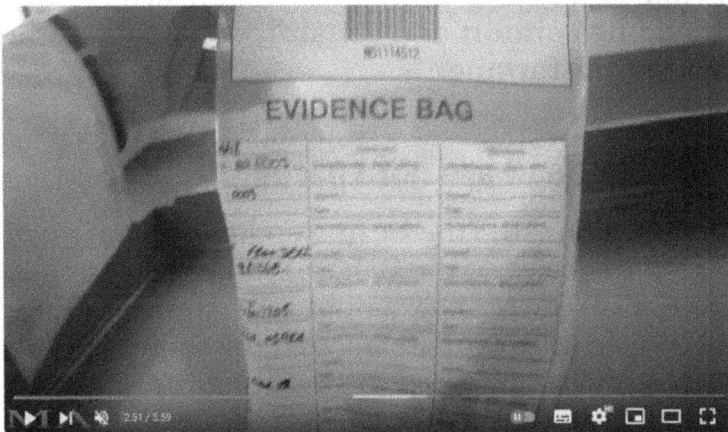

Figure 2.7: Evidence from the bridge collected and sealed in a plastic bag by the investigation team; a symbol of objective truth.

## Can this example serve as a ritual of learning?

For any learning to take place, you would expect an appreciation of: the social context; space for discussion; an acknowledgement of limitations and assumptions of the investigation process; dissent; engagement; critical thinking; questioning; humility; diversity of perspectives; and sharing of experiences. But in this ritual we do not see any of that.

What we see instead is formality, belief in objective truth (measuring tapes, log records, and plastic bags to seal the evidence), and an expectation for the crew to conform with rules. The ritual is framed as a monologue of obedience, control and fallibility, and a visual display of damage, destruction and disorder. There is neither dissent nor any attempt to engage with the seafarers' perspectives (in both the video and the accident report.) As the comments in the YouTube video were turned off, the opportunity to engage with the questions, comments and feedback from the community is clearly not considered important. **The purpose of this ritual cannot, then, be one of learning and sharing, but instead one of providing comfort and certainty to society in the wake of misfortune.**

## Even the dead are not spared

On 1 October 2015 the steamship *El Faro* went missing off the coast of the Bahamas after heading into the eye of Hurricane Joaquin. The crew of 33 was lost. The company that operated the ship, Tote Marine, stated in an email to CNN that the ship 'met all standards and certifications regardless of its age'.

In an interview with the CNN, three former crew members of *El Faro* described the ship as a 'rust bucket' that should have never been allowed to go to sea. Another crew member, Chris Cash, whose last voyage had ended months before the ship sank, had expressed concerns about the maintenance of the ship. 'They were bandaging the ship with extra steel all the time,' he said. 'It seemed like they didn't want to put any money into the ship. When things would break, they would just patch it up rather than really fix it.'

The crewmen had mixed feelings about their captain. While some considered him 'cocky and stubborn' others saw him as a 'good man' (Almasy & Khorram, 2015).

Just over two years after the accident, the National Transportation Safety Board (NTSB) conducted a detailed investigation and published a 300-page report. It is not my intention to provide a detailed analysis of this accident. What caught my attention was the first few sentences of the 'probable cause' of the accident that followed an exhaustive investigation process:

> The National Transportation Safety Board determines that the probable cause of the sinking of *El Faro* and the subsequent loss of life was the captain's insufficient action to avoid Hurricane Joaquin, his failure to use the most current weather information, and his late decision to muster the crew. Contributing to the sinking was ineffective bridge resource management on board *El Faro*, which included the captain's failure to adequately consider officers' suggestions. Also contributing to

the sinking was the inadequacy of both TOTE's oversight and its safety management system. (NTSB, 2015)

Notice the discourse – 'captain's insufficient action' and 'captain's failure'. How could an investigation team arrive at the conclusion that the captain's actions were insufficient or his decision to abandon the ship was too late when the ship had been lost and nobody from it, least of all the captain, was alive to share their version of the narrative?

Notice also, a series of conclusions of the formal investigation report below:

> 36. El Faro was receiving sufficient weather information for the captain's decision-making regarding the vessel's route.

> 37. Although up-to-date weather information was available on the ship, the El Faro captain did not use the most current weather information for decision-making.

> 38. Had the deck officers more assertively stated their concerns, in accordance with effective bridge resource management principles, the captain's situation awareness might have been improved.

> 39. The captain should have returned to the bridge after the second and third mates called him to gain a better awareness of the changing weather situation.

> 40. The captain did not take sufficient action to avoid Hurricane Joaquin, thereby putting El Faro and its crew in peril.

41. By failing to adequately consider the suggestions of the ship's junior officers to alter the passage plan and failing to alter his decision to proceed, the captain endangered El Faro and its crew. Source: (NTSB 2015, p.244)

Observe the choice of words above – 'the captain did ...; the captain endangered ..., and the captain did not', implying the agency of the captain and his crew members in making certain choices that led to the accident. In other words, the captain and his crew should have made better choices. Such an assumption implies that human beings consciously make errors and bad decisions; in this case, that the crew members of *El Faro* consciously made decisions that led to their death. Therefore, to avoid an accident people should learn how to make *good choices*.

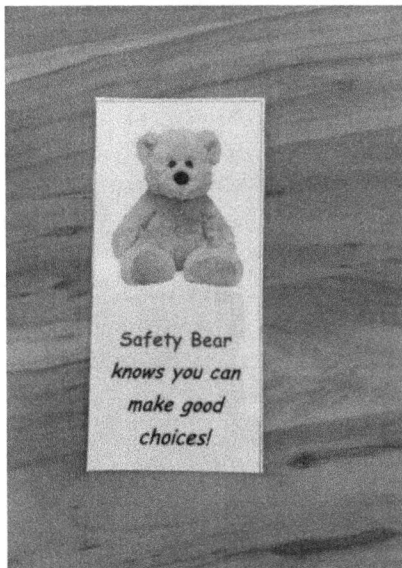

Figure 2.8: The above was handed to my six-year-old son at school. The picture symbolises denial of fallibility, search for perfection and the illusion of free will. Such an approach to education begins early in life.

The ritual of accident investigations is not about learning. It is more of a recipe to avoid killing our own selves, unlike those on *El Faro* who, according to the report, *chose* otherwise. In the ritual of accident investigations, even the dead are not spared. The ritual of accident investigations reflects rejection of fallibility and the delusion of certainty, comfort and control in making the world a safer place.

## The meaning in the ritual of root cause analysis

A popular myth in accident investigations is the quest for a root cause and corrective actions. I will begin with a personal story.

### There Are No Accidents Without a Root Cause

For the last six years I have conducted several workshops on Learning from Accidents using the *Costa Concordia* case. At the end of an intensive day facilitating the *Costa Concordia* workshop to a group of marine managers in Singapore, I thought I had done a reasonable job explaining Captain Francesco Schettino's perspective on the accident. As I was leaving the room a ship manager who had attended the workshop caught me in the corridor and asked, "Nippin, tell me honestly, okay – was a breath analysis test done on this captain just after the accident?"

I did not know how to respond to his question, but I thought hard about it for a few days and became even more curious about it. The thought that even though 32 people had died and I could not come up with a plausible cause for that was beyond imagination. Suffering must be located in a cause, or else what's the point in conducting an accident investigation? One can easily lose the credibility of an investigator by presenting an accident narrative without a cause. Without a cause, there can be no learning. Is root cause the outcome of all learning?

# Root cause

Figure 2.9: The incessant search for a root cause.

In E.E. Evans-Pritchard's book, *Witchcraft, Oracles and Magic among the Azande* (Evans-Pritchard, 1976), the social anthropologist explores how the Azande locate meaning in human suffering. The Azande are an ethnic group in the south-central and south-western part of South Sudan, and in south-eastern Central African Republic.

A myth goes around within the Azande community that a child becomes sick, very sick. One explanation is that the child became sick because of contaminated food, adulterated water or a viral infection. But for the Azande, such mechanistic causes do not explain what lies behind their suffering. Instead, the community believes that suffering is the result of witchcraft transferred from someone close to the sufferer – someone whom they may have offended or cheated in the past. Bad luck follows. One way of putting an end to suffering is to find someone who is not liked by the members of the community, tie a rope around their neck and drag them through the fields. The cause of the suffering is found not so much in epistemic explanations but in moral reasoning. In this way, the ritual of witchcraft hunting brings social conflicts to the forefront and resolves them openly within the community.

We in this so-called civilised world believe that the Azande are primitive and poorly educated, and an uncivilised tribe. But every time we are faced with an accident we do the same as the Azande. We like to think that we are objective, independent and scientific in our models and methods, but when we are faced with the same dilemma as the Azande we are just as mystified. As one CEO of an oil company whom I interviewed in Aberdeen put it:

> I've done everything in my capacity and still we had this accident. We've got all the procedures in place, the guys have all their training certificates valid, everything works, I don't know what else we can do. Why are we still having accidents?

> Later I came to know that the captain involved in the accident was removed from the company. It was not because he did something wrong. It was

simply because the company that hired their ships refused to work with this captain.

Just as the Azande turn to witch hunting, the ritual of root cause analysis is a quest to find someone or something to blame. In the end we follow the same ritual as the Azande: we dismiss people or send them for refresher training, and thus restore order within our workplaces. One person's witchcraft is another one's root cause analysis, all in the search for certainty, control and social order. Finding a root cause is foremost an existential need, and not necessarily a form of curiosity to understand what went wrong.

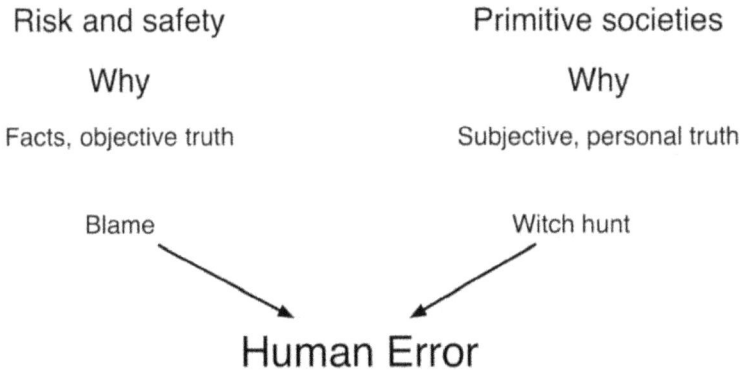

| Risk and safety | Primitive societies |
|---|---|
| Why | Why |
| Facts, objective truth | Subjective, personal truth |
| Blame | Witch hunt |

## Human Error

Figure 2.10: A comparison between the ritual of witchcraft and Root Cause Analysis.

The makeshift ritual in the bicycle accident was meant to mediate transition when a family was confronted by the sudden death of a young girl. As we observed, the ritual drew support from the community and served as an interim solution for the family to come to terms with a sudden tragedy. By contrast, if we think of accident investigations and 'lessons learned' to be seen as rituals of learning, we do not observe the key components of learning in the performance of the ritual. Instead, what we see is a tendency to seek comfort, certainty and order in the ritual by denying fallibility and dissent. We also notice in the ritual of accident investigations a propensity to find someone to blame under the pretext of 'science' and 'scientific methods'. How is the ritual of accident investigation any different from how our ancestors gave meaning to misfortune? In my view, our ancestors were more aware of the meaning and purpose of their rituals.

# 3

# The Narrative of Accident Investigations

What can we learn from the narrative of accident investigations? And more importantly, what can we learn about our assumptions, worldviews and beliefs in the way we narrate accidents? Are we really learning from our accident narratives? In this chapter, we will examine two examples – the Miracle of the Hudson River and the *Costa Concordia* disaster – to understand how we construct our narratives, and to establish what I have learned from those narratives.

> - Accident narratives as hero and anti-hero myth.
> - The example of 'Hudson River miracle' and 'the Costa Concordia accident'
> - The hidden patterns and assumptions in the making of the two narratives.

> - How helpful are those assumptions and beliefs when it comes to learning from accidents?
> - How should we think about accident narratives to promote learning?

Figure 3.1: A general outline of the chapter.

## The Miracle of the Hudson River

On 15 January 2009 US Airways flight 1549 took off from New York City's La Guardia Airport for Charlotte, North Carolina. While still in the climb-out from take-off, the aircraft struck a flock of Canada geese and lost engine power. The pilot, declaring an emergency, was given immediate clearance to land both back at La Guardia and at the nearest alternate airport, Teterboro in New Jersey. But the captain and his co-pilot, Jeff Skiles, calculated that the plane would not make it to either airport, and decided to ditch the aircraft in the Hudson River, alongside Manhattan Island. As it turned out, this was a good decision; all 155 people on board, passengers and crew, survived the accident. This was an American airliner, flown by two American pilots in American airspace.

More than six years after the accident, a newspaper printed a picture of Captain Chesley 'Sully' Sullenberger (Cook R. , 2016). Sitting bolt upright, Sully had represented the pride of an entire nation when he performed the 'most successful ditch in aviation history' (Olshan, 2009) and turned catastrophe into success. 'The Miracle of the Hudson River', as the accident was famously termed, made Sully a public hero.

# Chesley Sullenberger: an old-fashioned kind of hero

**Chesley 'Sully' Sullenberger became a global hero when he landed an airliner on New York's Hudson river in 2009. Now played by Tom Hanks in a film by Clint Eastwood, he talks about how the experience changed him**

📷 Former commercial airline pilot Chesley Sullenberger. 'I knew people would be debating whether I was right or wrong for decades.' Photograph: Suki Dhanda/The Observer

Figure 3.2: This photo of Captain Sullenberger was taken nearly five years after the accident. Source: Cook (2016)

In every accident there are elements of randomness and an unforeseen congruence of events that could not have been anticipated. Some of the events captured in the accident report would lie outside the imagination and influence of even a well-trained pilot:

1. A very experienced co-pilot, Jeff Skiles, who had recently completed type-rated training two weeks prior to the accident, was sitting alongside Sully;
2. An extremely cold day with temperature recorded at -15 degrees centigrade (5 Fahrenheit), meaning minimum marine traffic on an otherwise busy touristic river;

3. An air traffic controller who performed remarkably well in the situation, offering contingency plans and even backing those contingencies;
4. An emergency team that was readily available to conduct a rescue operation within minutes of the plane landing on the water;
5. An airplane that was '1 in 20 of Airbus A320s equipped as an EOW airplane in the US Airways fleet of 75 A320s', (NTSB, 2009), and which therefore carried lifesaving equipment such as passenger life vests, slide/rafts, and survival kit. Non-EOW planes are not required to carry those items.

Beneath this random congruence sits something far more sacred, which gives amplified attention to the captain and leads to the hero myth. Despite the unprecedented nature of his decision to land the plane on the water, there were no deaths and few injuries in this accident. All 155 passengers and crew members survived the accident – or should we say Sully saved the day? But would Sully still be the hero if a few people had died or had been seriously injured? I will return to this question later in the chapter, but first let us turn to the anti-hero myth.

## The shame of Italy

Consider another accident narrative, but this time at the opposite end of the spectrum: the anti-hero myth, which is also central to this book.

On 12 January, the passenger ship *Costa Concordia*, carrying 4229 persons, capsized off the Giglio Islands in Italy. The accident resulted in a death of 32 people. But this time it was an Italian captain on board an Italian ship, which belonged to an Italian company operating in Italian waters.

In a country that was facing one of the worst economic crises in the Eurozone, the capsizing of a ship was more than just an accident. For Italians, this accident became symbolic of 'national failure'. (Orsi, 2013)

**Captain Coward had his eye on English dancer: After claims he was distracted by a woman on the bridge, passengers and crew reveal Casanova antics of crash skipper**

Figure 3.3: One of the several tabloid articles accusing Captain Francesco Schettino of being distracted by the presence of a woman on the bridge during navigation. Source: Weathers (2012)

Within 48 hours of the accident, Captain Francesco Schettino became, in the public discourse, a murderer, a monster, a cartoon character, a crash skipper, a casanova, 'Captain Coward', a man without character, and a criminal. In 2013, an official accident report was released by the Ministry of Transport in Italy:

> It is needless to put in evidence that the case of the *Costa Concordia* is considered by this Investigative Body *(and we believe by everyone in the maritime field)* [my italics] a unique example for the lessons which may be learnt, despite the human tragedy and the Master's unconventional behavior, which represents the main cause of the shipwreck.
>
> (MIT, 2013, p. 9)

The *Costa Concordia* accident is a unique example in maritime history thus far, in that the captain of a ship is overtly declared to be the 'main cause' of the accident.

Beyond being simply the cause of the accident, Francesco Schettino became the *vergona* (shame) of Italy. Soon after the accident, both Italian news agencies and international journalists lined up behind him, and long before the official investigation had been concluded he was declared a criminal by the media. There could not be a more profound symbol of human failure in the history of human-made disasters. According to one news article:

> Some are convinced that he must have been drunk or ever so Italian distracted by a woman, a blonde Moldovan dancer was reportedly dining with the captain shortly before the disaster. Some former colleagues described him as a well trained professional and defended him. Others said he was a hot dog boat driver. (Reguly, 2012)

On 12 May 2017 the Italian court announced its verdict: Captain Schettino was sentenced to sixteen years in prison. He walked into Rebibbia Prison in Rome and handed himself over. The sentence against the captain included ten years for manslaughter, five for causing the shipwreck, one for abandoning the ship before the passengers and crew were clear, and one month for lying to the authorities afterwards. Meanwhile, Costa Crociere SpA, the company that owned the ship, 'sidestepped potential criminal charges in 2013 by agreeing to pay a €1m ($1.1m; £769,000) fine' (BBC News, 2017).

## The hero myth

What can we learn about ourselves from the two accident narratives? Let us begin with the choice of language. In the first accident, there is an unforeseen situation, an emergency, an unprecedented situation to land the plane on water in the face of a crisis, a miracle, and 'an old-fashioned hero' who saved 155 lives.

This is the hero myth (also called the monomyth). The concept is based on the work of Joseph Campbell: the protagonist, an ordinary person, is confronted by a challenge, which they accept; there are failures and setbacks on the journey until they find support (a coach, mentor or an inner force), turn failure into success, come home transformed, and become a force for change in society. (The final aspect of societal change is, however, often forgotten in individualist societies, because the hero takes all the credit for the success, and the journey often ends there.)

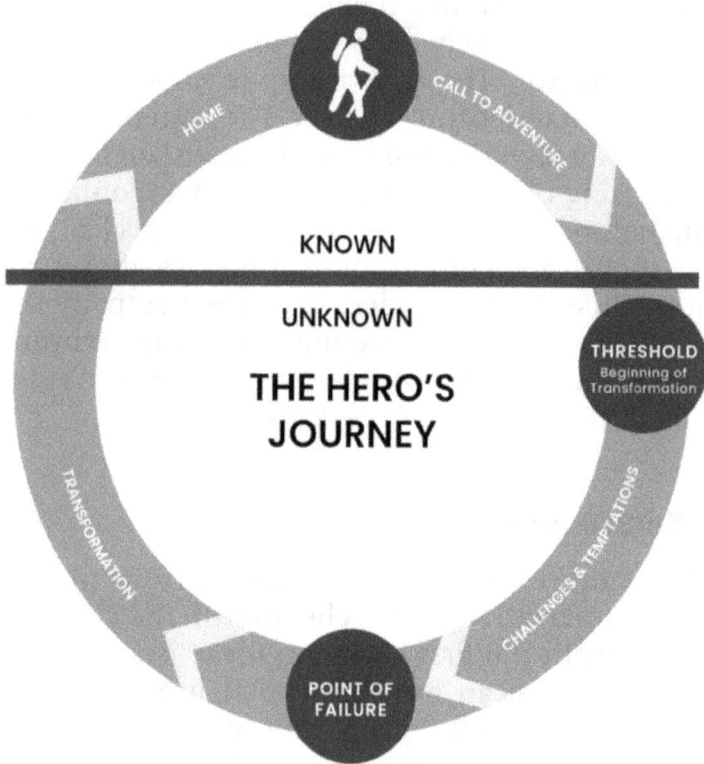

Hero's Journey

Figure 3.4: The Hero's Journey. (Campbell, 1949)

The hero myth, a recognised pattern in storytelling in the accident narrative, is intended to alleviate human emotions to the extent that there is no scope for reasoning, thinking or arguing. The mythical appeal in the narrative leaves little room for doubt. What is there to question in a pilot's decision that saved so many people from dying? It's interesting that some call this narrative a miracle and then search for answers to this miracle in human actions. The way to resolve this dilemma is in fact to accept that this is not an ordinary act but the making of a superhero. We see in this accident the same patterns of Greek mythology, with superheroes fighting against the odds in pursuit of justice and social order.

But can professionals ever be considered superheroes? Those working in emergency response teams and lifesaving, and in the teaching, helping and caring professions, would have difficulty buying into this 'superhero' narrative, because it does not align with the ethos of their profession (Egan, 2017).

When an act of caring and helping is made to appear extraordinary or supernatural, it is symbolic of an action that stands outside the reach of the average professional. The profession is no longer about finding communion, humility and equality in a relationship, but of giving support to the unequal other. It is a narrative of the oppressor and the oppressed, when the hero's job is to save the oppressed (Freire, 1973). In the absence of the hero, the oppressed is doomed.

My contention is not so much with the hero myth as with the imbalance in this narrative. If the hero myth offers participation and imitation, it is a narrative that inspires change in society. But if all that we experience is amusement, entertainment and passive admiration for a Hollywood-style celebrity, the accident narrative has failed to serve its purpose (Postman, 2010; Armstrong, 2006).

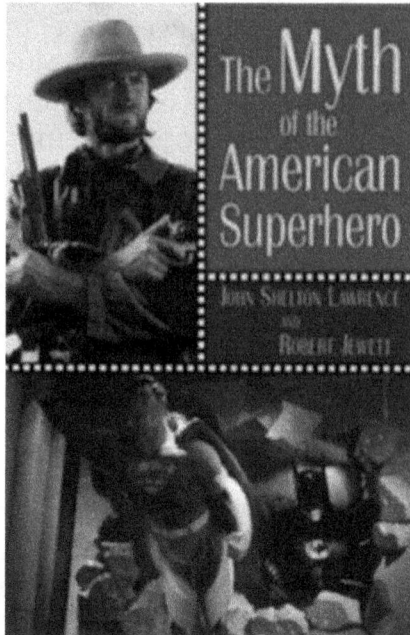

Figure 3.5: The Myth of the American Superhero by Jewett and Lawrence. The symbol of a superhero is the American hope for salvation and redemption in extraordinarily powerful people (sometimes by creating unreal characters) who can rise beyond our social and political institutions.[3]

## Success is all that matters

The image of the aircraft captain sitting proudly upright won him the title of 'old-fashioned global hero'. In that article, the captain made an honest confession about the outcome of his decision. This was an outcome which, Sully felt, could easily have gone worse than it did. The many environmental and social ingredients that came to work together in those ninety seconds were nothing short of a 'miracle': a competent co-pilot, the presence of EWS

---

[3]  https://en.wikipedia.org/wiki/The_Myth_of_the_American_Superhero

landing gear, the availability of lifejackets under the seats, the exceptional weather and the traffic conditions in the river on the day of the accident, and the quality of rescue and coordination services – all these factors are listed in the official report. But in a country seduced by the Hollywood culture, those details hardly mattered. What mattered was success in the face of the unexpected. The hero myth.

Consider also the choice of language in the formal investigation report, in the making of a hero myth:

> The *professionalism* of the flight crew members and their *excellent* Crew Resource Management during the accident sequence contributed to their ability to maintain control over the plane, configure it to the extent possible to control under the circumstance and fly an approach that increase the survivability of the impact [my italics]. (NTSB, 2009)

What could possibly explain an official government document making use of the normative expression 'professionalism'? What do we make of the term 'excellent'? Such is the power of this poetic language that it allows our own imagination to give meaning to these events. In the event that some people had not survived the accident, would the report still celebrate the heroism of the crew with the same vigour? What does this language tell us about the hidden unconscious in the narrative? The human need for superheroes is not limited to the calamities of pre-modern times or the superstitions of people in the developing world. Every time we are confronted by misfortune, what persist deep within us are miracles, magical whims and superpowers, in even the most advanced societies. Deep down, we are not as scientific and objective as we think we are.

## The anti-hero myth

At the other end of the accident investigation spectrum lies the anti-hero myth. This demonises a person or group in order to find some form of meaning in human suffering. In many workplace accidents, the labelling of someone as bad, incompetent, idiotic, ignorant, evil or a criminal happens long before the start of the investigation.

A large part of the *Costa Concordia* narrative was an attempt to undermine the captain's character. The media reports claimed that a 'blonde Moldovan dancer was reportedly dining with the captain shortly before the disaster'. In other words, the cause of the accident was attributed to the captain's character.

In the words of Professor Maurizio Catino, the entire investigation was framed as a 'moral, rather than a criminal, trial':

> ... the judicial investigation, first, and the trial thereafter, were both characterized by the numerous presence of third parties with respect to judicial procedures, and by mass media information that was extensive and, as will be seen, one-sided, at the same time. In this regard, the analysis of the media coverage of the Costa Concordia case, carried out with reference to the arc of time extending from the day of the accident (January 13, 2012) to the ruling of the Supreme Court of Cassation (May 12, 2017), brought some elements of partic-

ular interest to light. Out of a total of 292 articles analyzed, published by the two most widely circulated Italian national newspapers, *La Repubblica* and *Corriere della Sera*, about 90 percent (264 articles) focus exclusively on the individual factor and on the figure of the captain as the cause of the disaster. Only the remaining 10 percent (28 articles) investigate in some way the organizational factors and criticalities that played a role in the dynamics of the accident, as previous sections here have shown. Even before the evidence deriving from the inquiries was available, almost all of the articles featured an exclusive focus on the individual human factor, which were mainly based on the assumptions of the Prosecutor's Office, thus functioning as a kind of megaphone.

It is reasonable to believe that the extensive media coverage had an influence on the investigation and the trial, which saw the involvement not only of legitimately participating agents (judges, lawyers, defendants) but also of the general public. It was as if there existed not just the official panel of judges to answer to, but also a parallel panel of judges made up of this audience. This placed real public pressure on the magistrates, leading to the swift identification and sanctioning of the guilty, and raised many doubts with regard to the emotional poise of both investigators and magistrates. (Catino, 2023)

The official investigation report made the statement that the 'entire maritime field' was convinced that the captain's unconventional behaviour was the 'main cause of the shipwreck'. But without an opinion poll of the maritime community, how could such claims be made in an official report? The investigation report sought to persuade people by creating an anti-hero myth. Few would question the validity of such statements in an official accident report when the narrative seeks to address the fear and uncertainty that lies at the core of our existence.

Both the hero and anti-hero narratives are symbolic of a divisive world in every sphere of life, including politics, education, religion and climate change: 'If you do not agree with me, I will dehumanise you.' It is convenient to categorise people into groups – heroes and anti-heroes; conservatives and liberals; democrats and republicans; Black lives and White lives; good and bad; sacred and profane; and compliant and non-compliant. Once we decide who deserves to be labelled the hero and who the anti-hero, it is easier to both influence and understand the narrative of the accident.

## Are we learning from monomyths?

What is often missing in these oversimplified narratives is that people are more than just cardboard cutouts and superhumans. Each person, despite their actions and decisions, is worthy of dignity, respect and love. Schettino did not know that he was going to navigate the ship into a rock, or he would have been a kamikaze pilot on a path to self-destruction. Sully was hailed as a hero even when the successful landing on the river was perceived as a miracle. By calling something an accident, miracle, fatality, fate or misfortune, we unconsciously acknowledge the unknowable and the uncontrollable in an accident. But in attributing the cause, we bow to the heroes and witch-hunt the anti-heroes. What do we really learn from these narratives?

In a study of nearly 31,000 near misses and technical breakdowns, we observed a similar pattern of heroes and anti-heroes across reporting systems. Beyond simple stories of blame and fame, little desire to learn about the people themselves or to diagnose the situation was apparent. Such patterns can be observed as much in one-page safety alerts as in full-blown investigation narratives. Like any persuasive storyteller, the investigators weave together a complex combination of characters, events, time and space into a compelling narrative. Such recognisable patterns of heroes and anti-hero narratives, when told and retold several times, generate familiar rhythms that are intrinsically convincing to the reader's unconscious mind (Miller 1990; Postman 1987). But when familiarity and the comfort it is known to bring take precedence over doubt and critical thinking, then the cultural function of the narrative can only be to seek affirmation and reinforce the status quo whilst avoiding dissent and learning. Imagine the scale of manipulation when AI (artificial intelligence) starts writing investigation narratives ...

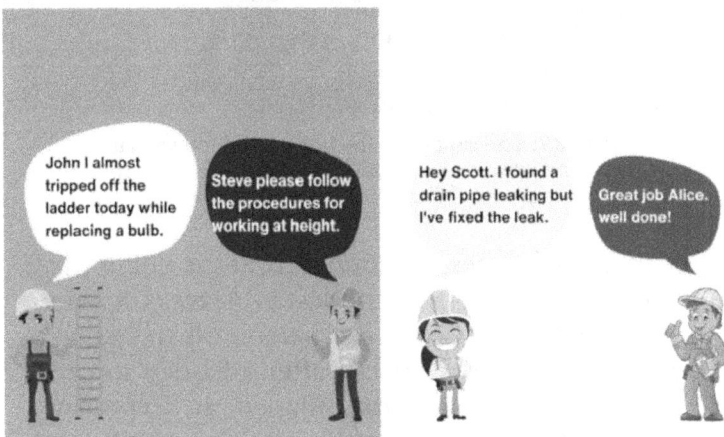

Figure 3.6: An everyday example of hero and anti-hero narratives in safety reporting systems.

You may be familiar with the occasional social media posts that can rev up to generate thousands of likes, shares and comments in little or no time. When the world is on the brink of collapse, an ordinary person confronted with death, destruction, chaos and uncertainty rises to the occasion to save us all. Here's one such example of a social media post from the maritime world.

Figure 3.7: The captain is the last person to evacuate the *Diamond Princess*. A symbol of salvation, superheroism, order out of chaos, and a happy ending.

In medieval times, #leadership meant being the first into a battle, and the last to leave. Captain Gennaro Arma was the last person off the gangway of 'Diamond Princess' after a 27-day forced quarantine in Yokohama, #Japan, in February 2020, after a #covid19 outbreak onboard. Of the 3,711 people on board, 712 became infected, and

14 died. Captain Arma vowed to stay aboard until everyone else had left safely.

Diamond Princess had departed from Yokohama on 20 January 2020 with 3,711 passengers on board. On 1 February, the first #covid case was confirmed (at a time when the world was just learning about a strange new illness called '#coronavirus'). By 4 February, the ship had 31 cases, and by 7 February it was at least 61. On 20 February, two passengers died. The World Health Organization declared that over half of the world's Covid-19 cases outside #China were onboard Diamond Princess.

Captain Arma had a reputation as a #master who cared deeply for his crew, his guests and his ship. His calm, dignified, eloquent professionalism in an unfolding crisis earned him a heroic reputation. His frequent, informative and caring updates made famous the phrase onboard 'Ladies and gentlemen, this is your captain speaking...' with a calm Italian accent. After 27 days of his passengers' sickness and deaths, Captain Arma was the last to disembark the ship.

Captain Arma started working for Princess Cruises in 1998 as a Cadet. He climbed the ranks, and achieved his command in 2018. After his return to #Italy, Captain Gennaro Arma and 15 Italian Officers from the Diamond Princess received a hero's welcome.

Captain Arma's leadership and professionalism in a world-changing crisis earned him several awards, including the highest honour of the Italian Republic – an Order of Merit – presented by the Italian Naval League. Bravo, Captain Arma.

(Livingstone, 2023)

As I read through this narrative, I noticed hundreds of likes and shares, and thousands of viewings. When a narrative appeals to so many people, one should question the underlying myth that touches humankind with such profoundness. What is the power of this narrative?

Observe the metaphors in the narrative. A battle to fight; an outbreak of a pandemic; death, destruction and calamity all around; a warrior as the leader; the last man to leave the ship; an unfolding crisis; the calm demeanour of a professional; and ultimately the hero who is awarded the highest honour by his country. In a narrative of just over 300 words, the term 'Captain Arma' is repeated eight times. It does not take a linguistics expert to locate the unconscious in that narrative. History will remember the successful evacuation of passengers from *Diamond Princess* as the heroic act of the captain.

But such a narrative leaves so many questions unanswered. What was the social context in this situation? Who else was on the team with the captain? What was their contribution towards the successful outcome? What were the choices and constraints faced by this team? What was the quality of support that the captain received from his employers? Who else was instrumental in helping the captain and questioning his decisions? What level of support was available to the ship en route to the destination? How many favourable outcomes were the result of the captain's decision making alone? Did the captain himself believe in this narrative? Does that matter? Once the myth gathers momentum, critical thinking and questioning take a back seat. The myth prevails.

Even if we were to believe in the superpowers of the captains and pilots, we might not always be so fortunate as to have superheroes around us in every situation. An organisation founded on the principles of mindfulness, critical thinking, respect and trust between ordinary people to carry out their duties is better equipped to manage the unexpected than an organisation that puts its trust in superheroes and miracles.

## What's the point?

A side issue in accident narratives that has always concerned me is the excessive use of reasoning, facts and empirical data – albeit done, understandably, to lay claim to the scientific nature of the enquiry. Copious resources are used, expert advice is sought and presented, and attention to detail is given to a series of small questions, to persuade the reader of the authenticity of the process. But as Tetlock (2017) rightly suggests, it seems to me at the time of writing that no one has dared ask: What is the big question we are attempting to answer? Or as Kay & King (2020) would call it, the 'diagnostic question': What is going *on* here? Without an umbrella narrative, all the probing and prompting, and the pedantic quest for micro-level details are of little use.

If we sift through the 175-page *Costa Concordia* accident report, there is no dearth of objective, indisputable data in it. However, despite accurate timelines, technical drawings, compliance certificates, black box recordings, factory acceptance tests, logbook events and official testimonies the reader is left wondering, 'What's the point'? In the end, the outcome of an objective enquiry has gone back to the same anti-hero myth and the denial of fallibility, which has existed since time immemorial, to give meaning to human suffering.

## Fate, God and the hero/anti-hero narrative

Is it possible to narrate the same accident differently?

When I told my mother, back home in India, about the US Airways 1549 accident, she responded '*Jako rakhein saiya maar sake na koye*,' which roughly translates as 'The one who is guarded by the divine cannot be harmed.' This is the myth of God.

Add a twist to this narrative. All the passengers on the aircraft were rescued by the emergency response service, but a small group of passengers met with an accident whilst being transported to their destination. That was their destiny. (In a way, the report acknowledges the role of fate in this accident by calling it a 'miracle').

Then we have three myths hidden in our narratives – Fate, God and the Hero. One could devote endless hours to sifting through the micro-details of the accidents to determine what went wrong and how. But ultimately, when faced with misfortune humans care less about the how and the what. What we really care about is *why* it happened. And more importantly, why *me* in this entire universe? Where should I go when a truck kills my young girl? In those moments, it is the myth within the narrative that gives us meaning in misfortune. 'Facts' and 'evidences' do not help as much.

# We need competing narratives

When we understand the hidden myths in our narratives, we realise that no single narrative has the potency to explain what is going on here. Don't get me wrong; I'm not suggesting that Captain Sullenberger did not deserve the credit for his presence of mind in averting the disaster, or that Captain Arma should not be praised for his wit or that Captain Francesco Schettino should be exonerated for what happened on the night of the accident. But to rely single-handedly on a narrative that slices and dices data and unambiguously connects selective events to produce a myth that is emotionally arousing and uncritically imbibed by the masses does not create opportunities for learning and reflection.

As in my own case at sea, realising that there is more than one way of narrating a human experience is liberating for those who, having become the subject of investigation, have ultimately become the object of humiliation and dehumanisation. For the investigators and the risk and safety industry, appreciating that there can be multiple and competing narratives is an invitation to learning and questioning the myths in science.

People involved in accidents are not heroes and anti-heroes. These are ordinary people, like most of us, who unexpectedly find themselves in out-of-the-ordinary conditions and undesirable situations. Is it necessary, for learning, to create narratives of superheroes and anti-heroes? Is it not easier to connect and learn with ordinary people by removing the boundaries that separate *us* from *them*?

# 4

# Learning Comes from Relationships

—⟨✦⟩—

This chapter illustrates the importance of relationships in learning. In investigating accidents, as a minimum we are expected to engage with people to understand their perspectives. Do we take the time and effort to understand and relate with people? Does it matter? Let us make an attempt to explore these questions.

---

- Why do relationships matter for sustained learning?
- Reflections on the importance of relationships from the Costa Concordia example.
- The common ways in which we relate with people.
- What kind of relationship is central to learning?

---

Figure 4.1: A general outline of the chapter.

73

## The power of relationships in learning

Through the years in her middle school, our daughter had developed a deep interest in science. She would come home each day, read her science books with interest, and finish her assignments without being reminded. Behind her passion for the subject was her teacher, Mrs Smith, who was equally enthusiastic and passionate. We discovered that she and Nakeeta had developed a special relationship. Even the occasional mention of this teacher would bring a big smile to Nakeeta's face.

One afternoon in the middle of her term, Nakeeta, along with three other pupils in her class, were removed from Mrs Smith's class and moved to a different section. The change came with a different science teacher. The school was experiencing an expansion with some new students joining in the middle of the term, and without consulting the parents or speaking with the children, the school made the change over the weekend. The principal's justification for the change was that 'it would be good for Nakeeta's resilience'. Our biggest concern was that Nakeeta would lose interest in the subject, but the principal maintained his 'resilience' narrative.

It is the second year since this change has happened. Our daughter has lost interest in the subject. What is most interesting is that when I looked up the principal on the internet, the first thing I saw was an interview from him in a news article. In the interview, the journalist asks the question, 'Why are you so passionate about mathematics?' His response: due to his relationship with his math teacher.

The essence of this story is realising that learning is nurtured through relationships. We cannot learn from another person if we cannot relate to them.

## From London to Sorrento

In every accident investigation, and during ship visits as an inspector, my focus has always been on relating with the crew members on ships. It was with this focus that I went to meet with 'Italy's most hated man', the captain of the *Costa Concordia*. It is often said that it takes time to build trust with another person, but in this case the reciprocation from the captain was felt quickly. What could be the reason? I can only offer reflections from my own experiences.

Back on 17 January 2017 Oessur Hilduberg, from the Danish Maritime Accident Investigation Board, and I had met up in London to plan workshops on accident investigations. During our meeting, the topic of the *Costa Concordia* came up. Oessur had dedicated a master's thesis to studying this accident. We both felt that a lot more could be brought to the surface if we could get the captain to share his version of the story. As we concluded the day, I committed to setting up a meeting with Captain Francesco Schettino.

While searching for him on the internet I found a familiar name, Arne Sagen from Skagerrak Foundation in Norway, who had been supporting the captain while he was under house arrest in his hometown, Meta, near Sorrento in south-western Italy. I contacted Arne, who passed me Francesco's details, and within the week we had set up a phone call.

Francesco agreed to meet me on Skype at 10.30 am on 23 January, but he did not turn up. At about 12.30 pm I received a phone call from him. He repeatedly apologised for missing my Skype call because he had overslept. (Later, I learned that his sleeping patterns had become disrupted after the accident.) It was only our first phone call, but at the end of the call we had already decided to meet in his hometown. He even offered to find us (Oessur and me) a place to stay close to his home. During the call, we laughed and joked, and he even cried when recalling one of his Indian shipmates who had not survived the accident. At the time of the phone call, my daughter was just over one year old. Francesco could hear her crying in the background. He ended the meeting by saying, 'I can hear a baby – do you have a child? I am a captain, and I am always alert.'

After two further phone calls, Oessur and I planned our trip to Meta, where we spent four days with Francesco. I must admit that even with a master's degree and a PhD, this was the first time I truly experienced the excitement of learning. Oessur and I sat for hours like vacuum cleaners sucking up every word of what Francesco had to say. From our first meeting at the airport when he came to meet us, Francesco was so eager to share his experiences. At one point, sitting in the car on the way from the airport, I became worried that he was spilling the beans so soon. I told him to wait until we were ready to 'capture' those moments on camera. When I look back, I often think how hurtful that comment would have been to someone so eager to share his experiences with us.

It was the first day of our interview. Francesco walked into the room dressed like a captain in a navy blue uniform sweater, so eager to share his story with us. We started off by asking about his background and his motivation to become a seafarer. As he spoke, we could feel the passion as his eyes locked with ours, then occasionally looking outside the window and drawing on his detailed recollections.

At the beginning he was careful not to deviate from facts and factual data. When his words drifted into feelings, opinions and views he would say, 'I need to check this,' or 'I'm not certain about that.' All this is understandable because of the nature of the investigations and interrogations he had been through. But slowly, as he felt more at ease, the conversation started to flow. In an interview that lasted for almost 12 hours (on record), Oessur and I would have spoken for no more than about 15 minutes. It was a journey of discovery and learning in a way that I had never experienced before. We listened and Francesco spoke, and when I try to make sense of it, it is naïve to think that there was some technique, a skill or a method to my listening. In fact, it was much more than just listening; it was the meeting of minds.

## Learning in the *i-thou*

We hear about deep listening and active listening techniques, and learn about personal development programmes. But listening is more than just a technique or a method (Ellul, 1964). The art of framing the questions and being present in the moment does indeed help, but listening requires the development of a relationship with the other person. This is where the knowledge of ethics, morality, philosophy, anthropology and philosophy come in helpful. **Listening is a disposition and an orientation to the other.**

Martin Buber (1937) speaks about two kinds of relationships: *i-it* and *i-thou*. In most relationships, Buber says, our participation is characteristic of i-it; we have a tendency to relate with others as if they are objects or a means to our end. If we don't see the benefit in it, if it hinders our goals and targets, if it does not serve our purpose, then it must cease to exist for us. I know of people who don't turn to others if they don't see the benefit. I also know of people who constantly search for the most influential person in the room. When they have found one they abruptly end the discussion they're in and walk away. To Buber, that is how most of us relate to the world.

| Relationship | How we see the other | Purpose of meeting |
|---|---|---|
| I-it | A means to an end | Goal, agenda; benefit; control; problem solving |
| I-thou | A being; a whole person | Discovery; learning about ourselves and the other |

Figure 4.2: A comparison between meetings (i-thou and i-it).

But there is another way of relating to the world, which Buber calls i-thou. This is when we see the other person as an equal other. We do not judge; we learn to suspend our agenda, surrender control, pay attention to them, affirm and confirm their being in meeting them. The famous physicist David Bohm in his book, *On Dialogue*, called it 'participatory consciousness', meaning a meeting of a whole person with another whole person (Bohm, 1996). **Buber stated profoundly that 'all life is meeting'.**

If our aim is to learn and discover from the other, particularly in relation to an accident, it is essential that we learn to practise participatory consciousness. Regardless of the errors made and crimes committed, we need to learn to see the other person as more than just what they *did do* or *did not do* on the day of the accident. As they are speaking, not to be pulled back into judgement but instead to experience a sense of curiosity to draw even more from their being. As they are speaking, not to be pulled back with dissonance by being revealed in our own ignorance, but to experience the joy of discovering the wisdom in our wholeness. As they are speaking, not to rush to interfere because it counters our authority, but to suspend our own agenda and listen with patience to enrich our expertise. One person at a time, one conversation at a time. That is how we learn. I did not travel to Francesco's hometown to find out why he ended up beaching the ship. In fact, I deliberately kept away from the official investigation report prior to our meeting. I wanted to hear with an open mind, and at first hand, from Francesco, about his experience of the accident.

A note on the hyphen in i-it and i-thou: the hyphen symbolises the umbilical cord in our relationship, i.e. in our connection with the other. For Buber, all learning is in this hyphen.

# 5

# The Role of the Embodied Mind in Learning

In this chapter, I will propose a model to illustrate how human beings learn, unlearn and make decisions. This model is based on the concept of the embodied mind. I will explain what the embodied mind means and how the model works in practice, using practical examples and stories. I am often asked the question: 'Do you have a checklist, a tool or a template for interviewing people in an accident investigation?' Towards the end of the chapter, we will discuss why we need a method and a philosophy, more than techniques and templates, to engage with people if we want to learn from them.

> - Disembodied Mind: the prevalent view about how human beings learn and make decisions.
> - Embodied Mind: a transdisciplinary view on how human beings learn, unlearn and make decisions.

- One Brain Three Minds: a proposed model of embodied mind.
- The application of One Brain Three Minds in learning and decision making.
- The application of One Brain Three Minds to obtain improved learning outcomes from accident investigations.

Figure 5.1: A general outline of the chapter.

Before we begin a discussion on the importance of the embodied mind for learning, it is worth beginning with what embodiment is not. For this, let us turn to one of the greatest educationalists of our times, Sir Ken Robinson, and hear his views.

If you were to visit education, as an alien, and say 'What's it for, public education?' I think you'd have to conclude, if you look at the output, who really succeeds by this, who does everything that they should, who gets all the brownie points, who are the winners — I think you'd have to conclude the whole purpose of public education throughout the world is to produce university professors. Isn't it? They're the people who come out the top. And I used to be one, so there.

And I like university professors, but you know, we shouldn't hold them up as the high-water mark of all human achievement. They're just a form of life, another form of life. But they're rather curious, and I say this out of affection for them. There's something curious about professors in my experience — not all of them, but typically, they live in their heads. They live up there, and slightly to one side. They're disembodied, you know, in a kind of literal way. They look upon their body as a form of transport for their heads.

(Robinson, 2006)

In that witty TED talk, Robinson (2006) provided a thought-provoking insight into the dominant model of education and schooling across the world. What Robinson referred to as people who 'live up in their heads' is a typical image of disembodiment. The idea of a disembodied mind was originally based on the work of René Descartes (sometimes referred to as the father of modern philosophy). Descartes' thesis, otherwise referred to as Cartesian dualism, viewed the human brain as separate from the body (hence, disembodied), even superior to the body, and the brain as equipped with the power to control the body. For Descartes, the body is a servant to the brain; the body follows the commands issued by the brain. All life is lived in the brain, or rather life becomes brain-centric.

The Cartesian philosophy sees the purpose of education and schooling as a matter of gathering intellect and strengthening our capacity to reason. Drawing upon Descartes' ideas, many scholars and business gurus have argued in favour of thinking, reasoning and evidence-based decision making as the most evolved form of human intelligence. 'Everything we *do* depends for its quality on the *thinking* we do first', says Nancy Kline, the author of the book *Time to Think* (Kline, 1999). If we can think well, we will do well in our lives.

According to Descartes, the existence of a person is fundamentally down to their ability to think; when you take away the thinking there is nothing left. There is a joke about Descartes having a beer in a bar: the bartender asks, 'You want another?' Descartes responds, 'I think not,' and disappears.

Figure 5.2: A Cartesian view of the brain–body relationship; the purpose of the body is to transport the brain. Notice, also the prevalent brain-centric worldview of how we greet the other person without involving our emotions.

### A visit to my daughter's school

Some years ago I ran a social experiment at my daughter's school. I was invited to share my views on learning with a class of about two dozen nine-year-old pupils. I started by asking them to give me five words or phrases that came to mind when they thought of learning. In the image are the main themes that emerged from this exercise.

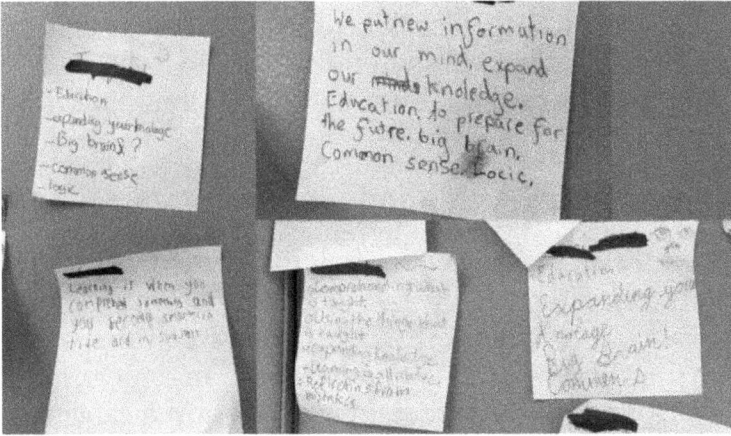

Figure 5.3: Post-it notes illustrating the metaphors of learning
(education, logic, expanding knowledge, Big Brain, common sense,
knowledge, putting information in mind, expanding knowledge,
education to prepare for the future, comprehending what is taught,
using the things that are taught, reflecting on mistakes).

My social experiment at the school revealed that nearly five centuries on, Descartes is still alive in our world. What came as a surprise to me was that such a brain-centric view on learning begins so early in life and, for most of us, it continues through our lifetime. In fact, when we talk about a corporate *body*, where a *head office* designs the strategy and a site office executes the operation, we see the same head–body relationship at work. Karl Marx referred to this as the separation of conception and execution which lies at the heart of modern capitalism. Thinking and doing can be separated in space and time. In fact, the discourse of the 'knowledge economy', i.e. how work is organised between high-skilled and low-skilled workers, is based on the same Cartesian view; only the privileged few are allowed to think, while the rest are kept busy doing the mundane stuff.

In contrast to the prevalent Cartesian, brain-centric view on learning, we shall now move to a discussion of learning through the lenses of the embodied Mind.

## Know-how is embodied

Many of those in skilled professions, such as ship captains, pilots, lawyers, surgeons, plumbers and nurses, are recognised (if not always compensated) for their know-how. When we meet an experienced professional, we can feel their know-how. Francesco, the son of a fisherman and the grandson of a marine engineer, was a seasoned seafarer who had spent all his working life at sea. I felt his know-how in the first few minutes of our meeting, as he was introducing himself.

> I started to be fascinated by the sea because as you can see, I live a few metres ... from the sea. My family there is a huge legacy regarding seamanship. My uncles, they were captains ... Since I was young I was helping my uncles with fishing in a small rowing boat that we used to fish. I remember some of his teaching when he used to tell me, 'You just keep the ship the position of the boat by keeping the position of the oars.' And I would ask, 'How can I do that?' 'Just see the reference on the shore by matching the church and the hotel. If you move from this position, we lose our fishing.' That was very fascinating for me to approach the sea. With this information it was very valuable with passing of the years when I became captain. Whenever the ship was docking or undocking, I had the reference, but still my eye was trained to watch the objects ashore. Since when I was young, I realised that was the beginning of my education at sea.

In a book co-authored with the Italian journalist Vittoriana Abate, titled *Le Verità Sommerse* (*The Truth Submerged*), Schettino wrote:

> My mother told me that as a girl with the canoe, very small boat, long and narrow, flat bottom, where she sits rowing the machine, it was usual to reach the adjoining port of Marina di Cassano, to take the water from the spring and take it home. Sometimes I told my officers that to learn how to maneuver a ship it is important to understand how a canoe moves on the water and how it reacts under the influence of wind and waves.'

(translated from Italian to English) (Abate, 2015).

Figure 5.4: Francesco Schettino and his brother Salvatore and mother Rosa. Source: Abate (2015)

Few seafarers during their career at sea move beyond their trade sector and specialisation. Schettino, on the other hand, had worked on oil tankers and ferries, and even on high-speed gas turbines. He had worked in shipyards and had assisted with building new ships. His work history on passenger ships included being a staff captain on passenger vessels for six years, and captain for five years. The know-how that this captain had accumulated as a seasoned mariner is exemplary.

Michael Polanyi (1966) once said that people know more than they can ever tell. This is true of all people, but all the more so when it comes to skilled professionals. As professionals, our know-how (that is, intuitive, tacit and embodied knowing) exceeds our ability to hold knowledge in our conscious minds through memory and recall. As we mature, through education, training and life experiences, our know-how becomes an integral part of our skills, habits, heuristics, gestures, routines, rituals, metaphors, myths and beliefs. In other words, know-how is embodied. This understanding is further supported in pioneering research in cognition and neurosciences (Damasio, 2003) (Damasio, 2000) (Damasio, 2021) (Lakoff, 1998) (Johnson, 2017) (Claxton, 2016). Understanding the source of this know-how is an appropriate place to begin a discussion on the pivotal role of the embodied Mind in how we learn and unlearn, and make decisions.

## The embodied Mind

The term 'embodied Mind' means that our whole body has its own Mind (hence the term 'embodied Mind' and the capitalisation). In other words, decision making is not restricted to the brain; our entire body participates in the process.

Think of the butterflies in our stomach when we get upset, the increased pace and shallowness of our breath when we are overwhelmed, the sweat in our palms when we get nervous, the goosebumps on our arms when we are excited, the dilation of our pupils when we get angry, our facial and muscle contractions when we feel stressed, the tears in our eyes when we are full of sadness, raised brows in shock and surprise – each part of our organism has its own Mind, independent of our overall consciousness. Thinking about how the mind functions based on topical studies in cognition and neurosciences brings a fundamental shift in our perception of how the Mind functions, and how we as humans learn, unlearn and make decisions (Claxton, 2016) (Damasio, 2021) (Johnson, 2017). As Claxton (1998) states so eloquently, the brain is not the control tower of our body; instead, the brain works like a coordination warehouse. The mind is embodied. In Social Psychology of Risk (SPoR) we don't speak of having a mind, we *are* our Mind!

Figure 5.5: 'The brain does not issue commands, it hosts conversations', Guy Claxton. (Graphic illustration by Dr Robert Long)

In SPoR we use One Brain Three Minds* (1B3M) as a foundational model to illustrate the embodied nature of the human Mind. Together, the three modes of being (head, heart and gut) represent the whole person – instead of the prevailing brain-centric view of humans.

Novice Mind 1          Beginner Mind 2          Expert Mind 3

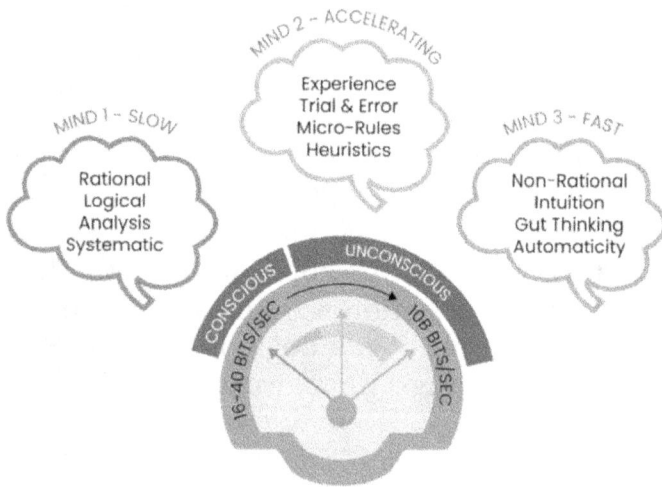

MIND 2 – ACCELERATING

Experience
Trial & Error
Micro-Rules
Heuristics

MIND 1 – SLOW

Rational
Logical
Analysis
Systematic

MIND 3 – FAST

Non-Rational
Intuition
Gut Thinking
Automaticity

CONSCIOUS    UNCONSCIOUS

16-40 BITS/SEC          10B BITS/SEC

Figure 5.6: One Brain Three Minds* (a model of the embodied Mind based on Social Psychology of Risk).

As with all models and semiotics, these diagrams are subjective and will be interpreted in different ways. They also have limitations and need to be understood with regard to their purpose. The use of a speedometer metaphor is only helpful to communicate the speed of human decision making. It is also important to understand the head, heart and gut as three centres of 'being'. All of these models need to be understood collectively.

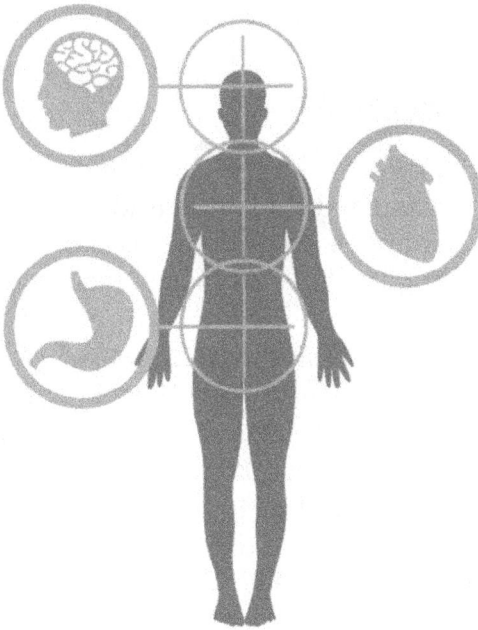

Whole Person Whole Mind

Figure 5.7: The Embodied Person.*

# One Brain Three Minds* (1B3M)

## Mind 1 (Brain Mind)

In Mind 1, we are in rational, logical and analytical mode. Think of Mind 1 as a state when we learn to follow the rules of the trade and slowly start to earn confidence and respect within our profession. When we follow a checklist, instructions or a procedure in order to carry out a particular task, we usually do it slowly and methodically. Decisions made in this mode are neither fast nor efficient. Even simple hand–eye coordination when using a tool can take months or years of repetitive practice.

## Mind 2 (Heart Mind)

Mind 2 is about thinking heuristically i.e. thinking that relies on learned shortcuts, and practised habits. This Mind state is in the process of developing into automaticity. This kind of decision making is essential for humans, in order for us to be fast and efficient. This is decision making based on patterns, trial and error, and habits that have become infused (embodied) into our thinking through experience, and it is triggered by perception, experience or memory. Much of this type of decision making does not involve any rational choice or analytical thinking. It is quick and efficient.

## Mind 3 (Gut Mind)

Mind 3 is about total automaticity, what Damasio (2000) states as non-conscious decision making. In this state, one is unaware of the process of deciding, thinking or rational processing. This is often referred to as gut thinking or intuition, and it is commonly understood as 'being on autopilot'.

# How we learn

Consider learning to drive, or an apprentice's experience when entering a trade. In the first few days, weeks and months, learning takes place in Mind 1. The **novice** driver/apprentice is slow, reading the rules, systematically following the process, and analysing their movements in carrying out the demands of the role.

Gradually, we move to a level of autonomy, automaticity and confidence in which frequent consultation of the rules and processes (both formal and informal) is no longer required. The novice is now a **beginner**, slowly settling into their role, learning the tricks of the trade, finding their own balance, comfort level and risk tolerance through trial and error, watching others and learning from the social surroundings – and only occasionally, when encountering novel situations, returning to rules, instructions and peer consultation. This is Mind 2.

Finally, we come to Mind 3. This is the super-efficient, superfast mind. As Polanyi suggests, at this stage the person feels and knows more than they can tell, because years of accumulated skills have become embodied within that person. Both repetitive work and novel situations can be comfortably and efficiently managed with little effort in this mode of being. In fact, in most skilled professions, becoming efficient in Mind 3 is a requirement to be considered an **expert** in the trade. (NB Most experts are not good teachers, because in needing to revisit Minds 1 and 2 effectively, they need to take specialised training to develop the relevant skills.)

## Why the speedometer?

The speedometer in the 1B3M model represents the speed at which we process information in the three different modes of being (Minds 1, 2 and 3). Mind 3 processes information at a speed of up to 10 billion bits per second, while Mind 1 can only work at a speed of around 16–40 bits per second.

In practical terms, this means that the non-rational Mind has already made a decision a few milliseconds before the rational Mind gets involved. In other words, our reflexes, impulses and gut reactions are the norm, not an exception, in the decision-making process – a trait that is understood and exploited by the sales and marketing world in persuading their target consumers to make instant decisions.

We think we have control over our decisions when in fact we are mostly governed by the automatic, non-rational Mind 3. American neuroscientist Benjamin Libet rightly described 'free will' as the illusion of humankind (Libet, Gleason, & Wright, 1983). Once we are conditioned to flow with our instincts and gut reactions in Mind 3, we are operating in our non-conscious Mind (Csikszentmihalyi, 2002).

## How we learn and unlearn

### A personal story of learning, unlearning and human fallibility

One of the challenges when I first took driving lessons in the UK was to unlearn the habits I had acquired in India. Those habits were neither good nor bad; they were simply not suited to the UK driving context. My first tutor, who I felt was racist, kept reminding me to let go of my 'Indian habits'. Instead of the joy of learning, I experienced a sense of shame, guilt and fear during my lessons. I failed my driving test three times. When I discussed this issue with my wife, she was quick to suggest that I change instructor. My new instructor, Rob Cooling – what a surname! – was a joy. He was patient and non-judgemental, and what I would now call 'open to fallibility'. I left him a feedback note, and at the time of writing, nearly 12 years after I passed my test, it is still on his website:

'I did more than 30 hours with another driving school in Nottingham and appeared for three tests only to realise that it was not working for me. Went to the internet and read some reviews about Apple driving school. Rob turned to be exactly the same as most people commented – very friendly, patient and positive. Rob's unique style is that he gives you a lot of freedom to make mistakes and learn from them. He makes sure that you know your stuff well before you are ready for the big day. Just two lessons with Rob, and I passed with four minors. I'd HIGHLY recommend Rob to anyone and everyone.'

Nippin Anand, Wollaton, Nottingham[4]

As I look back at my note on Rob's website, I am overwhelmed by emotions. This man had the wisdom that I find lacking in many professional coaches, seasoned mentors, teachers and leaders. He worked with me, clearly felt my frustrations, and embraced my fallible being, which gave me back the confidence I had lost with my previous instructor. All this was helpful not only in passing the test but in thriving when driving in a new environment. Despite spending so many hours with my previous instructor, I could not

---

[4] https://www.appledriving.co.uk/reviews-nottingham.html

come out of Mind 1 – slow, systematic, calculative, combined with the fear of making mistakes and being reminded of my national habits. But in less than two hours Rob encouraged me to experience the joy of driving as a whole person i.e. connecting Minds 1, 2 and 3. That is the essence of learning and flourishing, when we find someone who embraces fallibility and our whole being.

Rob also did something more subtle and powerful. By accepting me as a whole person, he helped me to bring to the surface the questions, hesitations, biases and assumptions that I had previously kept to myself for fear of being judged.

This lived example illustrates how we acquire learning and how we unlearn as a whole person when experience, habits, heuristics and rituals are no longer helpful for our survival and wellness. What is more, both learning and unlearning are achieved in the meeting of i-thou (in relationships).

This holistic approach to how human beings learn and make decisions is well documented in a range of studies in theology, mythology, analytical psychology, neuroscience, neurobiology, biology and evolutionary sciences (Buber, 1937) (Claxton, 2016) (Damasio, 2000) (Johnson, 2017).

NB: The embodied mind and 1B3M model should not be confused with Kahneman's theory of Systems 1 and 2, the fast and slow modes of thinking. What Kahneman proposes is a simple and dualist metaphor to illustrate how human beings make decisions, based on the principles of behavioural economics and hedonic psychology. A metaphor is not a replacement for a conceptual model of how the human mind functions. It does not attempt to understand the mind–body connection or the fact that the human body is itself a mind. Moreover, Kahneman's model excludes the idea of an intermediate, developing aspect of learning (Mind 2) that connects the novice (Mind 1) and the expert (Mind 3).

## Wrong questions and wrong learning outcomes

In this section, we will discover why our current approach to investigating accidents – even the way we ask questions to those involved in accidents – is not helpful when we fail to appreciate the embodied nature of decision making. For this, I will use some common examples of questions raised during investigations and the underlying assumptions in those questions.

1. **Why did you (*or* did you not) do this?**

In the investigation process, this is a common question. It begins with the assumptions that knowing precedes doing (in other words, that decisions are made in conscious awareness). But that is rarely the case in decision making. As research shows, if more than 95 per cent of our decisions originate from Minds 2 and 3, it is natural for people to be unaware of most of their decisions (Damasio, 2000).

Now consider the case of experts. The essence of all expertise is non-rational, intuitive decision making (in Mind 3); that is what experts are valued for. Why else should we hire experts and pay them so well, if it were not for their efficient decision making?

So it is unsurprising that during an accident investigation the experts involved struggle to articulate their decision making. And an investigator, unaware of the non-conscious nature of the embodied Mind, may become frustrated, and take that struggle as a cue of incompetence or deceit on the part of the expert.

Imagine if ...

Figure 5.8.

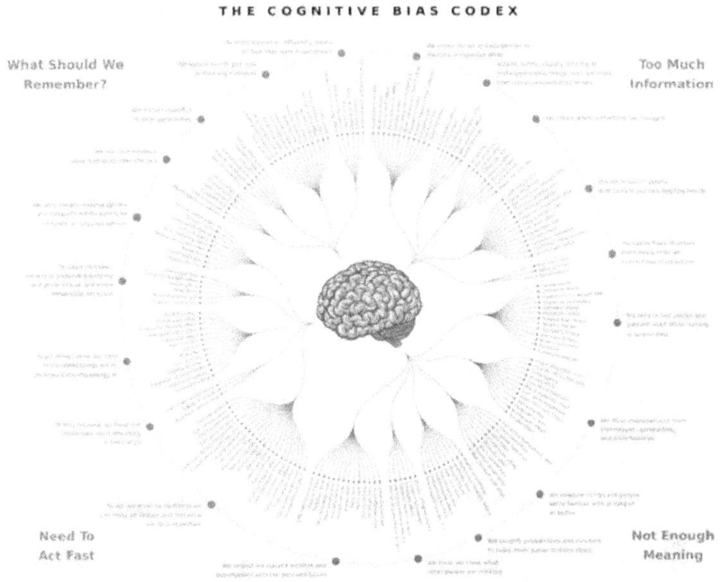

Figure 5.9: Cognitive Bias Codex. (Source: Wikipedia)

Cognitive Bias Codex: A list of human biases coded into categories. Biases, which are embodied in human beings, allow us to operate in Minds 2 and 3.

## 2. Answer my question, dammit!

When we are preoccupied with checklists, templates and questionnaires, and are determined to find out what went wrong during the investigation, it is easy to become frustrated when we don't get the desired response.

There are numerous examples of accident investi-gations and audits when people struggle to explain in their own words why they decided to act against a formal rule. The investigator would normally perceive this struggle as an indication of incompetence. In addition, it is a source of frustration to an investigator when people provide information not requested as part of the investigation process. **Such a view of learning gives little weight to intuitive, tacit, non-conscious, non-rational, and spontaneous knowledge, and the contextual nature of problems faced by the seafarer, because it does not fit with the investigator's agenda, check sheet, expectations and worldview.**

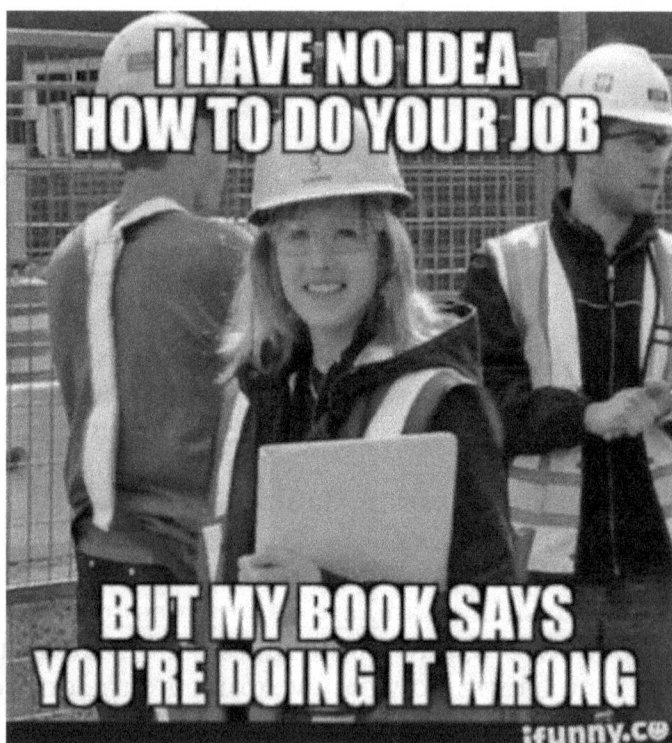

Figure 5.10: An inspector occupied with predefined rules may not be open to listening.

Through experience, seafarers and frontline staff regularly subjected to investigations and audits work out innovative ways of responding to investigations and audit questions. Success is not a matter of discovery and learning, but of working out how best to fly through the investigations and audits by managing the expectations of auditors and investigators. The success of learning is all about managing the measurable targets (zero findings and non-conformances).

Here, a story of a shipboard audit comes to mind. During an audit, a seafarer once told me how he negotiates his way through the expectations of the auditors:

> **Boxing and dancing**
>
> Every time they [inspectors] come on board, they have to find something. So, what I do, I'll put some paint cans in the engine room or remove a fire extinguisher from its location. Makes them happy when they find something, very happy. You should see their face. The moment they find something, they stop looking, so that makes my life easy.
>
> I call it boxing and dancing. The inspector wants to give a hard time to the seafarer in an audit, so the latter has found a way to keep the inspector entertained.

## 3. Why did you press that knob?

During a shipboard visit, I watched a seafarer being interrogated by an investigator. The investigator was puzzled by the seafarer as he was reviewing his actions on the electronic charts in playback mode. At one point, the investigator asked him, 'But why did you press that knob?'

During the coffee break, as I was chatting with the seafarer, he told me, 'If I'd told the inspector that I didn't think before I pressed that knob that'd be my last day at sea.'

This example illustrates that beyond a certain limit, people have difficulty answering questions emerging from deductive enquiry' methods, such as the 5 Whys. It is like trying to understand the intuitive and instinctive mind by using deductive reasoning. As though I'm given a bicycle repair kit to fix my car.

If you are an auditor or an investigator, you will have noticed how, when you ask a confrontational question, people make up a story and give you gibberish. And then, although you know it's an awkward explanation, you accept it. That explanation is more than often the rationalisation of an unconscious decision in hindsight. The explanation is neither fake nor untrue; it is a natural response to save face (and a job) in a rationalist interrogation. (See, for example, Sigmund Freud's theory on defence mechanisms.)

### 4. Why did you not follow the process?

This is where the Just Culture procedure – a protocol to establish guilt or innocence (and everything in between) and to evaluate an operator's behaviour based on pre-existing rules and independent peer reviews – does not seem to work in practice. How could a superswift intuitive decision made in Mind 3 make sense when evaluated in a slow, systematic and analytical mode?

**Just Culture in practice**

During the pandemic, I came across an incident
when a bosun on board a ship was put through the
Just Culture procedure. The accusation against
the bosun was that he had thrown a hammer with
full force at a bulkhead in his workshop. Mind
you, the bosun did not attack anyone, he was
only venting his frustration. But instead of sitting
down with this person to understand why he felt
such frustration, the company safety department
went straight into disciplining him.

# Methods and tools to engage with the embodied Mind

Francesco Schettino was an expert in his trade, and
much of his know-how and learned heuristics, like
that of all experts, had become embodied in his
habits, rituals, heuristics and language. If we want to
learn how and why certain decisions were made on
the night of the accident, we must learn to appreciate
the embodied nature of the human Mind.

### How to engage with the embodied mind

I was at the National Health Services conference in
Aberdeen, and I played a scenario where during a
hygiene inspection, a supervisor found out that a
colleague was not following the 'bare below elbow'
uniform policy.

Typically, when most people in a position of
authority spot someone not following a policy,

they go into telling and reminding mode: 'Why are you not following the process?' 'Can I remind you that we have a uniform policy?'

I invited everyone to reframe their question and ask instead: 'What do you feel (or think) might be the risk of not following this uniform policy?'

When a certain behaviour becomes normalised, it is primarily because it has made its way into the body (Minds 2 and 3). In those instances, telling and reminding only leads to self-defence and preservation. Nothing changes. But if we engage with the feelings, emotions, habits, gestures, heuristics, myths and beliefs in Minds 2 and 3 (see Figure 5.11), we create opportunities for reflection and change. Once people realise what has become embodied within them, they may also take ownership for change, because this realisation will have come from them and not from outside. That is the power of embodied Mind, which is often overlooked in safety investigations.

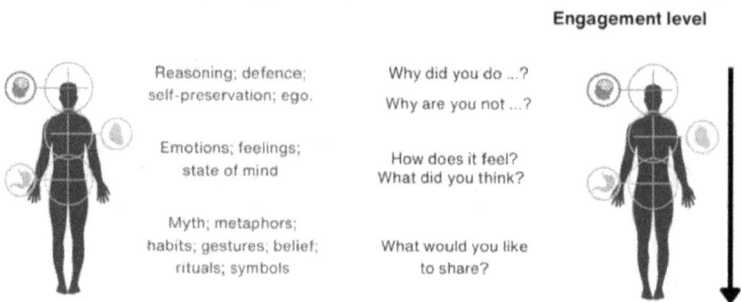

Figure 5.11: Engaging with the embodied Mind.

Simply starting off with a conversation when we have learned to surrender control, suspend our agenda, relate to the other person and ask open-ended questions such as 'Where would you like to begin?' or 'What would you like to share?' creates far more effective learning than predetermined checklists. To undertake such an approach, however, requires a new and different disposition from what is normally expected of auditors, inspectors and investigators. After all, who are we, and what do we know about the history, timelines, personal issues, social context and political influences that may have impacted the narrative of this person? The importance of asking open-ended questions, surfacing the embodied myths, metaphors, rituals, habits, gestures and heuristics, and helping the other person learn and unlearn, is central to the iCue listening and mapping of conversations (discussed in Chapter 16).

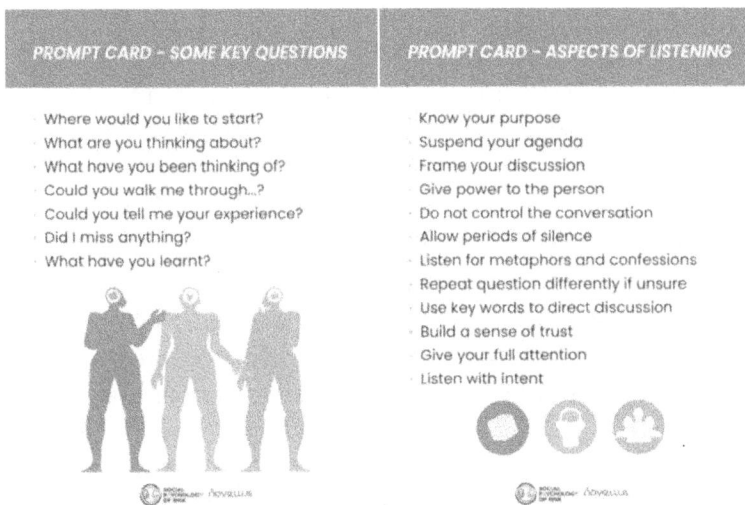

Figure 5.12: The iCue method* prompt cards used to facilitate and map conversations.

## The ethics to engage with the embodied Mind

'How can I suspend my agenda?' 'Will those prompt cards work for me?' I'm often asked such questions. To this I would say, listening is not a technique that can be adopted by following the instructions on a card. Yes, methods and tools can be helpful, but most important to bear in mind is the ethic of embodied mind. How do we relate with another person? (Recall our discussion on i-it and i-thou in Chapter 4). For this, we must learn to understand the philosophy of embodied mind and why it is so important to acknowledge and attend to the full person if we wish to learn from them. The One Brain Three Minds model is a representation of the whole person with a head, heart and gut.

Here's a story that should help to understand the ethics of engaging with the whole person. This story is about a ship I visited in Aberdeen to interview the seafarers, with the view to understanding the gap between their documented procedures and how they carried out their jobs. Such an exercise is often termed as 'learning from what goes well', meaning how can we proactively learn from everyday work to manage the risks, instead of focusing on accidents alone.

In January 2021, I visited a ship all excited to put my knowledge about 'learning from what goes well' into practice. I thought I knew perfectly well what I needed to make it work. Instead of focusing on accidents, I would focus on everyday work, pay careful attention to the context, observe the gap between documented manuals and 'real' work, and encourage people to talk about what really works. Simple.

Like an overzealous inspector, I approached an able seaman and asked, 'Raymond, can you talk me through how you lower the lifeboat from the start to the end?' After a long and uncomfortable silence, Raymond replied, 'I'll tell you everything about the lifeboat, but I want to share something else first if it's okay, sir. The company has introduced a new tax on our earnings. As seafarers, we never had to pay taxes on our income before and it's not small money. It's almost 30% of our earnings, and it puts us in a very difficult situation.' Raymond continued for a few minutes while other crew members joined us in the conversation. By now I was starting to get irritated. This was not really my question, I said to myself. I was there to learn from what goes well.

But I started listening to Raymond and then something happened that took me by surprise. Nearly 35 minutes into his moaning, Raymond looked into my eyes and said, 'I know you're here as a visitor. You can do nothing about our situation, but you care to listen. Thanks for listening; nobody from the office listens to us.'

In the weeks to follow this ship visit, I meditated on this experience. My first realisation was to become aware of the word 'worker'. What a loaded expression! When people come to work they are more than just workers. They are spouses, fathers, mothers, sons and siblings preoccupied with all sorts of challenges in their lives. How can people detach from their problems when they start work? I made a conscious attempt to start using the work 'person' or 'people' so that I could engage with the whole person.

Raymond's story also taught me that devoid of kindness and reciprocity, any initiative to 'gather data' is the continued legacy of the Industrial Revolution. Some would refer to it as Taylorism – viewing the worker as a mechanistic component in the production line. With modern technologies, Taylorism is repackaged and sold as digital Taylorism – more precise, scalable and efficient than its predecessor. It does not matter if we want to learn from what goes well or otherwise. **Without an ethic and a philosophy to engage with the embodied mind (of the whole person) there is no connection and therefore no learning.**

# 6

# Doubt is Essential for Learning

———————— ✦❦❧ ————————

We have discussed at length the human need for comfort and certainty in the rituals and narratives of accident investigations (Chapters 2 and 3). In this chapter, we will discover why creating space for doubt is essential for learning. Before I do that, I would like to share with you how I arrived at this position during the course of writing this book. Next, we will discuss why doubt is essential for learning. The chapter will end with some practical examples and techniques to create a culture of doubt.

> - How have I moved away from certainty and comfort towards doubt and reflection in my own learning journey?
> - Why I became inclined towards creating space for doubt in learning?
> - How can we promote a culture of doubt and critical thinking in our workplaces?

Figure 6.1: A general outline of the chapter.

In the days following the visit to the captain's hometown, I was inspired by the work of Woods and Cook (1998), about the 'first and second stories' of accidents. For a long time, I wanted to create a second story of the *Costa Concordia* accident, from the captain's perspective. So, what is a 'second story'?

## The first story

The orthodox view of an accident is often what Woods and Cook (1998) describe as the first story. That first story appears soon after the event. It is highly personalised, and is focused on the workers at the sharp end. It is low in complexity and context. It is a narrative of compliance and culpability. The first story is newsworthy and easy to understand – and in hindsight everything appears preventable and fixable.

To me, the official investigation and the public narrative of the *Costa Concordia* felt much like a first story. Within 48 hours of the accident, the CEO of Costa Crociere S.p.A. released a press statement:

> We cannot unfortunately, deny human error. The company cannot be associated with this behaviour. The Captain took a decision on his own which is contrary to our written and certified rules. This route was set correctly upon departure from Civitavecchia. The fact [that the ship deviated from this route] is solely due to a non-approved and unauthorised manoeuvre and which Costa Crociere was not made aware of. The procedures implemented after the ship hit the rock did not respect in any way the strict rules, procedures and training we have given our officer. (CEO press statement 15th January 2012)

> (Los Angeles Times, 2012)

Several sections of the official accident report held the captain and crew responsible for the accident. A bold assertion in the accident report is that the captain was the 'main cause of the accident'. Such an outright expression of blaming and shaming is rare even in the conservative maritime world. But the personalisation of this accident was taken to another level when the accident narrative extended beyond the captain and his professional judgement to include his character, morality and integrity. Stories of a 'blonde Moldovan dancer' on the bridge were linked with the captain in the tabloids and other news reports.

The self-righteous media outrage did not stop there. During our interviews, Francesco said:

> the accident has destroyed me, my family, my daughter, and my brother. My mother, who is 92 years old, asks me, When will you have a job?

When I contacted a family member of the captain, also a ship captain, nearly eight years after the accident, he told me that his family name still gets in the way of his finding decent employment in the maritime world.

At one point Francesco's Wikipedia personal profile read:

> present with him on the bridge during the collision was Moldovan dancer Domnica Cemortan, who has admitted she had been having an extramarital affair with Schettino. Before starting his prison sentence, Schettino lived in Meta in the Province of Naples. He is married and has one daughter.

Francesco told me that shortly after the accident even his family's Facebook accounts were made available on Wikipedia for some time. The brief Wikipedia description of the captain is not random. It is the dogma of Safety (as the archetype) that seeks to undermine the captain's character and his family as the source of the accident as an attempt to save society from evil and suffering.

It is the paradox of any accident that the people involved could not have foreseen the misfortune coming their way, and yet none of that matters when our society seeks meaning in suffering by demonising the people involved in that accident. At the time of writing, Schettino is serving the seventh year of his sixteen-year sentence.

## The second story

The starting point of this study was to go beyond the first story and create a second story of this accident. That is all about systems and system vulnerabilities. Some attributes of a second story are as follows.

It emerges slowly; in our case it took almost six years to research and write this story. The second story is low on personalisation, in fact, so low that once we have developed a rich context of the accident, it does not really matter who the people involved actually are. It is not newsworthy or sensational; it is insightful and informative. It offers few solutions and remedies. The notion of a second story, however, because it follows the first, is not to claim that the former is superior. It is simply an alternative version of the accident.

| First Story | Second story |
|---|---|
| Human error | System Vulnerability |
| - appears quickly after an event | - emerges slowly and after long delays |
| - highly personalized on sharp end workers | - lower personalization |
| - low in context and complexity | - high context, high complexity |
| - high in newsworthiness | - low newsworthiness |
| - easily preventable and fixable in hindsight | - no easy (and few) solutions and remedies |

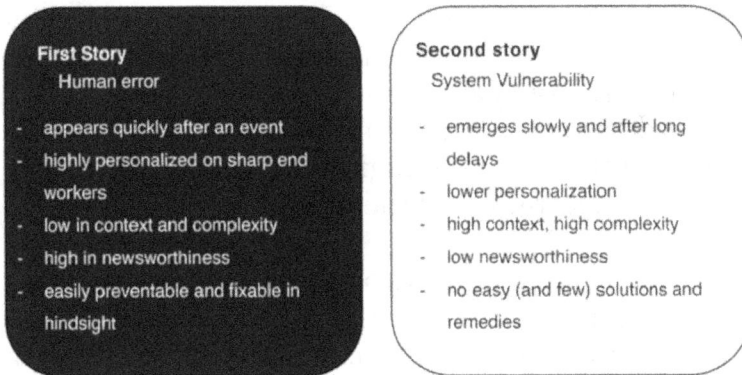

Figure 6.2: A comparison between the first story and the second.

(Source: Woods and Cook, 1998)

During the course of this study, I facilitated more than three dozen workshops to share the second story of the *Costa Concordia* with people from around the world. Most of the participants who attended the workshops appreciated the power of this story and recognised the various problems of organisational life in this story: recruitment and retention of talented people, design limitations, operational constraints, the goal conflicts of everyday work, the limits of deregulation, compliance and certification in risk and safety management – and how, when the system collapses, one person becomes the bearer of the burden. Few attendees, after listening to the captain's version of the story, thought that he was the main cause of the accident.

# First, second or alternative stories?

I realised during the course of this journey, that both the first story and the second are part of the same search for objective truth. Why one or two?

Does that mean that two is better than one? Why not as many versions of the accident narrative as possible? A large part of my workshops on the *Costa Concordia* accident was handing back control to the participants and encouraging them to draw from it their own learning and meaning.

What was frustrating throughout this journey was to find so few participants who would create space for listening and reflection. When people stopped, pondered and asked open-ended questions it was a refreshing experience. But if I were to summarise the experience in a few words, for most participants learning was someone else's problem. The most common responses were (and still are) that it is the captain who is to take the blame. As I stood back, listening to and observing the nature of responses and reflections, I heard some powerful themes beginning to emerge.

One afternoon, I came across a quote from the Dutch philosopher Spinoza:

> not to laugh, not to lament, not to curse but to understand.

There it was! The essence of my learning journey in a nutshell – even though with many seasoned practitioners I did not experience lamenting so much as a well-honed tendency to problem solve. Perhaps Spinoza was living in an era when lamenting was considered more appropriate than the present-day managerial instinct to fix all the problems of the organisation. I don't know, but every time I review the corrective actions and recommendations in an accident report, I get the impression that we want to fix the problem and move on, without realising the implications of our fixes.

## Learning as fixing the problem

As mentioned above, what I noticed in the participants' feedback during the workshops was an urge to fix the problem or to offer solutions for it. What I'd had in mind was learning and dissonance – but what I was actually starting to observe was a quest for certainty, order and closure, mainly to *avoid* dissonance. Here are some immediate responses from the participants:

• I think we need to consider organisational factors in this case.
• This is lack of accountability (commenting on the company's attitude towards the captain).
• At the end of the day, you have to hold someone accountable when things go wrong.
• There are limits to how much detail you can write in your procedures (commenting on the emergency procedures).
• I think we need to think about decluttering the procedures.
• What has the company done to support this captain?
• Poor quality of investigation (commenting on the official accident report).
• Unfair court trial.

Inherent within many of these responses is a common thread: learning is about projecting the problem; learning is for others. And there was also, to an extent, an absence of self-reflection and introspection.

As there was of course, that strong tendency to recommend solutions and fix the problem, common themes were: having conversations in the field to understand the work; designing fail-safe systems, because humans will always make mistakes; and writing processes that would enable work to take place and eventually reduce harm to workers. Some participants said they were left frustrated because I had spent a lot of time in helping them frame the problem and very little in offering solutions.

There were instances where people felt apologetic and ashamed about holding a low opinion of the captain and how attending the *Costa Concordia* workshop had exonerated him in their eyes. 'Now I know the real story,' some would end up saying. One woman cried and admitted to being shameful and guilty of not being made aware of the 'true story', and then she redirected her anger towards the media. In another case, a traffic controller wrote to me:

> My only meaningful comment on the *Costa Concordia* accident is that the captain has been unfairly treated. As the ship had lost power, I cannot see how much more he could have done. Additionally, his command to Port instead of starboard not followed, and, his heroic dive into the sea to help save a stuck lifeboat may have saved an additional 300 lives, and this seems to have been lost in the media. If there is some way to forward my sympathies to the captain, please do.

Workshop after workshop, I saw the learning outcome that I had contemplated slipping away from my original intentions. I wanted to create a space for people to think critically, embrace doubt, leave their session with a sense of newly opened space for thought and anxiety combined with the feeling that there was more to this accident investigation and human decision making than meets the eye. **But for the most part, when faced with uncertainty the participants filled the void with guilt, apologies, mockery and sympathy.**

I was aiming for a change within the participants, but for the most part, the need to join the dots (i.e. the gestalt principle) in search for certainty and control took over. A lot of people wanted the 'full story', the 'true story', the 'actual story' and the 'real story' from this workshop; clearly, they genuinely believed in the existence of an objective under-standing of the world. One ship manager wrote an elaborate email after being in my workshop. According to him, if my research was only about the captain's viewpoint, it was incomplete; I should have interviewed all the officers on the ship. That would make it a more accurate study, he felt. Such is the quest for objectivity and truth when we take an objective view of the world.

## Learning to entertain doubt

The objective of all genuine learning is the ability to feel doubtful before we make a decision. Recall the One Brain Three Minds model. Avoiding knee-jerk and reflexive decisions originating from gut thinking is essential to improving the quality of our decision making. That is where doubt helps in learning.

Figure 6.3: Aberdeen airport: on the steps leading to the exit are the words 'Take the first step in faith; you don't have to see the whole staircase. Just take the first step.' (Martin Luther King, Jr.)

I often think about the message at Aberdeen airport. It is rather ironic that in a city historically dominated by masculinity and risk aversion – granite quarries, fisheries, and now oil and gas production – a picture of faith and wisdom in the face of the unknown has survived for so long. I wonder how many people stepping up this stairway stop, think and reflect upon Dr King's words?

I am reminded of my own time on ships. On container ships, one of the most dangerous activities is in port, with stevedores and shore gangs hastily throwing heavy twist locks and bars onto the deck in their bid to ensure the timely departure of the ship. When walking in the narrow alleyways at night, your best bet, as you navigate the poorly lit deck spaces, is to whistle and shout loudly to signal your presence to the shore gangs. Will they listen? Even with all possible personal protective equipment (PPE), you can only hope that you will come out safe at the other end.

I learned early on in life that despite all the paperwork and risk assessments, the next step will always be into the unknown. I'm not suggesting that we should get rid of paperwork and PPE. Rather, my point is that we should acknowledge that all life is lived in uncertainty. The language of faith and doubt reminds us to become mindful of what lies ahead, and to view it with humility. One cannot learn and live in the delusion of certainty when there is none. Learning requires us to remain doubtful about ourselves or, as Hudson would say, in 'chronic unease' and as Robert Long often says, 'entertaining doubt'. Dr King's wise words are foundational to my own philosophy of risk.

A narrative will by its very nature, leave certain caveats and questions. Those gaps are not only inevitable but are also essential for self-reflection, self-awareness, learning and critical thinking. But in my workshops most participants, when faced with uncertainty, were prompt to fill those voids with their own assumptions, biases and experiences. Gradually, it became clear that it does not matter whether you create a first or second story: **the human need for certainty, culpability and control invariably takes precedence over learning.**

Whether you give people the first or the second story they want definitive answers and solutions (possibly in three to five silver bullets). It is a big ask to demand that people live with messy, incomplete accounts and half-truths, and then to leave them in doubt to think more critically in silence and discover their own truth. But that is how great educators encourage and evoke learning (Freire, 1973) (Parker, 1971) (Claxton, 2018). Learning in its true sense means appreciating that despite our best efforts, intellect and reasoning our stories will always remain incomplete.

One question that I would often leave with the participants at the end of my workshops:

> What did you learn from the last investigation (or audit, or site visit) that you did not know before you started the process?

I have since reframed this question:

> What have you learned about your own self from the last investigation (or audit, or site visit)?

## A biological view on doubt and learning

Many of our beliefs are an incomplete assumption of the world, and for the most part of our lives we live unaware of those assumptions. Leaving aside our social needs for belonging and identity, there are biological reasons why we are not prepared to let go of our beliefs. The Portuguese-American neuroscientist Antonio Damasio writes in his book *The Strange Order of Things* that our bodies consists of at least two worlds – the *old* internal world and the *new* outer world. The old internal world consists of the basic life processes that came earlier in the evolution of life on this planet. These are basic metabolic functions, and they include organs such as heart, guts, lungs and skin. Along with this old internal world there exists a newer outer world, consisting of our body frame (skeleton) and four sensing mechanisms (eyes, ears, nose and tongue).

According to Damasio, our internal world is subject to less manipulation than our outer world. When we feel heartburn, stomach ache, fatigue or oxygen depletion, there is not much we can do about it, because it is directly related to our survival. The new outer world is also concerned with our survival, albeit its functioning can deceive us. When we are threatened by what we hear or see in the outside world, we may have a heart attack or a nervous breakdown – but our senses can also alter our realities. Put simply, our senses were not designed to give us an accurate view of the world around us; they were meant to maximise our chances of survival in the short term. Come to think of it, it is the same principle that applies to our present-day approach to risk assessments. When the risk ranking exceeds the threshold of tolerance, we tend to manipulate the ranking instead of managing the risk (Muller, 2018). Our first instinct is to survive; learning and understanding takes a backseat when it conflicts with our survival.

## Encouraging a culture of doubt for learning

A healthy dose of doubt helps us become aware of the limitations of our beliefs. I'm not suggesting that you should become a pessimist or – back to Descartes – sit down and question everything you hear or see, in order to prove your existence. But if the aim is to create space for learning, we must look for methods and tools that encourage scepticism and doubt in our routines and rituals.

## An exercise on entertaining doubt

Here's a question worth asking every time a critical decision is being made by a group (during, say, a toolbox talk, a strategy meeting or an emergency response exercise): On a scale of 1 to 5, how confident are you about the decision we have made?

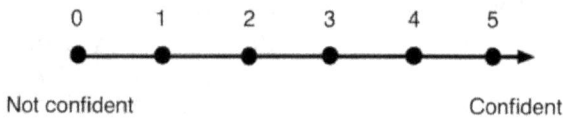

Figure 6.4: Scale of Confidence.

Those who respond with 4 or 5 should be asked to explain the basis for their confidence.

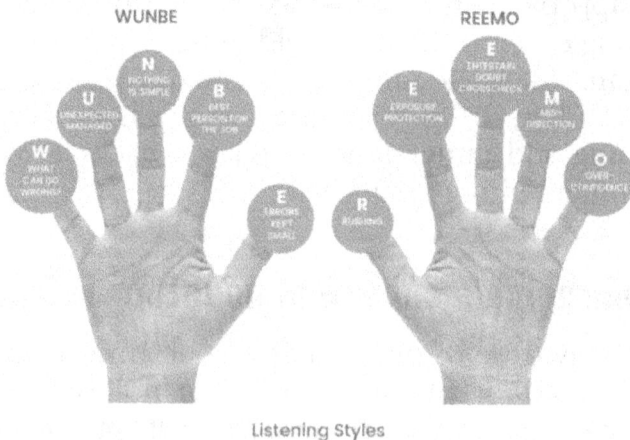

Listening Styles

Figure 6.5: Listening styles* to encourage doubt and learning in routine work: the prompts on the ten fingers can be used to encourage questioning, listening and critical thinking in a high-risk activity. (The words WUNBE and REEMO do not mean anything.)

The next time you are handling an emergency or entering an enclosed space, slow down and think what will help you make better decisions. The confidence that comes with ticking off all the tasks on the checklist? A predictive analysis run by a third-party software vendor? Or the anxiety and fear, and the ability to hold doubt, as you step onto the next rung in the ladder?

# 7

# Mocking is not Learning

In August 2019, soon after finishing a workshop in Qatar and heading home, I received a photograph of Francesco Schettino on WhatsApp from one of the participants. I have closely followed the media reports, so I have many caricatures and cartoons of the captain, but to me this picture stood out:

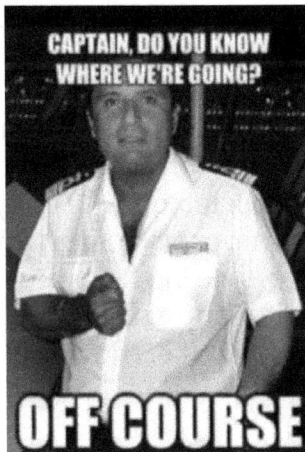

Figure 7.1: A meme of Captain Schettino; the paradox is that of a navigator and a captain losing their orientation, which goes against the ethos of the navigation profession.

The motivation to write this chapter triggered from this photograph. Why do people find this picture funny enough to share on social media? Why do some of us laugh at people caught up in an accident? How does that relate to learning from accidents? Why do humans, all of us so fallible, delight in behaving with such arrogance and self-righteousness? What can we learn about our methods, models and approaches from our tendency to mock at fallible people? We will reflect on these questions in this chapter.

---

- Why do we mock at people involved in accidents?
- Theories and perspectives on mockery.
- Henry Bergson's theory of mockery and its direct relevance to accident models.
- Why mockery is not helpful for learning?

---

Figure 7.2: A general outline of the chapter.

What makes this photograph so powerful is that it represents, amongst other things, a direct attack on the captain's social identity. Given that the captain's image has acquired centre stage mockery from the accident, it is worthwhile meditating on this question. It is not my intention to conduct a comprehensive literature review on the theory of mockery, but a brief outline may be helpful to understand why mockery takes precedence over learning when we face misfortune. To begin with, I am less concerned about laughing *with* and more focused on laughing *at* (i.e. mocking) those involved in accidents.

## Perspectives on mocking

In Western philosophy laughing is generally associated with negativity and considered a vice. Historically, the term 'laugh' was interchangeable with 'ridicule', 'comedy' and 'humour'. Plato made it very clear in *Philebus* that 'the ridiculous is a certain kind of evil, specifically a vice'. During that era, laughter – and more specifically excess laughter – was considered a sign of falling to the vice and losing self-control. Laughter was akin to mockery.

Aristotle, Plato and Descartes all held the view that we laugh at people because we believe we are morally superior, better looking, wiser or more righteous than them. A sense of superiority is also a trait of individualist and competitive societies, and the feeling that we are better, stronger, superior, or more fortunate than the ignorant, fallible and feeble who have become the subject of mockery. Children (and even adults) will not spare a chance to laugh at their friends when they accidentally stumble or land in a puddle. People who laugh at Francesco Schettino for losing control of the ship are likely to feel surprised and self-elevated at seeing Francesco being humiliated, but also feel at ease in not sharing his situation.

Sigmund Freud had a different view on laughter. To him, laughter occurs:

> if there is a situation in which, according to our usual habits, we should be tempted to release a distressing affect and if motives then operate upon us which suppress that affect in *statu nascendi* [in the process of being born] ... . The pleasure of

humor ... comes about ... at the cost of a release of affect that does not occur: it arise from an *economy in the expenditure of affect*. (Freud, 1905, p. 293).

When we first hear about the accident and the loss we may pity the captain. We may even build up an enormous sense of anxiety listening to the vivid and tragic story of the accident. But when we find out that the ship ran aground because the captain had lost his sense of direction, or that he was partying with a blonde dancer instead of attending to the navigation, our accumulated nervous energy may erupt as laughter. This is often termed 'Relief Theory'. Jokes and witty comments often fall into this category, where we suddenly experience an enormous flow of emotions pouring into our conscious minds as we go from climax to a steep fall.

There is also the Incongruity Theory, and its various versions. According to this theory, we laugh because what we experience may contradict our expectations. The thought that a captain could lose his sense of direction or jump off the ship before all the passengers were evacuated goes against our image of a ship captain.

## When the mechanical is mapped upon the living

Perhaps the most profound explanation of mockery comes from the work of Henri Bergson (Bergson, 1900). For him, our understanding of human life alternates between two main principles – vitalism and mechanism. Mechanism refers to the matter, or material aspect, of the human body. Think of mat-

ter as a kind of energy that holds our bodies together. When we think of life, and more specifically human behaviour, from a mechanistic perspective, all
actions can be reduced to matter and measurement.
We can explain human behaviour using reduction-
ist and mechanistic properties and breaking them
down to psychological attributes and physiological
anatomy. The ship hit the rocks because the captain
and his crew were fatigued, or they had lost situational awareness for a few moments.

Time is also measurable for Bergson. Time can be
measured in snapshots, and in this instance focusing
closely on events that preceded the accident can
give us an insight into human behaviour. The
living body is viewed as a rigid machine with inputs
and outputs, whose actions can be mapped and
evaluated in time and space. In this way, humans are
viewed like automata, i.e. they can be programmed
to behave like a machine.

Vitalism is the opposite of mechanism. **Vitalism is
about living, and vitality calls for elasticity, supple-
ness, flexibility, and being present and mindful,
and it is kindled in our soul.** Thinking of a human
as a living being, a soul with immaterial qualities, infinite boundaries, always in motion, beyond the laws
of mechanism or gravity that can limit, restrict, mea-
sure or hold us back, offers a different view of a human being. Far from a pre-programmed machine,
a human being is spontaneous, impulsive, intuitive
and organic, and is driven by moral principles.

According to Bergson, we laugh when we realise that
we have reduced the vitalism in a person, a human
action or situation to a mechanistic explanation. See-

ing the captain and his crew reduced to a rigid machine that became an absentminded object moments before the accident, when they should have been fully present and live in the moment, becomes a source of public mockery. During laughter, we witness what Bergson refers to as the 'momentary transformation of a person into a thing' or a static object. In other words, we laugh when we see how 'the mechanical encrusts upon the living'. Think about it. The navigation equipment cannot be comical, nor can the ship be; only a human being, who embodies both vitalism and mechanism, can be subject to mockery. Bergson refers to this as the 'mechanistic encrusted upon the living', which means we find ourselves mapping mechanical models to understand living beings.

**When the mechanistic is encrusted upon the living**

It takes just over an hour to fly from London to Aberdeen, where I live. On a busy Friday evening flight, I noticed this brief exchange between an attendant and a passenger sitting in front of me.

What would you like to have, sir?

A glass of red wine please.

Anything else I can get you?

Maybe later.

Later? Where do you think the flight is going, sir? Dubai?

The other passengers burst into laughter.

Figure 7.3: Attendant and passenger.

An incident or an event becomes an object of mockery when the material aspects of human behaviour take primacy over the *living being*. We laugh because of the mechanical explanation that the captain of the *Costa Concordia* became absentminded, or that he lost 'situational awareness' when we had expected him to be spontaneous, living and mindful of his actions. In the aircraft story, the passenger had momentarily gone into automatic mode (Mind 3), and the flight attendant brought him back to the vitality of living on a busy Friday evening.

When I read Bergson, I was left wondering about the differences between mocking someone, fixing them and cursing them. Does not our tendency to manage people, blame them or laugh at them emerge from the same principles? To this, Bergson says:

> Try, for a moment, to become interested in everything that is being said and done; act, in imagination, with those who act, and feel with those who feel; in a word, give your sympathy its widest expansion: as though at the touch of a fairy wand you will see the flimsiest of objects assume importance, and a gloomy hue spread over everything.

> Now step aside, look upon life as a disinterested spectator: many a drama will turn into a comedy. It is enough for us to stop our ears to the sound of music in a room, where dancing is going on, for the dancers at once to appear ridiculous. How many human actions would stand a similar test? Should we not see many of them suddenly pass from grave to gay, on isolating them from the accompanying music of sentiment? To produce the whole of its effect, then, the comic demands something like a momentary anaesthesia of the heart. Its appeal is to intelligence, pure and simple.

> (Bergson, 1900)

It is fair to say that cursing and laughter have much in common. Imagine an investigation method in search of objective truth. When we are in search of objectivity, establishing a sense of superiority, building a persuasive force in our narrative to establish human error, and setting up a divide between us (the investigators) and them (the investigated), we will end up mocking and/or fixing others under the pretext of investigating and 'learning from accidents'. The lessons learned turn out to be our proclivity to win and to prove others wrong. Mocking and cursing share the same tendency: our dominance and moral superiority over the other.

Where mockery distances itself from cursing or lamenting is when we experience temporary numbness towards the emotions and feelings in another person. In my experience on that flight, we laughed when we witnessed this passenger in an automated, absentminded mode. In that moment, laughter became a 'self-administered antidote'. We often laugh out loud because we have no control over the absurdity of a situation or indeed have any ability to correct it. The only correction is found *within* us, through a burst of laughter.

One last point that is relevant to our discussion about laughing at people involved in accidents: Bergson suggests that those unfortunate people are ones with 'separatist tendencies,' i.e. people who have gone against the norms of society, and their behaviour reflects extremist views and actions. The picture at the start of this chapter contradicts the public image of a ship captain who is typically seen in 'command and control'. Instead, Schettino violated the norms of the profession by navigating the ship close to the rocks.

Laughter, according to Bergson, is a psychological forgiveness of those 'criminals' with 'separatist tendencies' who pose a threat to the functioning of vital society and the maintenance of social order. Imagine the tension we would build up within us as members of society, if we did not laugh in such situations. Laughter is a human expression releasing the build-up of vengeance within a society. One can see Bergson's wisdom in the world of cartoonists, who are adept at using funny images to speak truth to power.

Figure 7.4: An illustration of the emotional effect of mechanistic models of investigating on understanding the vitalism of human life.

When we observe people involved in accidents being subject to mockery and ridicule, it is a reminder for us to revisit our own investigation process and ask:

*Have we reduced the vitality of human life into variants of mechanical explanations ('loss of situational awareness; procedural violation; complacency; lack of training')?*

*Have we turned human beings into absentminded machines?*

If you find yourself making fun of those involved in accidents, perhaps a question could be, 'How helpful for learning is it to mock another fallible person?'

# 8

# The Role of Emotions and Feelings in Learning

———————⟨⟨⟨⟩⟩⟩———————

Emotions and feelings have conventionally been considered a barrier to learning. In this chapter we will explore, using a biological framework, why emotions and feelings are the basis for all learning. I will begin by illustrating how we react when we are faced with dissonance (discomfort). Next, I will make an attempt to explain the biological basis for dissonance, and I will end the chapter with why understanding our biological being is essential for learning. The motivation to write this chapter mainly came from the reactions that I gathered from the participants during my workshops on the *Costa Concordia* accident.

> - What happens when emotions and feelings are overlooked in learning?
> - Understanding emotions and feelings.
> - Why emotions and feelings are essential for learning?
> - Strategies and tools for managing emotions and feelings in accident investigations.

Figure 8.1: A general outline of the chapter.

'Look at him, he has no shame. He does not even have the courage to face the camera,' said one of the participants when she first saw Francesco Schettino appear on the screen during one of my workshops.

To this I responded, 'There were two cameras positioned in the room. We took this shot from the side camera, and that is why you see his side pose.' When I look back, I realise my silliness: how naïve of me to respond to a non-rational question with a rational response. I have learned to ask a different question, 'What makes you feel the captain has no shame?'

Responses such as that by the participant were not uncommon every time Captain Francesco Schettino appeared on the screen to share his version of the story. What surprised me more was that the most unforgiving responses often came from people who work in the cruise sector. At first, I was puzzled about that, in that these people should know better about the systemic problems of the industry, the messy details of work and the pressure on a ship captain of a modern cruise carrier. Why, then, did they show so little empathy toward the captain?

I have also seen a perceptible difference between the non-mariners, who would mostly listen to the captain with an open mind and appreciate his views, and the mariners, who would reject him, criticise him and shut off as he spoke. It became obvious in this journey how, for many mariners, prior knowledge and experience gets in the way of understanding and learning.

*What was causing dissonance in these mariners?* I wondered – until I turned to neuroscience, evolutionary theories and biology, and recognised the centrality of the emotions in learning. Damasio's (2000) studies have played an influential role in my work, along with others including Johnson (2017), Slovic (2010) and Maiese (2010). Apparently Schettino, in the way he came across on screen, triggered the emotions of the mariners (unlike the non-mariners), and a lot of effort, which could otherwise be used on the topics of discussion, went into managing their emotions.

A second theme when the discussions would evoke excess emotions was related to the captain leaving the ship before all the passengers had been evacuated. In one of his earlier letters from prison, Francesco had told me that clarifying this misrepresented aspect of the story was central to the accident narrative, but I ignored his warning. I was convinced that most people would come to a workshop on learning from accidents with an open mind, in order to *learn*, and not to judge the captain's decisions and actions. I was wrong.

I found it both fascinating and frustrating to see how often the discussions would focus on the captain's 'Italian-ness', his 'arrogant' demeanour, his 'loud' voice, 'unapologetic' tone, and 'rude' camera etiquette every time he appeared on the video screen. Francesco's onscreen appearance apparently meant far more than his perspectives, insights and reflections about the accident. One woman, a seafarer, walked out of the workshop because she simply could not stand the captain's appearance on the screen: 'Shameless!' she said – and she never came back to the session.

**When emotions are running high ...**

In another workshop, an old ship captain announced, 'Stupid Italian!' and brought a very lively discussion in the room to a complete halt. Without being too excited or critical about why he responded in that way, I decided to leave the discussion there. In the evening, we met for dinner and I approached this captain to understand his viewpoint. We had an open discussion about why he felt so strongly about Captain Schettino. We did not agree on many things, but it was an enriching conversation. I'm not sure what he took away from this conversation, but I learned a lot. I realised that (1) when emotions are running high, it is easier to shoot the messenger than engage with the message, (2) when emotions are high, reasoning and convincing are the least helpful approaches (don't even *try* them!), (3) in a learning environment, winning arguments and tackling convictions hardly matters (in fact it is the opposite) – what matters is creating a space for people to think and reflect on their words and actions – and (4) non-rational behaviour cannot be understood by using rational methods.

For many, it was a turning point during the workshop to find out that the captain did not evacuate the ship in the way portrayed in the media. Every time this realisation became evident, I was intrigued by the power of emotions barricading learning, and how important it was for the participants to forgive the captain before they could listen to his story. (We will address the topic of the captain leaving the ship in Chapter 14.)

## Homoeostasis and emotions

Emotions are the physical manifestation, how our bodies react, when we are faced with threats, opportunities and everything in between. In familiar situations we can continue to function in automatic mode, but when we face an unfamiliar situation – a threat or an opportunity – our homoeostasis is disrupted. Homoeostasis is the bandwidth of tolerance within which our body can continue to self-regulate its life processes (the functioning of respiratory, immune, and nervous systems) without involving the conscious mind. The setting of energy in motion (e-motions) is a normal biological response intended to protect us when we unconsciously decide whether we want to fight or flee (Damasio, 2021).

Recall the discussion about the embodied nature of our Mind. Our skin goes pale as a reaction to bad news; our muscles contract when we face sorrow, defeat or surprise; our heart races in pride, and our pupils dilate when we are frightened or excited. In those moments, we are affected by emotion. When this happens, learning is not our default mode; the priority is to regain control of our life processes i.e. homoeostasis. When the mariners attending the workshop were overwhelmed by their emotions and their undeclared assumptions about social justice, they were losing their homoeostatic balance. Their prior knowledge and experiences were creating an enormous imbalance within their bodies and getting in the way of their understanding and learning. In those moments, it was natural for them to reject what they were hearing, because they needed to regain their homoeostasis. In those moments, agitated as they were, thinking and reflection was not on their minds.

## Emotions and feelings are essential for learning

For more than 300 years we have been conditioned to believe that reason is not only superior to emotions but also stands in opposition to them. René Descartes stated that while reason is situated *upward* in the brain, emotion is located in the body; thus he gave emotions a *downward* status. The Scottish philosopher David Hume reduced emotions to 'animal' and 'flesh'. Many of the technological advances following the industrial revolution have stood behind the supremacy of brain over body and reason over emotion.

It was Darwin, and later Freud, who gave a scientific status to emotions. New research in the cognitive sciences and neuroscience is increasingly making it evident that our understanding of the mind–body relationship is incomplete (Lakoff, 1998) (Johnson, 2017) (Damasio, 2000) (Claxton, 2016). Reasoning does not come from the supreme powers of heaven;

reason is a continuum of our emotions. Although life on this planet has existed for more than 4 billion years, the nervous system is only about 500 million years old. In the hierarchy of our evolution as a human species, emotions precede feelings, and reasoning flows from our feelings and emotions.

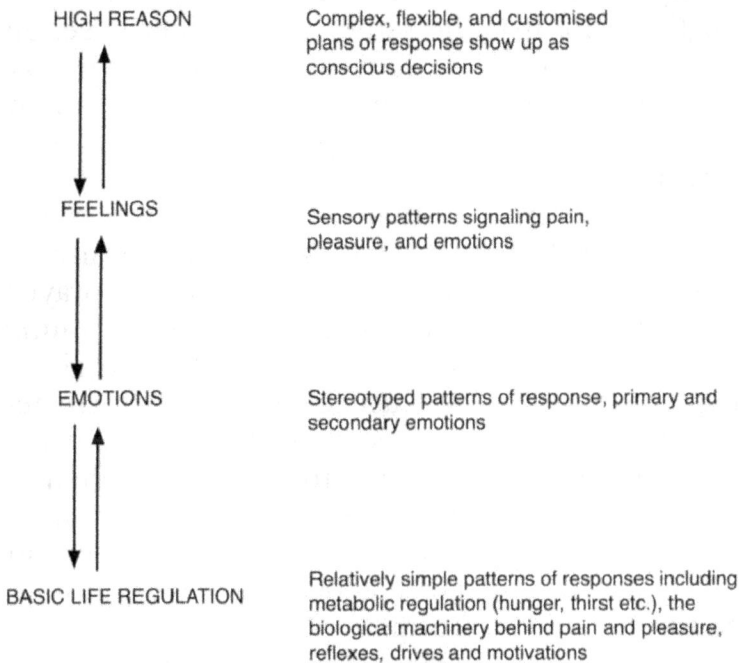

HIGH REASON — Complex, flexible, and customised plans of response show up as conscious decisions

FEELINGS — Sensory patterns signaling pain, pleasure, and emotions

EMOTIONS — Stereotyped patterns of response, primary and secondary emotions

BASIC LIFE REGULATION — Relatively simple patterns of responses including metabolic regulation (hunger, thirst etc.), the biological machinery behind pain and pleasure, reflexes, drives and motivations

Figure 8.2: Levels of Life Regulation
(extracted and modified from Damasio 1999).

We tend to conflate emotions and feelings, but there's a difference between them; you can hide your feeling of dislike for someone when you meet them, but you cannot control your emotions so easily. When your face turns red or your breath becomes shallow you will look agitated. Think of all emotions as 'e-motions' or energy in movement.

Feelings are the subjective representation of our emotions. You and I may be exposed to the same level of pain because of a cut finger, but our feeling of the pain will be subjective. I may, for example, shout and scream, whereas you may choose to occupy yourself in an activity to keep your mind off the pain. It is the same bodily experience, but felt and expressed in subjective ways. It is because of feelings that we develop a subjective sense of our lives. In fact, if you go deeper into understanding feelings and the power of feelings as the subjective representation of human life, you will find that feelings are the basis of all human culture (Damasio, 2000). Early religion, the notion of God, and prayers came from the fear of death, the feelings of trauma and grief to recover from the loss. Our moral and legal systems and our justice systems were created as impartial authorities that could be trusted when we *felt* we were being threatened or when we needed to threaten others. Feelings, as Damasio explains, can motivate intelligent responses not only from individuals but from entire groups and cultures. Large-scale disasters can evoke feelings of cooperation, collaboration and innovation in the face of suffering and opportunities. Empathy, compassion and even violence come from feelings.

Our capacity to communicate is helped by the formation of gestures, art, poetry, painting and the sophisticated use of language to express our feelings. We learn when we realise our emotions and we are able to express our subjective feelings through gestures and language until it becomes memory, adds to our experiences and shapes our anticipation. When we are not allowed to express our feelings, our experiences remain stagnant, our language does not evolve and future events are seen as a replica of the past. In such situations, people do not enrich their expertise, but simply pile up on the same experience. As decision expert Gary Klein shared with me on my podcast, 'Ten years in a profession becomes equivalent to one year of experience repeated ten times.' In the maritime industry, a typical response to an accident at sea from a seasoned mariner sitting ashore would be, 'I know the problem; we had the same issue when I was on board fifteen years ago.' Without emotions and feelings, there is little knowing and learning.

## Managing emotions and feelings in an accident investigation

When things go wrong, just your presence as an investigator or a person in authority will create an immense emotional burden on people being investigated. Chances are that your first question will send shivers down their spine, and may even become a threat to the existence of those whose livelihood (jobs, bonuses, performance targets) depend on the conclusions and recommendations of your report. In those moments of interviewing and trying to find out what went wrong, you need to remember the importance of helping people realise their emotions and express their feelings. Learning will inevitably follow from there.

People involved in accidents are known to sway you (the investigator) in different directions, at times even mislead and frustrate you, but it is also the case that once the same person connects with you emotionally, they will give you more than you had anticipated – often different from it, too. We act professionally, and that is quite understandable. But suppressing feelings, or denying emotions and expecting logical, rational responses according to how the investigation template is designed, is not a very helpful investigation and learning strategy.

Many of the strategies, methods and tools to help people realise emotions and express feelings are listed in the chapter on embodied Mind (Chapter 5).

# 9

# Learning is Surfacing the Unconscious

———— ❧ ————

This chapter is about understanding the importance of the unconscious mind, mainly based on studies in Jungian analytical psychology. (The difference between the terms 'unconscious' and 'non-conscious' is that while the former is based on humanistic theories, the latter is an evolutionary concept based on our biological being.) Together, we will explore how our everyday decisions are influenced by the power of unconscious. We will go deeper to understand the unconscious mind both at the personal and the collective level. We will explore how beliefs are formed and how we live those beliefs at the deepest level of our unconscious. Through several stories and examples, we will explore why surfacing the contents of the unconscious is essential to improve our creative capacities, healing, living and realising our full potential. The acknowledgement of the unconscious is largely absent in accident investigation models, methods and concepts. On the contrary, it is implicitly assumed that human beings are conscious and aware of their actions and behaviours.

---

- The power of the unconscious mind in everyday decisions.
- Understanding personal and collective unconscious.
- How the collective unconscious shapes our beliefs and worldviews?
- Why surfacing the contents of the unconscious is essential for learning?
- Why learning begins with healing?
- Understanding shadow: the dark side of the unconscious.
- Why understanding and surfacing the contents of the shadow matters in accident investigations?

Figure 9.1: A general outline of the chapter.

---

One evening, as Francesco and I were walking towards a restaurant, I asked him, 'What is the one thing you would wish for, if you were spared imprisonment?' I asked because he had indicated several times during the day that he might soon be sentenced to prison. Francesco responded:

> I would like to go back on ship even for one week or one month. It feels as if some lamp-post fell on my head. It was totally unexpected. I can understand and fully accept if it happened in dense fog, when gusting, but this was just a normal day at sea.

# A normal day

Francesco's words should sound familiar to the risk and safety industry, reaffirming what Perrow (1984) and more recently Le Coze (2020) have written about the banality of everyday decisions that can lead to accidents. In fact, when you read an accident report which states 'clear sky, moderate wind, good visibility', that is a metaphorical expression of a normal day at sea. There are in the risk and safety world colloquial expressions: 'understanding normal work', and 'learning from what goes well', meaning paying close attention to the compromises, choices and trade-offs that make up a day's routine. The assumption here is that since we are dealing with the same people working under similar conditions each day, behaviours present on an everyday basis will not be significantly different from those on the day of the accident. And so, if we focused on understanding the behaviours on a 'normal day', and worked to improve them, that would be a more proactive approach to managing risks than focusing on accidents alone.

What we refer to as compromises, trade-offs, choices and assumptions in decision making is the unconscious mind at work. Consider the start of a day at the office. You drive to your office, negotiating your way through heavy traffic, park your car and arrive at your desk – and you can't remember a thing about your drive. Have you ever wondered why? There was nothing unusual, nothing abnormal. So much of what happens on an everyday basis is taken over by the unconscious mind (Johnson R. , 1989). When there is nothing that attracts your conscious attention, then the heuristics, habits, routines, and rituals of the unconscious mind take control. Unless we understand how the unconscious mind influences our decisions, it is hard to appreciate a normal day at work or learn from an accident.

# Understanding the unconscious mind

Freud was one of the first neurologists to point out that our conscious thought is merely the tip of the iceberg. Since then, both neuroscience and cognitive science support the idea that more than 95 per cent of our decisions are made in the unconscious mind. If we want to learn from accidents, then, how can we lose sight of the unconscious? Let us shed light on the unconscious nature of decision making and how we can learn to surface the unconscious from accidents and everyday work.

In Social Psychology of Risk (SPoR), the foundation of all learning is acknowledging and bringing to the surface what is hidden in the unconscious.

## Personal and collective unconscious

Our psyche consists of three levels of consciousness: the conscious mind, the personal unconscious and the collective unconscious (see Figure 9.2). Our personal unconscious refers to individual experiences that we tend to forget through the course of time. These may include difficult childhood experiences such as being bullied by a classmate or punished by a teacher, experiencing abuse, or a tough relationship with a parent, friend or a family member. These are experiences of personal nature that were painful or traumatic, or simply became too much to handle, so they were pushed down into the personal unconscious. In Jungian studies such experiences are referred to as complexes. What we experience and learn through our lives, even when it is forgotten, stays in our personal unconscious. And then, sometimes all it takes is a prompt by a friend, a dream, a childhood picture or a visit to our old school for some of those unpleasant memories to come to the surface.

The collective unconscious extends beyond the personal space. While the personal unconscious consists of the forgotten and repressed past,

> the contents of collective unconscious were never in the consciousness and therefore have never been individually acquired but owe their existence exclusively to heredity (Jung, 1968, p. 42).

In studying human behaviour, both Carl Gustav Jung (1959) and later Joseph Campbell (1995) were intrigued as to how, irrespective of historical time and geographical distance, we humans have access to a collective memory that has been passed on to us by our ancestors and imprinted on our psyches. It is collective because, unlike the personal unconscious, its contents are universal, which means they are present in all of us – but to varying degrees, making each of us unique and different from others.

Jung's idea of the collective unconscious consists of the myths (stories) that we share as a group without being conscious of them. Collectively, our myths shape our worldview and influence our decisions. So deeply embedded in us are these myths that we do not even know they exist, and yet every moment of our lives we live by those myths (Midgley, 2003).

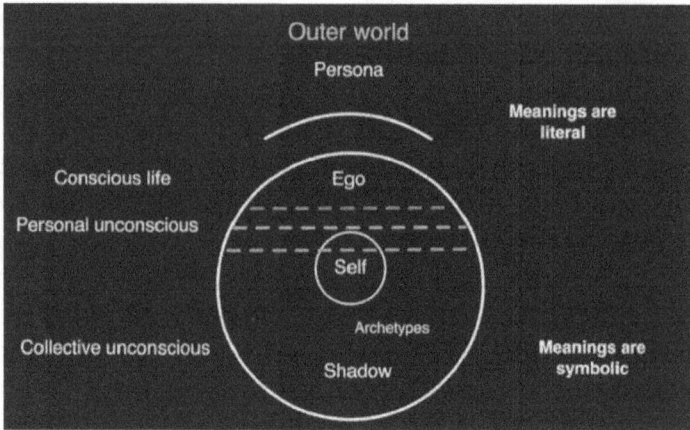

Figure 9.2: Personal and collective unconscious.
(Source: Carl Gustav Jung)

Why do some cultures believe that there is life after death while others don't? Why does an entire population believe that we should eat vegan while others don't? Why are some cultures keen on keeping the home organised while others can't be bothered? Why in some cultures are cattle eaten yet in others worshipped? The short answer is that every culture has its own myth about how life should be lived. For an illustration, I will turn to a personal story.

**Myths we live by**

'Hello there; let's start with your surname first.'

'Anand.'

'Your given name?'

'Nippin.'

Your son's surname?

'Of course it's the same as mine, Anand.'

'Well, that's fab – but nothing's 'of course', Mr Anand.'

This was the start of a conversation with the dental receptionist (let's call her Sue) to get our little boy booked in for a check-up, and I was left shocked; in less than fifteen seconds into this conversation, my worldview had been shattered.

*Now, where did that 'of course' come from?* I pondered. Upon reflection, I realised that it arose from my Hindu-generated monogamy myth: you marry only once, and the children of that marriage perforce have the same surname as their father. This is the belief I have for many years lived by at a deeply unconscious level. (Well, you could say that my wife's maiden name plus her married surname could also have been our son's surname, but that's as far as my reasoning took me.)

And where exactly did this realisation come from? I think there are images hidden deep in the unconscious which subtly but powerfully influence our decisions and shape our thoughts.

As I sat back thinking about this monogamy myth, so many stories and readings came to mind. The Hindu goddess Lakshmi left her husband Vishnu when she became angry with him, and Gauri did the same to Shiva for the same reason. But in those stories there was no mention of divorce, only separation, and the two gods then worked hard to bring their wives back home. Even today, one can observe sculptures of goddesses separated from gods in temples around India. The symbolism behind these stories is breathtaking. Women shared power; relationships mattered more than self-indulgence; and when conflicts arose both husband and wife made the effort to make their relationship work. When things did not work out, couples would separate in body – but they were still connected in their souls. These stories and sculptures are no longer popular in patriarchal, modern India. Instead, people in India (and, indeed, around the world) are every day being fed with narratives of masculinity and distorted history to serve political purposes.

In Hinduism (which can be seen as not so much a religion as a philosophy), marriage is not considered a contract. You do not need a divorce, because consent is not even part of a Hindu marriage. Marriage is considered a rite of passage, a commitment and an eternal bond between couples. Marriage does not end at death; relationships are meant to last for many lifetimes. As mentioned earlier, the concept of the afterlife does not exist in the same way as in Abrahamic faiths; in Hinduism there is not one life but many, and there are infinite chances to live, even within each lifetime.

Well, these are all myths, and things have changed over the years. While the idea of second and third marriages, civil partnerships and divorce are becoming normalised in modern India, my point is that, even so, myths and beliefs transcend time and space and trigger within us instinctively when someone challenges our values and what we consider so blatantly obvious.

How interesting that the tiny (but often loaded!) expression, 'of course', can bring to the surface a whole load of images, stories and memories that can reveal the moral principles and ethics of our everyday lives.

And how important it is to pay attention to these subtle expressions: 'of course'; 'definitely'; 'certainly'; 'obviously'; or 'that's normal'. Really? Did I even care to ask for whom?

Such is the power of language when we learn to listen with intent. It takes us back to understanding why one person's 'of course' is another person's no-no. It explains why everyday gossip, projections, scoffing, brawling and watercooler complaints that may seem so trivial on the surface are actually the result of tensions that exist so deep in our worldviews, ideologies, myths and beliefs.

We are driven by emotions and feelings, and trapped in our own myths and beliefs. The logical, scientific modern human fails to understand that as we go about our life each day we take in only a fraction of reality to make sense of the world around us. And when it comes to making decisions, the information that we use is even less. Now add just a tiny flavour of dissonance and time constraints, and you know what forms the core basis of human decision making – it's the myths and beliefs, of course!

Back in the dental surgery, when Sue posed the question about my son's surname, I could not see her beliefs and myths because I was so entrenched in mine. So often, when we are caught in a moment of reflexivity, we cannot see another person's belief, only curse or ridicule it. The problem is that what we resist will persist not because of some laws of physics but because our imagination struggles to grasp the mysteries of the universe.

In the moments when Sue confronted my beliefs by asking me for some information that I thought was obvious, my immediate reaction was to dismiss her behaviour as a mindless 'tick and flick' exercise. That's not just laziness, but it deepens my differences with Sue. What I have learned from this experience was that even after I have lived in the West for two decades my beliefs had not matured enough to absorb the possibility of a child having a different surname from that of their father, as they may be his stepchild. That illustrates now we live by our myths.

What I have also learned from this experience is that nothing that appears 'of course' is actually 'of course'. The first lesson in anthropology teaches us is to question the obvious, to make the familiar strange and the strange familiar.

The next time you laugh at someone, see their ideas as extreme, or see them as a threat to your own existence simply because they don't agree with what you consider 'of course', try slowing down, listening carefully and questioning your own worldview. Chances are that you may have reached the limits of your imagination.

This story serves as an illustration of how we live by our myths each day and how our collective unconscious shapes our worldview and influences our decisions. Certain images, or 'primordial images', as Jung (1968) would refer to them, sit deep in our collective unconscious, and persuade, even dictate, how we should live our lives. **Unaware of their profound implications for our lives, these images can lock our imagination forever.** By images, I don't mean just photos or visuals, but how we envision the world in dreams and reality. What images attract us? What images do we hold so deeply inside us about our morals, values, beliefs and ethics, and how we should live our life? Sometimes all it takes is the language of absolutism – 'of course', 'absolutely', 'definitely', 'certainly', 'this is right', 'perfect', 'flawless', 'I know', 'it's okay', 'that's usual', 'it's always been this way' or 'this is normal' for us to visualise the boundaries of our imagination. And then all it takes is a gentle nudge from someone like Sue to bring it all to the surface. Let's delve a bit deeper into this topic.

## Surfacing the unconscious

Over a few days, I meditated on this story and asked myself how we can surface the contents of the collective unconscious. Where do we even start? It is all too easy to say we should learn to listen better, but the question is what should we listen to? In my view, becoming culturally sensitive holds the key to accessing the contents of the collective unconscious. In fact, as Long (2012) describes it, 'our collective unconscious is our culture'.

Think of the habits, rituals, attitudes, values, patterns in our stories (hero and anti-hero ones), history, artefacts, symbols, slogans and mantras, and the language and metaphors that make up a belief system. Where do they originate? None of these operate at the level of the conscious mind; they are seated in our collective unconscious. Learning begins when we can surface the contents of our collective unconscious. In fact, the real potential of learning lies in doing so, because we have even less control over it than the little we do over the personal unconscious.

In Social Psychology of Risk, we use the metaphor of a cloud to represent the collective unconscious. We cannot observe a cloud from the inside; we can only feel the turbulence when we are caught up within it. To observe a cloud, we must learn to see it from a distance. The same principle applies when it comes to understanding and surfacing the collective unconscious within a culture. Think of the habits, metaphors, behaviours, attitudes, values, beliefs, narratives, artefacts and symbols of the culture of safety. For instance, 'ticking and flicking' paperwork; the language of zero; slogans and mantras such as 'safety first' or 'safety moment', the icons of circles, pyramids and triangles; the dominance of warnings and reminders, black, white and red; the use of objects to represent safety; the hero and the anti-hero narratives; and so on.

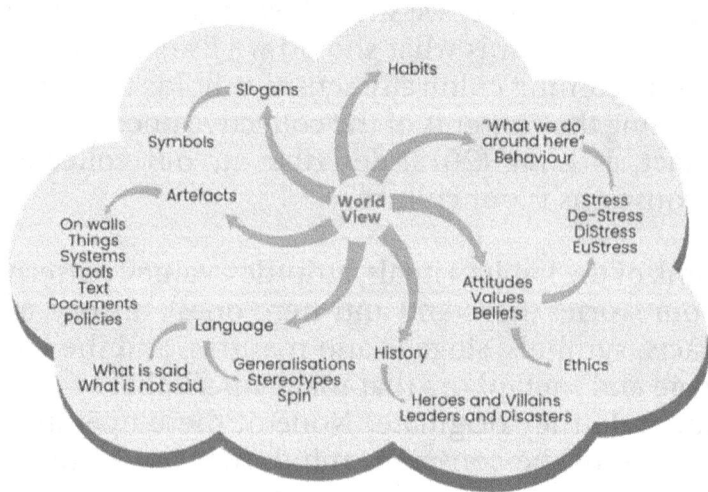

Figure 9.3: The Culture Cloud.*

When we observe the culture of safety from a distance, we can also start to discern what is *not* present in the cloud. To represent safety we rarely come across: slogans that might evoke critical thinking and questioning; pictures of people and relationships; icons representing care and love; the shape of flowers, petals and leaves; asymmetrical shapes; the colours purple or pink. These contents of the Culture Cloud work together to influence the collective unconscious of an entire industry. Later in this book we will apply the Culture Cloud in practice, and learn what is hidden in the collective unconscious of the cruise industry.

## The archetypes of the collective unconscious

Within every culture there are familiar patterns of human behaviour, which Carl Jung referred to as archetypes. The term 'archetype' means 'first pattern'. In the context of collective unconsciousness, it means the first pattern of human behaviour in the history of that culture. Myths of every culture reveal the archetypal patterns of that culture. Some of the familiar ones include: the wise old man who saves the world from being destroyed; the lover who sacrifices his life for his beloved; the father who expects his child to fulfil his dreams; the mother who becomes overprotective of her son; the man who becomes a serial killer because of his abusive childhood; and, in the context of this book, the anti-hero who is put behind bars to end the suffering of the world. These are recognisable patterns of human behaviour, revealing, guiding, inspiring and even deciding how we should live our life each day.

Archetypes, unlike learned behaviours, are not the result of our personal experiences or the learning from our own lives. Instead, archetypes are the instincts and reflexes of our collective unconscious passed on to us by our ancestors, below the level of our awareness. This is an important distinction to make. Think of the archetypal qualities: bees know intrinsically how to build hives, and migrating birds know where to fly to. The knowledge of archetypes can help us understand how people behave instinctively in a culture and how their behaviours are interpreted intuitively by the members of their culture. When you see the picture of a captain proudly sitting on his chair and another one being handcuffed and taken into prison, it does not take thinking and questioning to understand what is being communicated in the accident narrative. The archetypal pattern of behaviour intuitively makes sense.

Examples of archetypes include the Jungian personality types, the Greek gods and goddesses, tarot card characters and zodiac signs. Many of these archetypes are used in creating brand identities and marketing strategies. The technology company Apple uses the logo of an apple as an archetype of innovation, knowledge and the quest for perfection. The well-known sports brand Nike is based on the archetype of the Greek goddess of victory, representing competition and success. The same is true for a range of successful brands such as Coca Cola (the Innocent), Harley Davidson (the Outlaw), TED conferences (the Sage) and so on. Archetypal branding motivates and regulates human behaviour, pushing consumers to pick the brand whose archetype resonates with their behaviours. Common archetypes of safety include behaviours representing intolerance for error, denial of death, rule-following, hubris (overconfidence), masculinity, condemning people operating in automatic mode (loss of situational awareness or complacency), a search for objective truth, a search for perfection, heroism, the myth of salvation, and a quest for objectivity, certainty and control. But the archetypes of wisdom, helping, caring, femininity, humour, creativity, thinking and imagination are less common in the culture of safety.

## Why is healing part of learning?

To answer this question, I will reflect on my own life story. After experiencing a near collision at sea I lost confidence in my abilities, and for a long time I felt that I was genuinely responsible for the mishap. But when I met with Francesco and many others who were involved in accidents and listened to their stories, my experience felt like a familiar pattern of human behaviour. The knowledge of this archetype gave me a sense of normality and perspective.

Until that point, I had experienced an over-identification with the archetype of perfection: 'I cannot afford to make any more mistakes'; 'I should have checked and re-checked everything'; 'I'm not good enough'; 'I have to be careful.' I found myself caught up in these inner voices and drawn into a negative spiral of guilt, shame and loss of self-esteem. Back then, little was known about the effects of accidents on the human psyche. I first became aware of my own trauma and distress when I enrolled for a PhD, and even then it was not a direct awareness. It was through anthropology that I realised the power of narrative construction and how the same narrative can be reconstructed in different ways. 'You're *not* alone; it's *not* your mistake only; and there are others who are also responsible for this outcome.' Multiple stories, shared accountability; competing versions of the same experience and plural realities can liberate us from becoming over-identified with the accident outcome, for which we feel wholly responsible.

Times are changing. Studies in trauma and healing are bringing the awareness that the knowledge of the archetypes gives us the comfort that we are not alone in going through an experience. Even knowing that there are others who have been through the same experience, and that the trend may well continue after we are gone, can produce a healing effect (Johnson R. , 1989) (Johnson R. , 1991) (Levine, 1997). Knowing this, I could take control of my life and thrive once again; I could detach myself from the archetype of perfection and infallibility and focus instead on realising my potential. But I am aware that many people, once they have experienced an over-identification with an archetype, may not be able to set themselves free so easily. Guilt, shame, worthlessness, lack of confidence and low sense of esteem can sit deep in our unconscious forever. **To a large extent learning is healing, and our investigation methods are not always helpful in generating healing through the process of learning.** Often, one comes at the expense of the other.

Once again, the *Costa Concordia* accident serves as a relevant example. During our visit, Francesco told us that following the accident the entire team was awake through the night attending to the crisis. The next morning, he was summoned to the police station for an interrogation. When he told the police officers he had a headache, he was given two parac- etamols and fifteen minutes to shower before the interrogation commenced. If this was an attempt to understand the captain's perspective, it clearly showed little appreciation for what it means to be a human being faced with trauma in a crisis.

Note: Should you wish to enhance your under- standing about archetypes and the collective un- conscious, I recommend starting by listening to Dr Kevin Lu's podcast, 'Archetypes and the Collective Unconscious'; Dr Lu's humble and erudite style of presenting the work of Carl Jung in a series of short sessions is commendable.

## Learning as assimilating the shadow

We arrive in this world as innocent souls with a psyche. As we mature, we are enculturated into our society, and our psyche becomes less than the whole. We learn to wear a persona like an article of clothing, so that we can fit within the decorum and order of our society. We learn to say 'Yes, please' to an invitation to a birthday party, to please our bosses, and 'You may also wish to consider ...' when we don't want to upset our colleagues with our disagreement. Finding harmony with decorum is necessary, or there will be no civilised society. Along the way, we develop a conscious sense of who we are, which we call 'I'. The 'I' is our ego; although it is the tiniest expression in English writing, it forms the centre of our consciousness. As far as we are consciously aware, our ego is who we are.

As our ego develops, there are also neglected and unacceptable parts of our personality that we feel need to be put away. History shows that neighbours, peers, colleagues and society, and even our parents and spouses, will not accept our authentic personality, so as we mature we realise that authenticity has its limits. What we choose not to reveal does not disappear; it collects in the darker corners of our personality. Over time, this stored energy gathers a life of its own and becomes our shadow. The more we reject our dark side, the more darkness is collected in our shadow.

Carl Jung wrote extensively about the shadow and how, if not dealt with, it gets in the way of our personal growth and relationships. He wrote:

> everything that irritates us about others can lead us to an understanding of ourselves.

Contempt for others mainly comes from the animosity we have developed for our shadow without our awareness. We have a tendency to project our shadow onto something or someone so that we do not have to take responsibility for it.

### A short story of projection and shadow

Some years ago I attended a safety conference titled 'Just Culture: learning from accidents' organised by a shipping company. As part of the ritual of learning, a captain was asked to present to us how he had lost control of his ship while entering the Suez Canal. He started off with the details of the ship, the navigation and the weather information, the voyage itinerary and the location of the accident, and then went into an admission of a detailed list of errors made by him and his team, which he believed had led to the accident. He concluded by saying, 'I'm sorry, I made a mistake. I should never have entered the Canal knowing that the weather was outside the limits of safe operations.' For a few seconds, there was complete silence in the room.

The panel then invited everyone to ask questions and comments. Many of his peers were openly critical of the captain's actions and decisions, considering it an 'unnecessary risk', which none of them, faced with a similar situation, would have taken.

But later, during personal discussions with a few of the seafarers, the common themes that emerged were 'This was waiting to happen' or 'This could have happened to any of us'. It was interesting to observe that people will say one thing in public and quite the opposite in private. It was a good example of how we disown our shadow and project it on to the others.

I can relate with this experience at a personal level. When we were young, when my father had had a bad day at work he would cane our dog. The dog, in turn, would dig and scratch at the earth in frustration. Each of us has our own way to project our shadow. Forget humans and animals; if you sift through your near-miss data, your accident and maintenance reports, you will notice that when it comes to exposing our failures to the world we don't even spare machines, spanners and tools. In the story above, the men who in public criticised the captain for running the ship aground were projecting their shadow onto him. While in private they were able to confess their empathy and support for the captain, in public their personas were overpowered by their own shadows.

The animosity that Francesco Schettino and his family had to face from the public is a reflection of how accident reports and public narratives feed our shadow outwardly. So intense was the hatred that Francesco found it difficult to cope with public anger even in Meta, his hometown. So he bought a Napoleon mastiff, Leon. I have never seen a dog that looked more depressed than Leon. The dog's 'eccentric appearance', said Schettino, diverted attention from him as they walked around the town.

Figure 9.4: Francesco's dog, Leon.

Despite all the problems in the ship's design, the dubious regulatory and certification business, the questionable quality of the lifesaving equipment, the ambiguous safety management systems, the substandard training, and the recruitment of inexperienced seafarers, combined with a rising trend for cruise holidays – a trend that's driving an entire industry to the brink of collapse – the official accident report declared Schettino to be the 'main cause' of the accident.

The organisation, the investigation team, the safety department, the press, and society at large found in this accident a way to disown its collective shadow. No one asks the questions: What would I do differently if I had been in Schettino's place? Why did we not see this coming? What are we doing under the pretext of audits and inspections? What can we learn from this accident about our own way of managing the business risks? As Robertson wrote, 'projection is always easier than assimilation' (Johnson R. , 1991, p. 32).

## The creative capacity of our shadow

Not everything in our shadow is pejorative. When my eight-year-old son admires his elder sister, his shadow craves to emulate her character. People are known to find their inner creativity, their hidden potential, and their element when they learn to assimilate their shadow with their ego (Johnson R. , 1991). Francesco's life story is a telling example of how misfortune can help us realise our hidden potential. While waiting for his prison sentence, Francesco was the first to design the world's lightest canoe; it weighed less than 10 kilos and measured 5.4 metres. He later obtained a prototype for the design, and set up a successful business for his daughter so that the family members could sustain themselves and make a living while he was in prison. In his letters from prison, he often questions the assumptions about the principles of ship design. For instance, why do we have such powerful fire pumps but low-capacity bilge pumps? In other words, how well do we understand the nature of emergencies in designing and constructing ships?

Figure 9.5: A kayak prototyped by Francesco Schettino.

## Tragic optimism

The Austrian psychiatrist Victor Frankl coined a term for the creative capacity in our shadow: 'tragic optimism' (Frankl, 1962), defining it as:

> the human capacity to creatively turn life's negative aspects into something positive or constructive. In other words, what matters is to make the best of any given situation. Hence the reason I

speak of a tragic optimism and optimism in the face of tragedy.

It is disturbing that we spend so much time writing and distributing 'safety flashes' and 'lessons learned' when we should instead be finding ways to assimilate the shadow and learn something meaningful by unlocking the potential of people involved in accidents. Why not include people involved in accidents, to share their experiences without guilt or shame?

With so much hidden in the mysteries of the unconscious, it is appropriate to ask what our role is as an investigator. Like a mirror, our role is to show to people their unconscious and bring them closer to their shadow and their archetype. But by projecting our own archetypal qualities and shadow onto others and failing to see theirs, not only do we overburden a traumatised fallible person, but also we lose the chance to learn and transform ourselves.

In the final chapter of this book, we will illustrate the use of the iCue mapping as a method to surface the contents of the unconscious mind using the example of an accident report.

# 10

# Learning is Embracing Fallibility

Finally, I am discussing a topic so close to my heart and life experiences. In this chapter, we will explore why are we humans so unforgiving about errors and mistakes? While there is an extensive body of literature on human error, there is little discussion in the culture of risk and safety to understand the basis for human fallibility. So, what does it mean to be a fallible human? And why instead of rejecting or controlling fallibility, we should consider the idea of embracing fallibility when it comes to learning? Towards the end of this chapter, I summarise my approach to learning in this book. (I will switch between the terms 'error', 'mistake', and 'failure' as metaphors of human fallibility without being too technical.)

- Understanding human fallibility.
- The risk of denying and controlling human fallibility.
- The transformational power in embracing fallibility.
- Embracing fallibility as an investigation philosophy.
- Summarising learning.

Figure 10.1: A general outline of the chapter.

> You are the first two people who came to talk to me at a professional level. Nobody has spoken to me from the industry, apart from the lawyers.

Those were Francesco Schettino's first words when we met him in his hometown. I still ponder on this statement. When I first heard him say that, it almost felt as if I'd discovered a goldmine, but I didn't know its worth. Why *wouldn't* anyone want to speak with this man? What is the risk? What is really at stake? Am I missing something?

The aviation world relies on black boxes to learn from accidents, because it's rare that pilots will survive the crash. Now, here is Schettino, a living black box with a wealth of insight, willing to share everything about what happened on the night – but no one wants to listen to him. We talk of designing resilient systems of the future. What better way could there be to lay down the foundations of a resilient future in shipping than by incorporating his embodied experiences? You could reject everything that he has to say – but I'd suggest you lend him an ear, at least. But as we will discover, it's not that simple.

## The stigma of failure

Children find out early in life that despite all the pep talks from their parents, failure is not an option. In India, where I was born and spent the first seventeen years of my life, at least one student commits suicide every forty-two minutes. The country recorded 9,478 student suicides in 2016, which increased to 10,335 in 2019 and 13,089 in 2021 when it was 8 per cent of all suicide cases. In 2021 alone, during Covid, the total number of suicide cases rose by 20 per cent over the same period: from 131,008 in 2016 to 164,033 in 2021. For most of these students, according to the National Crime Records Bureau (NCBR 2021), the reason for suicide was 'failure in examination'. In other parts of the world things may not be as bad, but the stigma of failure is scarcely any different across cultures and geography.

During my career at sea I learned that organisations insist that failures and errors should be controlled – and if not, then we should at least learn to manage them. The risk and safety industry does not realise how deeply it is caught up in the myth of error avoidance. Few people in the industry question the source of human error, and even fewer realise that fallibility is an intrinsic part of our being. One cannot manage error without understanding that fall-ability is our first nature as unconscious beings.

## Why do humans err?

Let us raise a question that often remains unaddressed in safety studies: 'Why do humans make errors?' Paul Ricoeur (1960), going further, asks why people commit crime. I am referring to his book *Fallible Man*, the second of his trilogy The Philosophy of the Will.

According to Ricoeur, we are in part voluntary but in large part involuntary beings.[5] The voluntary being is free to decide, to move and to consent. When we live in a free society we can decide what we want for ourselves; we can move when we feel the need; we have a choice whether or not to agree with others. However, all three modes of freedom – decision, movement and consent – are subject to the involuntary constraints that arise from our biological needs.

When we *decide* something, we may be in a conflict with our desires and needs. I can decide not to eat, but at some point my body feels hungry. Or I need to feed my children, but if I am motivated by selfishness alone, I may choose not to do so. Similarly with my bodily movements, which are not completely within my voluntary control, I am driven in one sense, but my (involuntary) habits, my emotions, my physiology and my basic survival needs can make it difficult for me to exercise my will.

On the issue of our freedom of *movement*, a few years ago I had a conversation with decision expert Gary Klein, who asked me a wonderfully thought-provoking question: As we get older we may become more experienced, but how good is the experience if the body cannot move? He was referring in this case to

---

[5] He uses the terms 'voluntary' and 'involuntary' as against 'conscious' and 'unconscious', which begins to make sense once we arrive at an understanding of our fallibility.

mountaineering, but the same could be said of any profession: our limitations affect the function of our being as a whole. What good is a firefighter's or a surgeon's experience if their body does not enable them to do their job? The idea of a skilled worker or an expert cannot be reduced to the proper functioning of mind alone or body alone; an expert is an embodied person.

Reflecting upon Klein's humbling question, I find that Ricoeur's thesis makes a lot of sense. As I watch my parents getting older, I can see how our freedom of movement is limited by our own biological constraints. For example, I intend to write, but I am sick and I need rest; can I, then, write? I may have to work on a night shift, but my body is tired, so I must push myself to stay up; should I drink more coffee? I am navigating close to a rock, so I must check the position of the ship more frequently – but my body (i.e. my embodied Mind) has learned through experience that such a manoeuvre is safe. Should I go back to check the position, or can I rely on my heuristics and save the effort? Such a conflict between the freedom of will and the constraints of our (unconscious) necessities sets up an ongoing tension within our own selves. That ongoing tension is characteristic of all human life, and negotiating between our will and necessity runs deep within our existence. It induces fragility, error, temptations, desires, vices and the possibility of failure.

In direct opposition to the Cartesian notion of *cogito, ergo sum* ('I think, therefore I am': the rational thinking person who learns to doubt everything around them in order to prove their existence), for Ricoeur, thinking alone is not enough to evoke change in society.

Eventually, we must do something to bring change, and to enact change we need our bodies. Here Ricoeur is challenging the Cartesian view of mind and body separation at the basic level of existence.

Why do people make errors? Why do some good people turn evil? From Ricoeur's point of view, evil and error do not come from outside, but are embedded within our own existence. We are fallible, and fallibility is something we are born with because of the incongruence between our freedom (will) and necessity (body). We all make errors.

## Fallibility and behaviourism

One immediate thought that arises here is the limitation of the philosophy of behaviourism. The idea of behaviourism – the temptation to simplify an individual's behaviours into a single trait – is not very helpful for learning. By saying that someone is alcoholic (greedy, complacent, negligent, lazy, inefficient, careless, callous, or complacent) means that we are taking apart the whole person. In so doing, we are lacking a holistic understanding. On the other hand, the ability to see the other person as a whole helps us appreciate that we are all fallible beings – and that in our fallibility we are all connected with each other. We have the tendency to take the person involved in an accident so far along the behavioural spectrum that no one dares to relate to them; and then, when no one can relate to them, no one will behave like them. Does that really work? When I met with Francesco, I saw in him glimpses of a caring father, a respected community member, a pet owner, and a craftsperson. I have drawn from those glimpses during my workshops, and some participants, seeing themselves in Francesco's situation, have said, 'Next time, it could be me.'

## The risk of denying and controlling fallibility

If you are a risk and safety manager you may be thinking: Should I start to allow mistakes to happen? If so, where does that leave me? If you have a sloppy team member, a lazy co-worker, or a colleague or a friend who you think never takes responsibility for their actions, it is difficult to imagine the idea of *embracing* fallibility in practice. Organisations work under intensive financial pressure, and we all have expectations of qualified professionals. It is reasonable, therefore, to think about how to prevent errors and seek a path towards infallibility: zero accidents.

But embracing fallibility, or error, is none of this. The idea of embracing fallibility is to reflect upon our instinct, to prime our unconscious mind to listen before making a judgement, even when 'human error' seems like an obvious answer, a familiar pattern of rule violation or a mistake repeated by someone. No matter how familiar the error sounds and how well we know the person who has made the error, we must learn to see every situation afresh and every person anew, irrespective of their history. Such a fundamental change in our behaviour does not come from reading self-help books or by following a technique or listening to a few podcasts, although those things do help. It comes from articulating our philosophy about how we should live and relate to fallible humans, and by repeatedly practising our philosophy each time we respond to an error (Long, 2018) (Claxton, 2016).

Consider for a moment the practical implications of our knee-jerk reactions in denying and controlling fallibility – trying to make people work perfectly by punishing them for every error, and plastering our crippling safety management systems (SMS) with yet more controls and checks. Further, we have those Just Culture models, setting up courtrooms in our organisations to decide between guilt and innocence, even though we have no qualifications as lawyers. We examine facts, but we don't really know how to read, deconstruct and make meaning of those facts until a professional lawyer pulls back the curtain, revealing that we are out of our depth in our fear-driven reflexes to managing risk.

The internationally acclaimed Health and Safety lawyer Greg Smith, with whom I have had the privilege of facilitating several workshops and podcasts, makes compelling reading in his book *Paper Safe*. Smith's (2018) wisdom, supported by a number of case studies, is enlightening, yet often ignored:

- do not overburden your safety management system with unrealistic controls;
- if people on the ground cannot cope with the burden of those checks and controls, it is not only counterproductive to safety but also detrimental to the reputation and survivability of your organisation;
- compliance does not mean much if your paperwork does not align with its intent and purpose.

The *Hoegh Osaka*, the car carrier we discussed earlier, provides a classic example of Smith's wisdom. Within a span of four hours in port while the ship was discharging cargo, its crew were expected to carry out 232 checks according to the company procedures (Anand, 2016). Storkensen's (2020) research shows that we are seeing a new pattern in maritime accidents; ships run aground, collide and catch fire not despite but *because* of the ever-proliferating regulations and controls. What is the source of the unrealistic nature of controls that we have created in our organisations? The delusion of infallibility.

A deeper problem of 'controlling' fallibility lies in the shared unconscious of the entire risk and safety industry. Many safety managers I have interacted with are convinced that their primary role is to prevent people from being injured or killed. This is understandable when you think of workers as unthinking beings who can harm themselves if they are not controlled. But that view of human behaviour is by far the most profound distortion, and one that does not even coincide with the legal perspective. Both Smith (2018) and Ashurst et al. (2016) remind us that our role as risk and safety managers is not to protect people but to give them a sense of ownership and critical thinking in order for them to identify the risks, then tackle them.

The law does not expect us to achieve 'zero harm'; the legal position is in fact to ensure that we maintain the ability to manage the risk in order to make it as low as reasonably practicable (ALARP). **This is a radical shift in not only the role but also the identity of a risk and safety manager; that is, from someone accountable for saving lives to someone** who adopts a critical and mindful approach – and, when it comes to managing risk, asks searching questions to those in positions of power (who may find them difficult to answer). It is in the latter that we begin to appreciate the ecosystem in which the business operates and can devote our resources to meaningful work. It is also in the latter that we create space for people to take ownership of their processes so that we don't end up in an erosion of trust.[6]

## The transformational power in embracing fallibility

Existence is fallible; we are born imperfect, and we remain vulnerable throughout life. I would encourage you to read Dr Long's book, *Fallibility and Risk* (Long, 2018).[7] How eloquently he brings us to a different worldview of fallibility: in our imperfection and vulnerability lies our social dependence for learning, evolving and risk taking. There is no learning when there is no embracing. I would also recommend you read researcher Brene Brown, who talks extensively about vulnerability and imperfection in her book *The Gift of Imperfection.*

When Francesco said that no one spoke with him after the accident, it became clear to me that silence was a manifestation of the collective unconscious of an entire industry, which is struggling to embrace the fallibility of this person. No true maritime

---

[6] https://www.humandymensions.com/product/risky-conversations/
[7] Free for download in an accessible format.

professional deliberately cuts connections with people involved in accidents, yet it seems that in the world of shipping no one has recognised the potential for learning from this fallible person.

When I was planning to meet with Francesco, I had the same hesitation. I wondered what would happen if I learned something new about him. What if he was not the 'main cause' of the disaster? What if I were to see glimpses of my own life story in this accident? Participation and understanding are risky for me, for they may change my mind forever. It would be much safer for me to have a low opinion of 'Captain Coward'. Hatred would allow me to preserve my anger and project my fear onto him. Hatred is easy: love takes effort. Deep down, we have not learned to embrace fallible people. To underline the point, we are in essence more belief-ridden, more primitive, and more mythical than we like to think.

In the world of risk management, our role should not be to manage fallibility but to embrace it. Contrary to popular belief, the first question we actually ask after an accident is not the what, how or why, but the who. Who was involved in the accident? What do we know about this person? What would it take to connect with this person's unconscious?

Brene Brown defines connection as:

> the energy that exists between people when they feel seen, heard, and valued; when they can give and receive without judgment; and when they derive sustenance and strength from the relationship (Brown, 2018, p. 19).

It is through this connection that we experience the joy of living, learning and flourishing. If the mysteries of the unconscious provide the treasure for learning, it is the embracing of fallibility that is the key to unlocking the treasure chest.

In my interviews with the captain, which lasted for many hours, I experienced at first hand the power of embracing fallibility. In the following chapters, you will be able to perceive the depth of learning that followed from those interviews. In them, barely any questions were asked, no probing took place. All that was required was a desire to embrace fallibility, and a genuine meeting of minds in the i-thou.

## A side note on imperfection

When I was planning to interview Francesco in his role as captain of *Costa Concordia*, it took us hours to select the most appropriate background (you could call it the sickness of perfectionism). We were looking for a plain wall with good natural light, and at last we found one. It was against this spotless white wall that I interviewed Schettino.

But when I came home and watched the recordings, I noticed a thin crack running right through the middle of the wall, from top to bottom. What could be a more powerful symbol of imperfection?

## Embracing fallibility as an investigation philosophy

These days we often hear about the importance of a shift in our language as a solution to improving learning from accidents. Once again, that focus misses the point that language is metaphorical and embodied. If the investigation philosophy remains embedded in brain-centric, disembodied methods and models, it does not matter if we use the term 'human error' or 'human performance'. It does not matter if we modify the labelling of our investigation to a 'learning review' or an 'event analysis'.

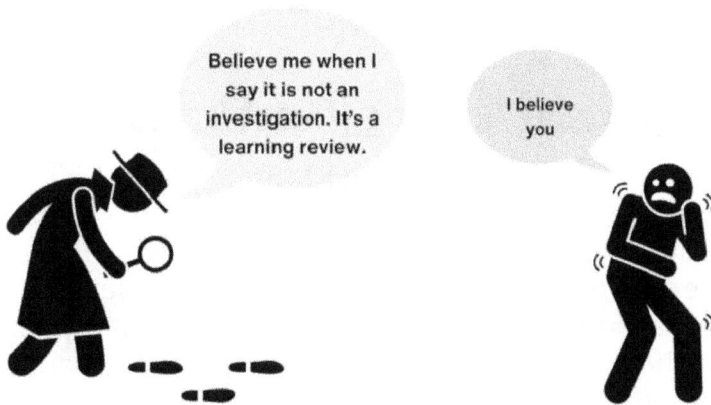

Figure 10.2: A change in language requires a change in our orientation, or we face the risk of reverting to our default.

A sustainable change in language begins with questioning our investigation philosophy. How do our methods, models and questioning styles engage with the fallible person? What are the common metaphors of accidents and learning in our organisation? How consistent are our metaphors with the common narratives, artefacts, slogans and policies, and our immediate response to an accident? Even though we can be seduced by mantras such as 'we want to learn from mistakes' or 'humans are fallible', when an accident actually happens we may end up doing exactly the opposite.

So a change in language must begin with an articulation of our ethics and moral principles. How do we respond to errors? How do we relate with fallible humans? Do we share a common view about error and fallibility? **Without this knowledge, we end up with an investigation report that is nothing but a post-hoc justification of the conscious (threatened) mind.** What is there to learn from the outcome of such an investigation? Perhaps how not to conduct an accident investigation.

## Summarising learning (Chapter 4 to 10)

As I have gone through the hundreds of feedback notes and takeaways from my workshops, I have noticed that at the end of the workshop most attendees are still locked in the same mindset: better training programmes, fewer processes, sympathy for the captain, vengeance against the organisation, 'poor leadership', or sloppy top management. Their frustrations were mostly projected outwards, as were their solutions.

Occasionally, though, I met people who clearly felt the need for change within. One of the greatest gifts of the pandemic was the way I was forced to change the format of the workshop. From a day's in-person session, I switched to a series of four two-hour sessions online. So a typical face-to-face workshop that had lasted for a day could now stretch to a month.

In New Zealand, where hundreds of participants joined one of the series, I was told that many people would take time off from work to join the sessions.

They became excited as they watched the story unfolding each week. One woman told me that after the workshop each week she would wait all day for her husband in order to tell him about what she had learned. In another series in Singapore, a ship manager in Hong Kong, who had been highly critical of Francesco in the first session, experienced a shift by the time the workshop series came to an end; he said, 'Life will never be the same.' Another wrote, 'I cannot continue like this any more.' It was because the workshop lasted for a few weeks that these people were experiencing a shift within themselves.

Recall our discussions on One Brain Three Minds. Week after week, as the participants kept returning to the sessions, the story was bringing their unconscious to the surface, and that shift was being felt in their bodies. The learning was first met with dissonance in Mind 1, but slowly it penetrated into Mind 2 and Mind 3 in the same way as unlearning was surfacing from Minds 2 and 3 into Mind 1. Through this learning and unlearning experience, the participants gradually felt a movement within.

When Shakespeare said 'the antithesis of love is not hatred but indifference', he was right. You can only draw close to someone if you feel the emotion. Without the energy in motion, there is no movement and therefore no learning.

Michelle Dykstra, a woman of Dutch origin, wrote:

> Dear Nippin, I just want to express the respect I have both for you and for the ship's captain. I find myself moved to tears when seeing the captain go over how events unfolded and realising he is

a victim of the accident too. I do hope you get more fruit from your work in the form of a kinder outcome for the captain. Warm regards.

Respect, hope, kindness, fruit, movement, and tears. What better metaphors for learning and change? It is not as if the participants uncritically embraced everything they had heard and seen. On the contrary: many of them were critical, and stuck to their original viewpoints. During my trip to New Zealand in August 2023 I met Michelle, and she shared her life story of fallibilities with me. The difference with Michelle and the ship manager from Hong Kong and a few others was that they felt a movement within. They were not apologetic or sympathetic to the captain; instead, they saw in his vulnerabilities and imperfections a glimpse of their own lives, and they were drawn to his archetype. When they felt the discomfort within and the dissonance with their worldview, they were ready to take their next step in Faith. They took their chance. **Learning begins when we feel the dissonance. Learning begins with a step beyond reasoning in our own worldview and a movement in faith and doubt to experience the world anew.**

Through this journey of self-reflection, I summarise learning as:

- the meeting of a whole person with a whole person, as against individual learning;
- creating space for faith, doubt and subjectivity, as against a search for objective truth and certainty;
- realising the power of emotions (e-motions), as against denying or disowning feelings and emotions;

- surfacing the tacit, implicit and unconscious, as against focusing on the explicit and conscious;
- assimilating the shadow, as against projecting it;
- embracing fallibility, as against denying or managing error;
- and experiencing an embodied movement towards the other, as against the disembodied and brain-centric model of education, schooling and training.

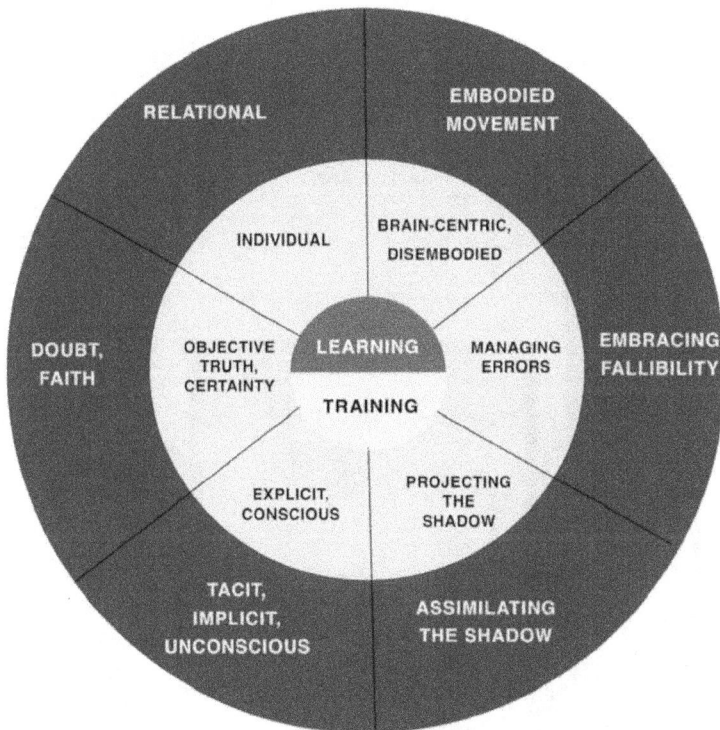

Figure 10.3: A dialectic between embodied learning and disembodied education and training.

It is against this framework of learning that we turn to the next three chapters, where, in search for a more holistic understanding of the accident, we meet with Captain Francesco Schettino, listen to his unconscious, and compare his views to the official investigation report and public discourse. I encourage you to remain doubtful yet open-minded, critical yet empathetic, and unconvinced yet forgiving as you too meet with this fallible person. I encourage you to be like the lion on the book cover. Let us learn to be patient and discerning, and listen to the fallible mouse.

Figure 10.4: The lion and the mouse.

# 11

# The Accident

———————⚬✦⚬———————

> - The details of the ship.
> - Background to the Costa Concordia accident.
> - Public perception about the accident.
> - The outcome of the accident investigation.
> - The impact of the accident on the captain of Costa Concordia.
> - The questions to be addressed in the following chapters.

Figure 11.1: A general outline of the chapter.

The *Costa Concordia* was a ship of 114,000 gross tons, 13 decks high, 290 metres (951 feet) in length and 8 metres in draft, owned by Costa Crociere, a subsidiary of Carnival Corporation. Built in 2006, the ship could carry up to 3780 passengers and 1110 crew, a total complement of 4890. In addition to being the largest Italian passenger ship of its time, the ship had four swimming pools, a casino and a large spa. At the time of the accident, the ship was on a regular route around the Mediterranean, from Civitavecchia to Savona, Marseille, Barcelona, Palma, Cagliari, Palermo and back to Civitavecchia. That's seven ports in seven days, a demanding voyage.

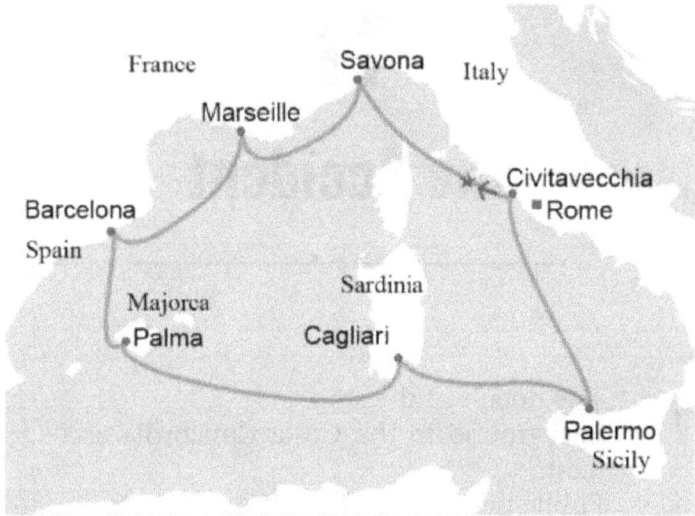

Figure 11.2: Map of *Costa Concordia* voyage plan. (Photo: Wikimedia Commons, photo credit Soerfm, date 29-11-2021)

## The accident

On 13 January 2012 the *Costa Concordia* sailed out from Civitavecchia bound for Savona. About two hours after departure, the ship collided with Le Scole rocks off the Giglio Islands, off Tuscany. The contact with the rocks resulted in a 53-metre gash in the ship's side, leading to progressive flooding and capsizing of the ship. The gash had unfortunately proved to be in a particularly vulnerable location. According to the official report:

the immediate flooding of five contiguous watertight compartments, where most of the vital equipment of the ship was located, makes the *Costa Concordia* casualty quite a unique event, because of the extent of damage is well beyond the survivability standard applicable to the ship according to her keel laying date

(MIT, 2013, p. 3).

Furthermore:

The vessel immediately lost propulsion and was consequently affected by a black-out. The Emergency Generator Power switched on as expected, but was not able to supply the utilities to handle the emergency and on the other hand worked in a discontinuous way. The rudder remained blocked completely starboard and no longer handled. The ship turned starboard by herself and finally grounded (due to favourable wind and current) at the Giglio Island at around 23.00 and was seriously heeled (approximately 15°)

(MIT, 2013, p. 4).

Within 48 hours of the accident, the company CEO issued a press statement:

We cannot unfortunately, deny human error. The company cannot be associated with this behaviour. The Captain took a decision on his own which is contrary to our written and certified rules. This route was set correctly upon departure from Civitavecchia. The fact [that the ship deviated from this route] is solely due to a non-approved and unauthorised manoeuvre and which Costa Crociere was not made aware of. The procedures implemented after the ship hit the rock did not respect in any way the strict rules, procedures and training we have given our officer. (CEO press statement 15 January 2012)

(Los Angeles Times, 2012)

Coincidentally, on the same day a former captain and a safety expert appeared on television, making the following statement:

To hear talk of being 300 metres from dangerous rocks is very worrying. In my long career I have never heard people talk about such situations in terms of metres, it is always in terms of miles, so I do not understand how this can suffice as an argument. ... The weather was favourable, there was good visibility and this was a familiar route, so it is very perplexing how an accident of this kind occurred.

(15 January 2012, Sky TV UK)

As with most maritime accidents, culpability and criminality were determined in the public view long before the formal accident investigation was concluded.

A year later, the official accident report was found to align with the public narrative:

The ship was sailing too close to the coastline, in a poorly lit shore area, under the Master's command who had planned to pass at an unsafe distance at night time and at high speed (15.5 kts).

(MIT, 2013, p. 11)

Amongst other things, the captain was criticised for his casual attitude towards formulating the ship's voyage plan, sailing 0.5 miles too close to the coast, and 'disregarding to properly consider the distance from the coast'.

In 2017, the Court of Cassation, Italy's highest criminal tribunal, sentenced Francesco Schettino to sixteen years in prison: ten for multiple manslaughter, five for causing the shipwreck and one for abandoning his passengers. In contrast, while the Costa Cruises unit of Carnival Corporation paid a fine of €1 million (US$1.3 million at the time), the prosecutors accepted plea bargains from the five officials concerned.

The following chapters are dedicated to answering the questions:

1. What explains the captain's motivation to sail so close to the Giglio Islands?
2. What can we learn from studying this accident about the construct of psychological safety and error management?
3. What can we learn from this accident about the effectiveness of plans and procedures in managing a crisis?
4. And finally, why do we feel the need to blame someone in an accident?

# 12

# It's a Normal Practice

If there's one image that most people instantly recall when we discuss the case of the *Costa Concordia*, it would be the captain navigating the ship too close to the islands. In the cruise industry, this manoeuvre is famously referred to as a 'sail-past' but to an outsider it appears as a case of violation of safety rules in keeping the ship at a safe distance from the shore. What explains this mismatch? How can we understand it?

---

- The captain's motivation to sail close to the Giglio islands (sail-past manoeuvre).
- Understanding the normal practice of sail-past.
- How 'normal' practices evolve over a period of time.
- What / who empowers 'normal practices?'

---

> - Understanding normal practices through cultural lenses.
> - A legal perspective about what is considered 'normal.'

Figure 12.1: A general outline of the chapter.

We asked Francesco, 'Tell us, what was your motivation to navigate close to the Giglio Islands?'

To this, his response was:

> In general, we are performing a salute with a cruise line in reducing the speed, calling the manoeuvre operation, taking the bow thruster on the bridge, we slow down the engine, perform the salute at 5, 6, 7 knots maximum. This was not any kind of restricting navigation. This was simply a passage at 0.5 nautical miles from shore. It was not any special practice. We didn't have time to lose, to slow down the engine to go very close to the land. This is the same passage that you can perform when you go from Savona to Barcelona and you pass at 0.4 nautical miles from shore, or even when you navigate at full speed in Copenhagen where you are at 0.2 [nautical miles] on each side from the land and you are in restricted water. This was not the practice that you perform.
>
> Let's say you pay tribute to the island or make the passengers happy, to offer an additional value to the cruise. Obviously even if you are passing by at 0.5 nautical miles still it's interesting for the passengers to see that they are on the island; this was normal practice to pass close, but 'close' is relatively close, because we are talking here about 1000 metres away. Obviously, if we talk to

a captain of a tanker of a very large crude carrier when they never see the land, even when I was an officer on a very large crude carrier, you have different parameters to establish the distance. When you are a cruise ship captain and on a daily basis you navigate through the Venice channel, the fjords of Ushuaia, it was nothing so special just to make a course deviation on the waypoint at 0.5 nautical miles, with a bathymetric of 10 metres from the bottom. So it was not difficult.

I reflected upon Francesco's response over many months. When I had first listened to the captain, his words almost felt like a grounded message: 'This is my identity, my world; and this is what I do day in, day out. Why would you punish me for doing my work? How can you accuse me for existing?' But there is a powerful expression here that I was emotionally and anthropologically drawn to: 'This was normal practice.' While the world, including the leading industry experts, are pointing their finger at the captain for being negligent, five years later the man is still convinced that he did nothing wrong by taking the ship close to the island. You and I can debate what is normal and abnormal, but an understanding of our differences requires a wholly different approach. To understand Francesco's normal, we must be prepared to let go of our own.

When something appears normal to you, it is because that's the way you see the world. It's your normal. In this chapter, we will learn how 'normal practices' are created and maintained in an organisation, and how we can understand the normal through the lenses of culture. Recall our discussion on collective unconscious and culture in Chapter 9. We will use the

Culture Cloud framework (Figure 9.3) to understand the culture of the cruise industry. We will study the rituals, ethics, artefacts, language and the history of past successes and failures to understand the assumptions, beliefs, and myths hidden in the normal practice of sail-past.

Before we end this chapter, we will also briefly discuss the legal view on normal practices. What would be the legal position when sail-past becomes a normal practice, particularly when it does not match with how the risk is captured and managed in the documented processes? A framework to help us understand what has become normal to the insiders but remains a distant reality to the outside world can improve our capacity to tackle risks and allocate our resources to where it is most needed.

Let us start with an understanding of how the famous 'sail-past' was planned.

## The deviation from the plan

A week before the accident the ship's maître d'hôtel had approached the captain, saying, 'Given that I am due to sign off, I would be grateful if you could pass by Giglio for a sail past' (Court of Grosseto, 2012). This was the second time the maître d'hôtel had made the request. The first time, the weather had not been favourable so the captain had refused, but on this occasion the captain felt 'obliged' to fulfil the expectations of the maître d'.

During our interview, the captain told me:

The maître was asking me to perform the manoeuvre so I said OK, I will come to the bridge. It was kind of reward as this man was good and also there was a former captain at Giglio so I thought I will make happy both of them.

(Interview notes March 2017)

Based on a second request from the same maître d', the captain had asked his second officer:

Have a look to see what speed we need to get out of here and approach Giglio. We've got to sail past this fucking Giglio right, let's chart the route, then.

Is half a mile OK, Captain? There's [enough] depth of water [there].

This exchange of words between Captain Francesco Schettino and the second officer on board the *Costa Concordia*, at 18:27 on 13 January 2012, was recorded in the interrogation report. Following this exchange, the passage plan was amended by the second officer and approved by the captain for the ship to perform a sail-past.

## The sail-past ritual

Seafarers have always been thrilled by sighting the coast after a long sea passage. Before the presence of our technologies and with the desire to connect with their families and the outside world, seafarers would look forward to phone calls, television and radio signals from the shore. After living at the mercy of nature for months, the sighting of land would be bliss for any sailor. From my own days at sea, I remember returning home and walking barefoot on the grass after months of strolling on steel plates, and while sailing along the coast of United States, staying up all night to listen to songs on FM radio. The sight of a beach or the shoreside was always a symbol of hope, connection and positivity. As a mark of respect, seafarers would often sail close to the coast and greet the inhabitants with their foghorns. Sail-past is sometimes also referred to as a salute, although the latter has its origin in naval customs.

To find out how this age-old ritual has arrived at an alternative meaning today, let us come back to the *Costa Concordia* case. According to the German news source *Spiegel Online*, the maître d' on board was a native of the Giglio Islands (Stanek, 2012). The newspaper *Il Tirreno* stated that the maître d' had called his parents on Friday afternoon and told them that he would be passing by their house, on the island's west coast. The paper also quoted a comment from his family member:

> In just a little while the Concordia is going to pass really close. A big hello to my brother, who will finally disembark at Savona to enjoy a bit of rest!

Shortly before the ship was due to pass the island the captain invited the maître d' to the bridge to show how close they were navigating to it. The captain was honouring his commitment to his shipmate. How do you refuse a sail-past to your maître d'? That would mean depriving him of the reunion, and the love and affection from his family. In fact, twice in our conversation on this topic Schettino used the term 'deontological'; it was his 'duty of care' towards his shipmate to perform the sail-past.

## What empowers the sail-past myth?

Beyond a sailor's love and affection for his family, I discovered how through the rise of tourism in the cruise industry the sail-past has taken on a new meaning, and has become a ritual for entertainment.

During follow-up correspondence two weeks after our meeting in Italy, I called Francesco to ask why he felt the need to deviate the ship's course on request from the maître d', to which he replied:

> Fleetwide was induced a sort of mentality to reward the hotel managers on board by paying attention to them. His request was not an exceptional one since the island was on the route, and passing close to any island is normal practice for a cruise ship.

Why would an organisation want to reward the maître d' in particular, or pay any more attention to that person than to other crew members on board? Thinking about this question generates another question: Where is the power located in the ritual?

While it may be simple to pin down the survival of an organisation to a single metric of profitability, to achieve that, given the multiple and conflicting goals within any organisation, is not always straightforward. The problem is even more pronounced in large or-ganisations, which consist of business units, sub-units and so on. It is here that the divide between the revenue-earning and the resource-exhausting units within an organisation merits investigation. While the operations and sales divisions are considered a source of revenue, the technical and safety units are generally considered a burden on resources. I can't see any company admitting this openly, but in general the resource-exhausting units often struggle with power and autonomy compared to the revenue-earning departments. In deep-sea drilling, for example, the production teams enjoy more privileges than the marine department, and the same is the case with the crane technicians on heavy lift vessels and with the subsea engineers on specialised offshore vessels. On luxury cruise vessels the catering department enjoys similar privilege in terms of departmental supremacy.

Sifting through some of the cruise line websites, it is not difficult to understand this dynamic. Some of the world's most famous chefs are appointed on cruise ships to showcase their culinary skills. A job advert seeking to fill in the role of a maître d'hôtel on a cruise ship job read:

> I am a Department Head and so responsible for reporting to on-board management and the main office, scheduling of all my personnel, disciplinary action within my Department, public relations with guests and taking care of any special needs, such as specific dietary requirements.

'Public relations with guests' explains the vital nature of this role. After all, dining is a core business of cruise lines. It is understandable, then, that any request from the maître d', given the power of that position, could not be taken lightly by the captain.

## Why normal practices should be understood and not controlled?

In all cultural dynamics there are dominant groups and subservient ones. In this case, the dominant group, whose purpose is being served by the 'normal', defends the ritual of sail-past as a matter of business necessity and survival. The subservient group that bears the consequences learns to accept it as their new normal (Bourdieu, 1972).

The chief executive of Costa Cruises condemned the captain for his non-approved plan to sail close to the coast. But on the other hand, he told the Italian Senate Committee, during questioning, that carefully planned 'touristic navigation' was 'accepted by laws, and it enriches the cruise package'. It helped drive business, he said. 'We do it because it is desired by passengers and we are competing on the world market' (Dinmore, 2012). In other words, sail-pasts are a business requirement in cruise companies in order for them to remain competitive.

Reading through the news articles, I found several expressions such as 'not a new trend', 'a nice tradition', 'touristic experience', 'maritime greeting' and *'normalissima'* ('very normal indeed') associated with the sail-past.

Figure 12.2: The tradition of sailing close to the shore was considered 'normal' by the local press. Photo: Stanek (2012)

Michael Lloyd (2019), a noted maritime freelance author, wrote:

> In court at Grosseto, Simone Canessa, the ship's navigating officer, said a former captain employed by the ship's owner, Mario Palombo, 'had successfully sailed 100 metres from the island's coast in a different ship in 2005'.

Many instances have highlighted the common practice of large cruise liners, including the *Costa Concordia* itself, cruising unacceptably close to the coast. It is notable that legislation has to be enacted rather than relying on the cruise operators to respect normal prudence and caution.

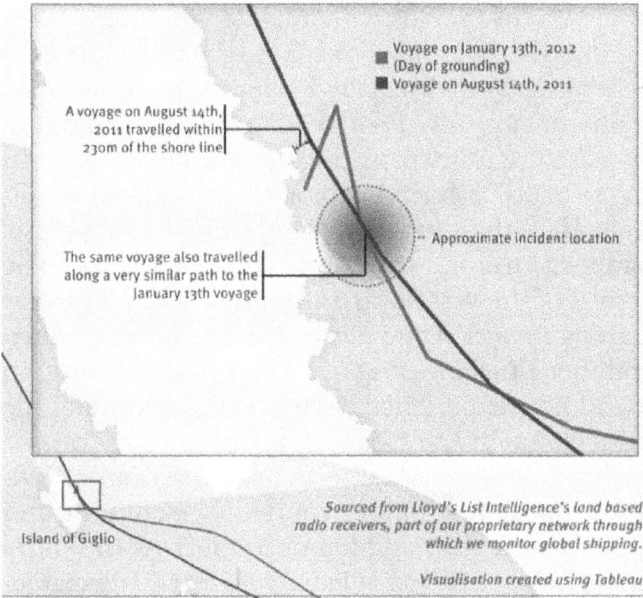

Figure 12.3: *Costa Concordia*'s previous near miss on 14 August 2011, a voyage track similar to the disastrous one in 2012. (Source: Lloyd's List, cited in Lloyd (2019))

Maurizio Catino, in his book *Scapegoating*, wrote:

An aporia emerges from Captain Schettino's testimony: on the one hand, he was criticised for not having notified the company and the authorities of the ship's deviation from its course; on the other hand, he was publicly praised by the company for making a similar sail-by salute on August 30, 2010, in front of the island of Procida. On the very same day as the disaster, on the company's website, the following post appeared (and was later deleted):

On August 30, 2010, before arriving in Naples at around 13:00, the Costa Concordia paid homage to the island of Procida with a salute and brief stop in the bay of Corricella, all thanks to Captain Francesco Schettino from Meta di Sorrento. An emotional moment not only for the island's inhabitants but also for the numerous tourists present who, from motorboats, fishing boats and boats of all kinds, welcomed the huge, imposing ship with applause, banners, music, trumpets and vuvuzelas. The arrival of the vessel was announced with 10 mortar rounds to which the Costa Concordia responded with her ritual greeting of 3 siren whistles. Surely a joyful new experience for everyone, including the passengers on the Costa Concordia, ready on the external decks with cameras and video cameras to immortalize that unique moment, celebrating and saluting with flags and handkerchiefs. As the ship's first officer – a native of Procida himself – declared, "It was a real celebration, a gesture of affection and a tribute to the maritime tradition that the folk of Procida and Sorrento have imbedded in their DNA".

(Catino, 2023)

It would be simplistic to think that such normal practices can be abolished through regulation and procedural controls when they have been embedded in the rituals and myths of the industry. New regulations (penalties, new regulations, criminalisation of offenders) will create new problems. And when an entire industry is seduced by the myth of the sail-past, there is not much that any individual company can do to resist the commercial pressure. The fact that both the captain and the CEO had normalised the sail-past in their world shows that normalisation is neither deliberate nor conscious. Rituals, myths and archetypical norms are the by-product of the history and legacy of the culture, which means that normal practices can remain unspoken and unchallenged forever, but at the same time become even more deeply embodied.

When it comes to influencing a culture we tend to attribute far too much power to the leaders and the CEOs. But when a myth becomes embodied, the CEOs and leaders can become helpless. How much of an influence do you think the President of United States can possibly exercise over gun control? In the cruise industry, what could a new CEO or rebel leader possibly do to discourage the practice of sail-past? The thought that leaders can change the culture of an organisation usually comes from viewing them as heroes and organisations as top-down structures, and seeing rewards, incentives and punishments as mechanisms to influence their culture. It is true that leaders can have an influence on the culture – but there is an extensive body of knowledge showing that human actions are motivated by intrinsic meaning and purpose far more than by carrots, sticks, rewards, awards and structures (Higgins, 2011) (Moskowitz & Grant, 2009).

At some stage, the ritual of sail-past may have been initiated out of necessity or as a pragmatic solution to seafarers being away for too long from their families. But over time the ritual of sail-past took on an entirely different meaning for the culture of cruise shipping. It became an unspoken demand by cruise passengers and an implied expectation by the powerful people in the organisational structure. Once that happens in any culture, anyone who becomes part of the group will be unconsciously primed to conform to the norms and practices of that group, and they will automatically accept this as their own normal. It requires much effort from any individual in the group to realise the power of the unconscious, let alone raise the courage and persistence to challenge it.

Do you notice a paradox here? It is the habits of the group that have attracted others to participate in that group in the first place. How, then, can someone who belongs to the group disapprove of a practice that gives solidarity to the group? The acclaimed sociologist and a pioneer in cultural studies Pierre Bourdieu called it *Habitus* (habit-us) i.e. 'a set of dispositions, skills, styles, tastes and behaviour that is shared by the members of a community, class or culture' (Bourdieu, 2023). In this way, an entire culture learns to develop the (unconscious) habit of not questioning what has become normal within the group (Bourdieu, 2023).

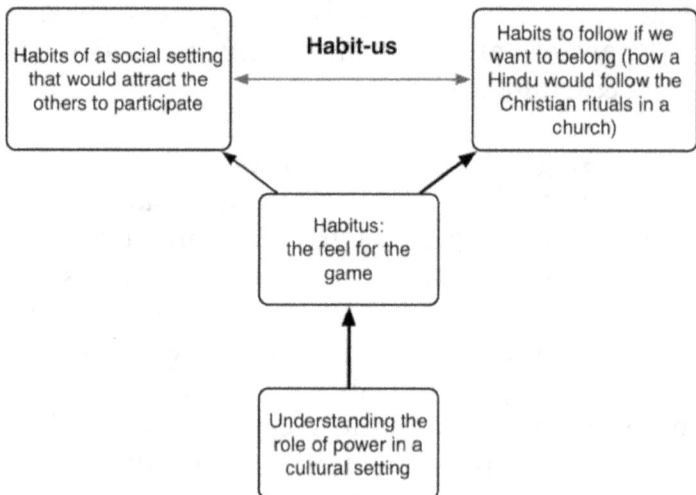

Figure 12.4: An illustration of Habitus based on Bourdieu (1982).

## The alternative values and ethics of normal practices

Why did the captain choose to go 'so close' to the island? Why did he deviate from the approved plan? Why did he not consider maintaining a 'safe distance'? Why was he making the ship go so fast? What was the rush? The framing of these questions is replete with value judgements. It is as if decision making is about an individual's binary choices between safety and efficiency goals – in this case maximising pleasure for the passengers whilst keeping the ship at a safe distance from the coast. But when I asked Francesco about his motivation to manoeuvre the vessel close to the Giglio Islands, his response reflected a strong sense of giving back to his community. He said, 'I thought I will make happy both of them' (i.e. the maître d' and his friend, a former captain, who lived on the island).

It was a captivating insight into the ethical and moral values that underpinned Francesco's normal. From one viewpoint the idea of making a crew member or a close friend happy by putting the ship in danger sounds ridiculous. It goes against the professional conduct of a ship captain who, in the modern Western world at least, is expected to conform to a set of rules and standards (code of ethics), and exercise judgement in their vocation. But this may not be true of other societies in which skills, finesse, charisma, artistry, heroism, and courtesy may be valued more than meticulous conformity to a code of practice (Elias, 1939).

When we think of ethics within the risk and safety industry, we are largely (but unconsciously) drawn into the imagery of rule following and duty of care (deontological) ethics. Where does this idea originate from? And, what are the alternative ways to think about ethics?

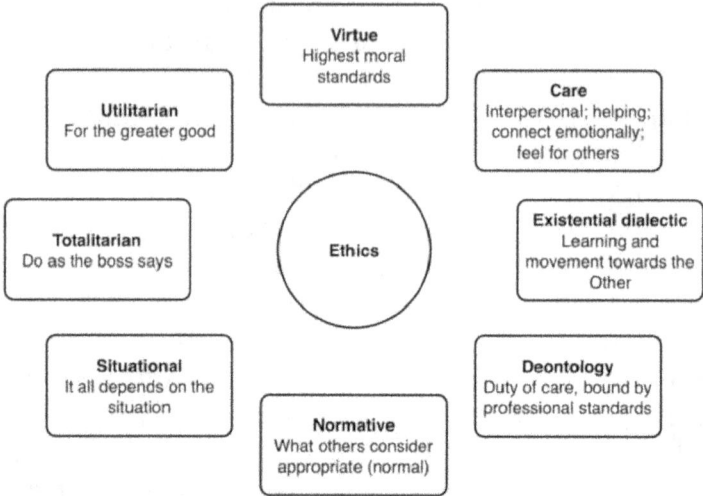

Figure 12.5: Examples of 'schools' (methodologies) of ethics.

Expressions such as 'rule following', 'ethical conduct' and 'duty of care' are the by-products of the monotheistic religions. In them, a good life lived is about following the word of Jesus, Mohammed or Jehovah. The details can vary, but the idea is that God created a perfect world, and human beings, born in sin, are tempted to fall prey to error and fallibility. And so the purpose of human lives is to seek perfection by following the word of their God. The Ten Commandments, for example, offer guidance about how to live and behave in the world – and then on Judgement Day it will be decided whether you have lived near enough to the expectations of God. Based on your thoughts, words and deeds in this life, you will, or won't, be granted a place in heaven in your afterlife.

Followers of polytheistic religions on the other hand – and Hinduism is a prime example – believe in multiple gods and goddesses (with a small g). There is no single preferred way to live life. Different deities symbolise different characters, and everyone is free to choose how to live their life. Human behaviour is not governed by a set of rules; in contrast, the underlying basis of human life is *dharma*, i.e. seeking harmony with existence and the laws of nature. Human subjectivity is celebrated in polytheistic religions. What is correct for a woman may not be correct for a man, and the idea of right and wrong shifts at different stages in one's lifetime. Reading the epics of the *Mahabharata* and the *Ramayana*, one gets the sense that the ethical basis of life is found in acting virtuously, for instance how those in positions of power should live their lives, and why the mighty should care for the meek. Society is thus held together by morality, not the rule of law.

It is natural to become frustrated when, despite our best efforts, the root cause of an accident almost invariably ends in a determination as to which rules have been breached. But in those instances, we should learn to recognise that it is much more than just the reluctance of an institution or an organisation to search for answers beyond rule compliance. It is the ethics of risk and safety.

What is fundamentally right and wrong at a basic level of the culture of safety industry? The industry is anchored to the same monotheistic myth of one God, one truth, and one set of rules as the guiding principles of life (otherwise referred to as the Safety Management System.) **As an industry, we have not**

**evolved to appreciate what other cultures would consider right or wrong.**

For example, the decision of the captain of the bulk carrier ship *Wakashio* that went aground off Mauritius shook many seasoned investigators in the risk and safety world. The captain was condemned for deviating the ship from its course by navigating close to the land. Why did he do this? Because he was trying to find a phone signal to help his crew members communicate with their families (Panama Maritime Authority, 2023). Maritime investigators stop their questioning beyond the point where rule violation is determined, without questioning the competing values and ethics, ie. those that do not align with the rule-following ethic. So, the root cause? – 'Procedure not followed'; period.

There are many instances from around the world where the ethics of rule following simply don't make sense if viewed through the framework of rule-following ethics. In 2008 a senior pilot in Cathay Pacific was sacked for flying a passenger jet barely 28 feet above the ground at the Boeing headquarters in Seattle, in a stunt to entertain a group of VIPs on the plane for its maiden flight. Later it was found that on maiden flights such stunts were common practice, intended as a 'bit of a jolly' for executives. More recently, Pakistan International Airlines came under attack on at least two occasions where 'unauthorised' guests were allowed into the cockpit by the pilot while the aircraft was airborne and during landing (Huffpost, 2017). A New York air traffic controller who attended my workshop told me that 'on a less busy day airline pilots often request a fly-around the New York City before leaving the airspace to provide an additional value to the passengers'. In Australia, planes flying into Ayers Rock/Connellan airport loop Uluru before landing, and stories of 'low passes' and fly-bys can be found in Zimbabwe and at air shows.

These examples illustrate a direct conflict between the duty of care (deontology) ethics strictly based on rule following in the culture of safety, and the alternative forms of conduct in professionals such as nepotism, favouritism, virtue, finesse, courtesy and care, based on ethics intrinsic to other cultures. We struggle to understand the diversity of human culture when all behaviour is judged through the lenses of the rule-following ethics. When Francesco talks about obliging his shipmate as the reason for performing a sail-past on the night of the accident, at that moment we are offered a rare glimpse into his worldview. We have a choice. We can dismiss Francesco as an irrational being, or we can choose to learn something new from another culture and enrich our worldview. I am not suggesting for a minute that this behaviour should be accepted. But the first principle of influencing behaviour, as any social scientist will tell you, is to learn to appreciate it, not dismiss it. Here is an important lesson in leadership: **understand before you want to be understood**.

# What is the history of successes and disasters of sail-past?

History is never a collection of neutral and objective facts; it is a social, cultural and power-laden narrative from a particular point of view. This is affirmed by studies in historiography and hermeneutics

(Ricoeur, 2016). How an organisation creates and shares stories of successes and failures plays an important role in shaping and influencing what is considered normal within its culture.

In 2005, Costa Cruises had another accident of a similar nature. The *Costa Fortuna*, with 3500 people on board on her passage along Capri, off the western coast of Italy, was performing a salute (sail-past) to entertain the passengers.

The maritime lawyer Jim Walker, who has devoted a lifetime of working on litigation cases involving passengers and crew injury and assault on cruise ships, wrote on his blog about this case (Walker, 2013):

> that the ship [Costa Fortuna] cruised into shallow water during what is called a 'sail-by' or 'salute' to entertain the guests. Just like the Costa Fortuna Cruise Ship Sail By Concordia, the Fortuna's hull was ruptured by rocks in the shallow waters and the cruise ship began to take on water.
>
> The Italian newspaper writes that the Master and officers of the Fortuna did not report the incident to the Italian Coast Guard or any maritime or port officials. The officers then ordered the use of pumps at maximum effort to keep the water from sinking the ship. The Fortuna was able to make it to the port of Palermo in Southern Italy. Once back in port, Costa had the hole repaired and then continued the cruise the following morning with all of the passengers.
>
> The only thing reported by Costa was that there had been an abnormal rise in the temperature of an engine. After making this false report, Costa 'buried' the incident.

The incident came to light as part of the investigation into Costa following the 2012 Costa Concordia disaster. One of the photographers who worked in 2005 on Fortuna reported the incident to the Master of Palermo. His story has been verified. Investigators said that there is 'numerous and insurmountable' evidence to support the photographer's account. The incident was a 'real critical situation,' and it was only favourable weather conditions that avoided a disaster.

Another Italian newspaper, *La Nazione*, covered this story and has additional information. The reference to the 2005 incident is contained in a 700 page report about the Costa Concordia which focused on prior 'sail bys.' On page 619 of the report, there is a reference to the Costa Fortuna cruising 300 meters from the coast near Sorrento when it hit a shoal and began to take on water, 'just before a greeting to the island of Capri.' The impact caused a gash in the hull 'deep and ten meters long.' Passengers were disembarked from the ship in dry dock where the ship was repaired during the night by Fincantieri workers and set off on the morning of June 15 2005. The Master, Giuseppe Russo, did not report the incident, and the ship officers falsely stated that while cruising from Naples to Palermo there had been an unexpected rise of temperature.

*La Nazione* explains that there was never any indication of the incident to the maritime authorities until January 18 2012, when the wave of emotion caused by the sinking of Concordia and of the 32 victims, caused one of two Costa Fortuna photographers, Roberto Cappello, to come forward.

This story was first reported last year by the UK press. *The Sun* reported that Fortuna ship photographer Cappello was on board the ship when he felt and heard a 'loud bang' during the 'sail-by'. The ship then rolled from left to right. Cappello later photographed damage to the cruise ship's keel and broken propeller blade. However, Costa demanded and confiscated his photographs. Costa later claimed that the ship had 'struck a whale.'

Shipping companies are known for underreporting accidents and passing the blame on to the seafarers, to avoid liability and preserve their public image (Anderson, 2003) (Ellis, Bloor, & Sampson, 2010) (Gekara & Sampson, 2021). But here is an important lesson – manipulating and underreporting accidents comes with its own set of problems. When stories about critical failures are shared as if these are normal occurrences, tolerance for failures increases until it becomes the new normal (Vaughan, 1997).

So when you make the choice to underplay an accident or ask one of your employees to hide a problem from the regulator, think carefully. What message are you sending? What history are you writing? The same could be said about successful sail-pasts. Each success story is hailed until it becomes embodied within the *body* corporate. And once the behaviour is embodied, it is normalised.

## When a picture tells a thousand words

On our last day in Italy, Francesco shared with us a large collection of photographs taken on cruise ships. As I looked through those pictures his view about what is considered normal made a lot more sense to me.

The normal is not a threat to be controlled and managed; when the normal has become a prerequisite for the survival of your business, it is to be embraced and understood.

Figure 12.6: *Costa Atlanta* navigating close to land on a routine basis; photo shared by Francesco Schettino.

Figure 12.7: Cruising near the coast of Ushuaia.

As one participant observed during a workshop, 'No one pays a fortune to travel on a cruise ship to look at the boring sea. People want beautiful sightseeing the moment they open their cabin curtain.'

When photographs such as those in Figures 12.6 and 12.7 are put up on the walls of our offices, alleyways and board rooms, their power is immense. Little do we understand how such artefacts influence the unconscious mind, thence all human motivations and decisions.

Figure 12.8: The priming of the unconscious mind by advertising and publicity agencies: an example from the London Underground.

In summarising the normal practice of sail-past, I describe it as:

- a ritual of the cruise culture
- a delicate balance between customer expectations and the safety of navigation
- a reckless and irresponsible action, but, when observed through the lived experience of the captain, one that illustrates the banality of everyday work.

Figure 12.9: The embodiment of risk (in this case, balancing safety vs customer demand) by a lone professional, i.e. the captain.

# What is the legal perspective about normal practices?

Before we conclude this chapter, I have one last question. What is the legal perspective relating to normal practice? Can we really cover up such normal practices in documented processes, pretending that we have controlled the risk on paper, and then, when things go wrong, transfer the negative externalities of the risk to the end operators? What can we learn from the *Costa Concordia* accident?

For this, let us go back to the process of plan amendment at the start of the voyage. In response to the request from the maître d', the captain requested the second officer to amend the plan. While the original route kept the ship 13 miles from the coast, the second officer prepared an amended plan to take the ship at a distance of 0.5 nautical miles from the shore (see Figure 12.10). The captain is expected to approve this plan prior to departure from port.

A sail-past involves navigating close to the coast, clearly a risk to the safety of the ship. Appropriate measures should be taken, such as keeping the ship at a safe distance from the shore, slowing down, using large-scale charts and terrestrial aids to navigation, and so on. Let us observe how the risk of deviating from the plan was managed by the captain and his team. Di Lieto (2015) captured the details of the process succinctly in his book on the *Costa Concordia* accident.

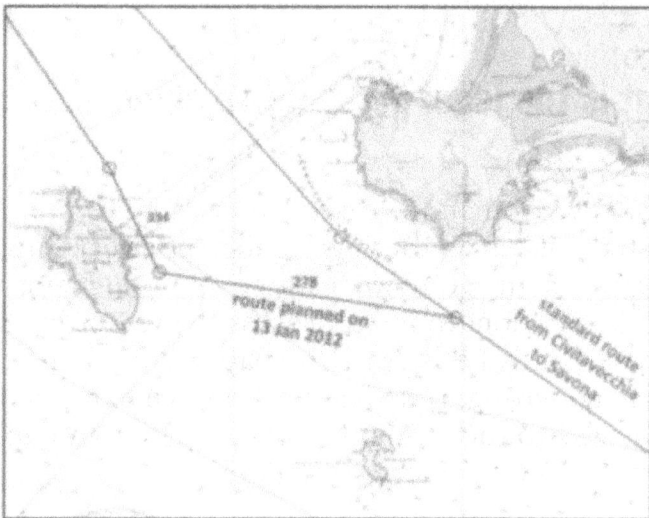

Figure 12.10: The deviation from the original passage plan.

De Lieto raises the following concerns about the process of deviation:

1. There were no specific company policies about sail-past except 'the formalisation of business objectives such as brand promotion and passenger entertainment, as well as precautionary measures concerning sail pasts'. (Di Lieto, 2015, p. 33).

2. The nautical chart used for navigation was not appropriate for coastal sailing. As De Lieto (2015) wrote, 'the nautical chart used for planning was the coastal chart IIM N°6 by the Italian Hydrographic Office with a scale of 1:100.000 (see figure I-7). Half a nautical mile on a chart scaled 1:100.000 would show up at around half a centimetre. If we consider that the width of a pencil line is 0.5 millimetres it is clear that the safety margin on such a chart would be viewed quite inaccurately. There was another nautical chart on board, the IM N°119 with a much larger scale (1:20.000), which, however, was never considered during planning.' (p. 33)

3. Since the vessel is equipped with electronic charts as well, the route plotted on the paper chart is then transferred to the electronic charts.

4. At the time of the accident, the electronic chart was not the primary means of navigation but an aid. Officially the paper charts were to be used as the primary means of navigation.

5. In practice, however, even though the traditional paper charts should be formally used, the electronic charts were used as the primary means of navigation.

6. Since the electronic charts were not a primary means of navigation in those times, there was no regulatory requirement for the formal training of officers in the use of electronic charts.

7. Neither the captain nor the officer who transferred the route on the chart had received any formal training on the use of electronic charts. This means that the 'captain probably wasn't able to check the officer's planning work, who also may have learned to use the instruments by himself.' Di Lieto (2015, p. 35)

8. The only form of training considered necessary at this point was a *familiarisation* checklist with bridge equipment. This consisted of a list of functions for the various instruments, 'which officers must be familiar with when they step on board a ship for the first time (or when returning from a period of absence)'. (p. 35)

9. The electronic chart system is part of an integrated system (Electronic Chart Display and Information System), which is not present on this checklist. The proficient operation of the Integrated Navigation System requires a training course in a simulator. In other words, a familiarisation checklist is a solution to a training problem.

10. The captain, who is formally responsible for checking and approving the deviation from the passage, has not received any formal training on the use of the navigation system used for planning the passage.

If you are struggling to follow the technical jargon of a marine navigation process, Di Lieto provides a simple analogy from the aviation sector. Imagine this scenario:

> The Captain of a modern airliner delegating the programming of the flight computer – which he himself is not capable of operating – to his First Officer, who is self-taught in its use without any formal training.'
>
> (Di Leito 2015, p.36)

The example of the deviation process is illustrative of the fact that although in theory no rules are breached, in practice rule compliance should not be mistaken for managing the risk. That much is understood and explained well, but Di Lieto, focused on error management here, has missed an important point: this was an Italian company, an Italian ship, and an Italian captain operating in Italian waters, a rare occurrence given the global nature of the maritime industry. The company was fortunate to avoid the liability of this accident by allocating the blame to the captain. However, in another jurisdiction such a casual approach to the formal approval of voyage plan deviation may not necessarily be treated so lightly.

In his book *Paper Safe*, Greg Smith (2018), drawing on a wide range of legal cases from around the world, warns us that most organisations do not understand the meaning of Due Diligence. From a legal perspective, it is not the documented process to manage risk that matters. What *does* matter is how the regulatory requirements are interpreted and how the risk management is demonstrated in practice. So in this case, regardless of the checklists and procedures, as the captain and the second officer had not been formally trained on the use of the electronic charts used for navigation, the company should be held responsible for not following the principles of risk management.

In a legal sense, what matters is how the process is implemented in practice, which can only be validated by understanding what is considered normal in a given situation. The normal cannot be found in ring binders and management systems; the normal is best understood by engaging with the myths, beliefs, rituals, narratives, habits, heuristics, symbols and metaphors of those who have come to believe those practices as *normal*.

## Culture cloud

Too often, we hear the expression 'it's normal'; 'this is routine'; 'this is how it's always done'; 'it's always been this way'; 'no worries'; 'we can deal with this'; or even a subliminal sigh of relief – 'that's okay.' These are all metaphorical expressions of what has become normal within a group.

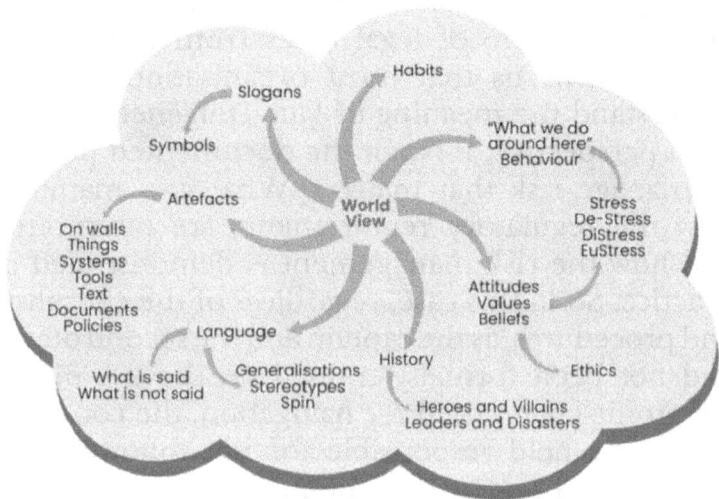

Figure 12.11: Culture Cloud, based on Social Psychology of Risk.*

In such situations, ask yourself the following question: What is considered normal within my culture but can come as a surprise to another person? And then ask: What is normal to another person but appears surprising in my world? Those are your cultural indicators.

At the heart of the Culture Cloud lies our worldview. When a practice is considered normal, it is because that is how we have started to perceive the world. Your normal is your worldview because it sets the limits of your imagination.

# 13

# Why Don't They Speak Up?

Through framing, we create the realities to which
we must then respond.

Gail T. Fairhurst

> This is unbelievable! A ship with at least 5–6 peo-
> ple on the bridge, and no one speaks to the cap-
> tain even when they are heading straight into the
> rocks. Why don't they speak up?

The above is a typical reaction when I share the
voyage data recording[8] of the accident to those participating in the workshop.

Why don't people *speak up* even when it is obvious
they should have? How we frame our questions
reflects the limits of our imagination. In the first

---

[8] The voyage data recorder on a ship is the equivalent of a black
box on an aircraft, its purpose being to keep a record of the
navigation and voice data of the voyage.

half of this chapter, we will explore the beliefs, assumptions and biases hidden in the 'speak up' myth. What does 'speak up' mean? Why do we believe in this myth? What are the dominant theories and 'scientific' concepts that have shaped the myth of 'speaking up?' Many of us do not realise that once we have framed our words, we can remain trapped in those words forever.

The next half of this chapter will illustrate how reframing our questions brings us to a wholly different point of view. Sometimes, letting go of the idea that the nail is our only problem because all we have is a hammer can lead to a shift in our perspectives.

- What can we learn about ourselves through the framing of our questions?
- The hidden assumptions in the framing of the question, 'Why don't people speak up?'
- Understanding the framing of 'psychological safety', 'soft skills' and 'crew resource management.'
- How reframing brings us to an alternative worldview?
- Reframing: a practical exercise.
- An alternative view about 'why people don't speak up'.
- New insights, methods and tools to rethink 'why people don't speak up?'

Figure 13.1: A general outline of the chapter.

## Moments before the accident

Allow me to narrate the situation on the bridge of the *Costa Concordia* moments before the accident.

On the bridge there are three officers, one helmsman and the captain. The ship is approaching the Giglio Islands for a sail-past. The captain is looking out of the window, two officers are monitoring the electronic charts, a third officer is at the navigation console, and the helmsman is at the wheel.

Figure 13.2: The positions of the officers on the bridge. (Shared by Francesco Schettino, for illustration only.)

Moments before the accident, the captain can be overheard correcting the helmsman at least twice for misinterpreting his orders. On one occasion, the captain even chuckles when the helmsman mis-reads his order. The captain then says, 'Pay proper attention, or we go straight into the rocks.'

In light of this context, I empathise with anyone who asks, 'Why did no one speak to the captain or warn him of the looming danger?' I too was confronted by that question when I saw this manoeuvre for the first time. But over the years I have realised the power of 'framing' our questions. If we are not conscious of our framing, we will remain locked in our worldview. It is my intention in this chapter to surface the unconscious in our questions and, more specifically, to explore why the re-framing is essential in addressing the assumptions behind why people don't speak up even when it is so obvious to many of us from the outside that they should do so.

Think of frames as glasses we wear. Just like those glasses, frames act as a mental structure and influence the way we see the world. When we realise how we frame our narratives, we can more easily recognise our hitherto hidden expectations and goals – and, more generally, our beliefs and myths. Figure 13.3 shows why framing is important, how language can be misunderstood and how assumptions in our everyday language are hidden in framing. My teenage daughter and I carry very different frames of 'apples' and 'tablets' in our minds. This is what Lakoff (2014) refers to as the 'unconscious, automatic, effortless inferences' of framing.

Figure 13.3: How our framing can affect our perceptions.

In the question 'Why don't they speak up?' there are at least three levels of assumption:

1. Culture: What metaphors, terms, beliefs, generalisations, stories, arguments and narratives do you use to describe 'speak up'? Now notice how your colleague from another culture or boss may describe 'speak up'? (Recall the Culture Cloud).
2. Mental model: What are your most deeply held images about 'speak up'? These are pictures in our mind about other people, situations, objects, and events. Sometimes these images are clear to us and on another occasions they are scanty.
3. Framing: What communication patterns do you use regularly to describe 'speak up'? (Policy, models, concepts, tools, jargon, frequently used words, phrases etc.)

These components are elaborated in detail by Fairhurst (2010):

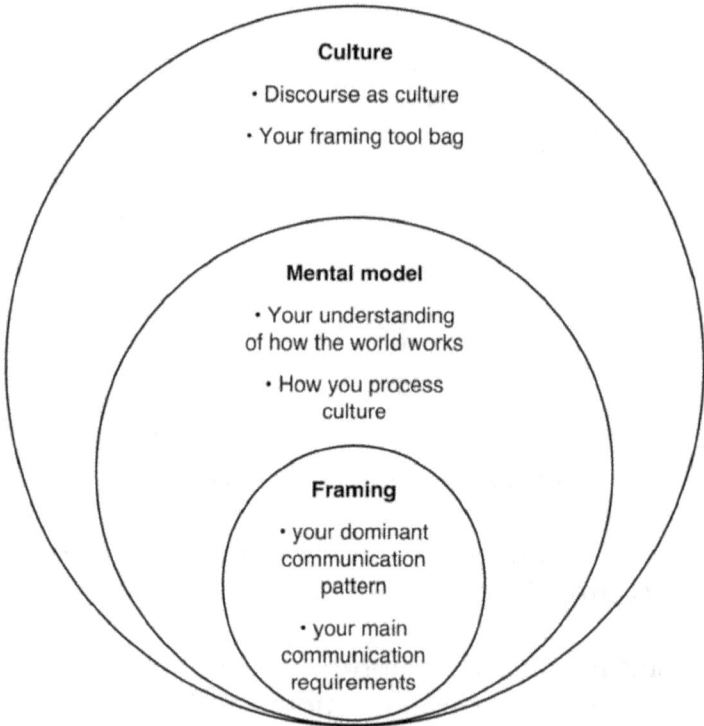

Figure 13.4: Components of framing (Fairhurst, 2010).

When we say 'Why don't people speak up?' what might we be assuming?

**Culture:** People don't speak up; fairness; justice; equality; fair culture; just culture; when we speak up we will improve things for everyone; is it safe to speak up; speak up at work; you have the right to speak up; your rights; safety.

**Mental model:** A distressed person; a lone person; loudhailer; horn; speaker; microphone; silence; employee; voice.

**Framing:** Psychological safety; crew resource management; stop work authority; stop the job; report; reporting error; sharing ideas; raising concerns; whistleblowing.

Let us now examine the unconscious biases in our frames.

# Psychological safety

The first concept that comes to mind is of 'psychological safety'. Harvard professor Amy Edmondson (who I interviewed on this topic) believes that people don't speak up because of a lack of psychological safety: a 'belief that one will not be punished or humiliated for speaking up with ideas, questions, concerns or mistakes'.

Figure 13.5: A rating on deck speaks **up** to the captain on the bridge.

What is the unconscious bias in this framing? For a start, speaking *up* means the vulnerable and powerless raising concerns to someone in a position of authority. Secondly, speaking up is a relational issue, because it takes at least one other person for the speaker to speak *with*. However, with any exchange there is the possibility of an imbalance of power, and in any act of speaking up this implies issues with ethics, hierarchy and justice. Most 'speak up' courses, models, and images I have reviewed do not address the ethical assumptions and power relations. More on this as we manoeuvre through this chapter.

Next, what does 'speaking up with ideas, questions, concerns or mistakes' involve? How does that happen? While ideas require imagination, questions and concerns are shared only when there is trust between people. But speaking up about mistakes goes back to the familiar concept of detecting and reporting errors. Once I realise that I've made a mistake, I should own my mistake and talk about it; a culture of realising, owning and reporting mistakes will lead to better learning and improvement (i.e. a reporting culture). But inherent within this egalitarian idea is that the environment needs to be perceived as psychologically safe, or else I'm in trouble for exposing my vulnerabilities to others.

Two questions come to mind: How is psychological safety different from trust between people? Second, are the two constructs mutually exclusive? For example, could there be psychological safety but no trust in the same space? I will share what I have learned in my journey so far.

## Crew resource management

When we review the cause of the accident, we find the same unconscious inferences and assumptions as when we were discussing entailing psychological safety – errors, mistakes and questions that were never raised by the bridge team to the captain.

In the official report the following contributing factors were highlighted as the cause of the accident:

- keeping a high speed (16 kts) in night conditions is too close to the shore line (breakers/reef);

- Master's inattention/distraction due to the presence of persons extraneous to Bridge watch and a phone call not related to the navigation operations;

- Bridge Team, although more than suitable in terms of number of crew members, not paying the required attention (e.g. ship steering, acquisition of the ship position, lookout);

- Master's arbitrary attitude in reviewing the initial navigation plan (making it quite hazardous in including a passage 0,5 mile off the coast by using an inappropriate nautical chart), disregarding to properly consider the distance from the coast and not relying on the support of the Bridge Team;

- overall passive attitude of the Bridge Staff. Nobody seemed to have urged the Master to accelerate the turn or to give warning on the looming danger.

Therefore, the accident may lead to an overall discussion on the adequacy, in terms of organization and roles of Bridge Teams.

(MIT, 2013, p. 11)

The same report also proposed that

regarding the competency, not having attended a training course on Bridge Resources Management course[9] - BRM, (not mandatory at this stage) could have represented a weakness in terms of competency (human factor as bad human performance) in this casualty. In fact, none of those deck Officers on duty before the contact (Master and all the Bridge Team) had attended a BRM course.

(MIT, 2013, pp. 161-62).

We are again caught up within the same frame of mind. To quote a participant who once attended my workshop and wrote back to me:

This sounds like a very familiar pattern:

- The disaster occurred because the co-pilot did not question the judgment of the pilot.

- The co-pilot knew the correct course of action but did not feel psychologically safe to question the pilot.

---

[9]  Bridge resource management is a mandatory training course in the maritime industry (akin to crew resource management in the aviation sector) with the aim of detecting and rectifying errors in communication during critical team operations.

- The co-pilot would die rather than question the authority.

- If the co-pilot had spoken up the crash would not happen.

- We now train our people, we even have protocols for them to speak up and when they don't, we reprimand them.

Crew resource management is embedded within the same discourse as psychological safety. If we can detect, report and manage errors, we can improve our chances to learn from those errors. Encouraging people of a lower rank to speak up, practise assertiveness, exhibit 'good communication skills', and challenge those in position of power is considered the solution to this problem.

If a crew member on the *Costa Concordia* had, on detecting the captain's error, raised their concerns and questioned his decisions, the disaster might have been averted. As part of this journey, I reviewed the bridge resource management courses provided by nearly three dozen service providers. Their common metaphors included: situational awareness, language barriers, cultural differences, crisis management, decision making, workload management, communication and assertiveness.

As I went deeper into my analysis of these service providers' training curricula, two themes stood out: 'good communication' and 'assertiveness'.

**Course Duration:** 3 days
**Course dates:** On Demand
**Course Fee:** £ 1800/-

**Course Eligility:**
Minimum OOW COC

**Course Description:**
The course is design to meet the bridge resource management requirements detailed in Table A-II/I of the 2010 Manila amedments to the STCW Convention and Code. This course is a mix of the theory case studies and simulation exercise covering topics below.

**Course Content:**
- Resource managment: Situational Awareness
- Attitudes: Cultural Awareness
- Communications and brefings: Short Term Strategy: Authoriy & Assertiveness
- Management Styles: Workload
- Human Involvement: Judgement & Decision Making
- Automation Awareness

Figure 13.6: The content of a bridge resource management course.

# Non-technical skills

Another issue that caught my attention was a simplistic divide between technical and non-technical skills in the course structure. While technical skills include practical ship handling, the collision regulations (also referred to as the Rules of the Road / COLREGS), and knowledge of the weather and the nautical sciences, everything related to the cognitive and behavioural aspects of training was bundled into a package titled 'non-technical skills'. One service provider who joined my workshop said, 'You have to be innovative with your words. If you are trying to sell soft skills to a technical industry, you have to use the word *non-technical skills'*. That tells us a lot about the power of framing, mental models and culture in general.

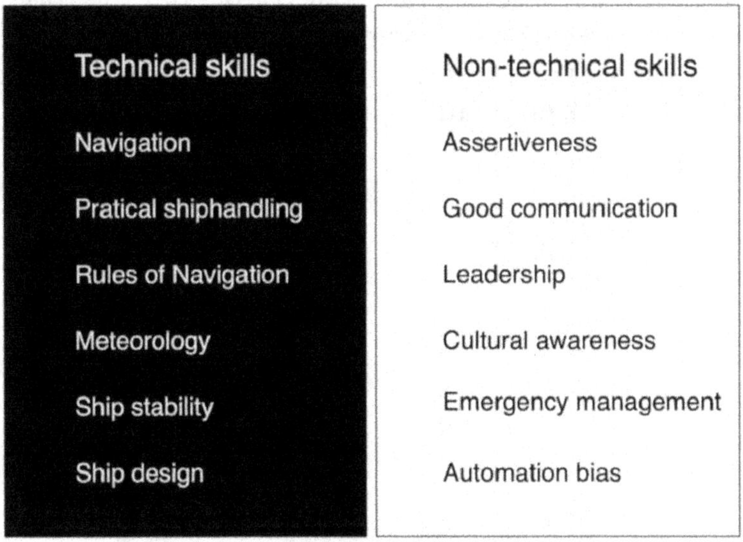

| Technical skills | Non-technical skills |
|---|---|
| Navigation | Assertiveness |
| Pratical shiphandling | Good communication |
| Rules of Navigation | Leadership |
| Meteorology | Cultural awareness |
| Ship stability | Emergency management |
| Ship design | Automation bias |

Figure 13.7: Technical and non-technical skills.

Before we begin exploring the power of reframing, let us take a minute to observe the question, 'Why don't they speak up?' The question is framed negative. What happens when we approach a problem with a negative frame of mind?

## Negative framing

My eight-year-old son enjoys eating mangoes so much that he won't leave a single slice of a mango for others to eat. I too enjoy eating mangoes, and over the years I have learned *never* to remind him that he should leave at least one slice for me.

This example works at every stage in life, including when you see a road safety sign that warns you: *Kill Your Speed Not a Child*. As Lakoff (2014) suggests in his book, *Don't Think of an Elephant*, 'not only does negating a frame activate that frame, but the more it is activated, the stronger it gets.' Think what would happen in your mind if I asked you to not think about a pink elephant.

Figure 13.8: A road sign in the UK with negative framing.

When we ask the question, 'Why didn't you speak up?', we activate certain frames in the other person's mind. Their immediate response is fear, guilt, projection and self-defence.

## The power of reframing

We underestimate the power of frames and mental models, and how worldviews are shaped. One way of making someone aware of their framing of a situation and helping them realise the limits of their worldview is by asking open-ended questions: 'What would you like to share?'; 'Where would you like to begin?'; 'What has your learning been?'; 'What do you think?' etc. Such open questions allow the other person to bring forth their assumptions. It gives them the opportunity to tell their version of the narrative without being overly selective about what the interviewer wants to hear. At the same time, it allows the interviewer to bring forth and realise their own assumptions. The conversation is less about validating or negating and more about discovery and learning.

### A framing exercise

I often start with a simple exercise on framing during my workshops. For instance, I would give people a scenario such as one listed below, then note down their responses on a whiteboard.

Figure 13.9: Scenario cards involving framing exercises.

Responses that I typically receive in relation to the scenario illustrated here:

1. Who is responsible for updating the board?
2. How often do you update this notice board?
3. Why has the notice board not been updated?
4. When was the safety board last updated?
5. How can we improve the process of updating the notice board?

Notice the hidden assumptions in the responses: a quest for control and measurement; binary questioning; locating responsibility; negative framing; and looking at a problem that needs to be fixed. The interesting thing about this exercise is that even the most senior leaders cannot escape the idea of relinquishing control and problem fixing to engage in an open conversation. Isn't it a paradox when we expect leaders to fix problems?

I then encourage the participants to reframe and ask open-ended questions.

1. What is the risk of displaying outdated information on the whiteboard?
2. What is the normal practice of updating the board?
3. What does 'outdated information' really mean to you?
4. I see the information on the safety notice board is outdated. What are your thoughts?

The first two questions are meant to engage the embodied Mind of the other person. The third question is focused on understanding our cultural differences (as we have seen in Chapter 2). And the idea behind the last question is to state the obvious (the shared view) and end with an open question – one of my favourites!

When participants practise open-ended enquiry, they are often shocked by the responses they receive. A few minutes into the workshop, the participants will have realised how the framing of their questions can entrap them in their own biases and assumptions. But as Lakoff (2014) warns us, reframing is not a technique or a search for magic words; **reframing is about honesty, integrity and a commitment to learning with an open mind.**

## Reframing the concept of *speaking up*

From the outset I deliberately never asked Francesco why he had not created the space for his officers to speak up, nor did I question him as to why no one had reported to him that the ship was running into a danger. Instead, apart from occasional probing and prompting, I asked him just three questions during our conversation: What was your motivation to join the industry as a seafarer? What was your motivation to go close to the islands? and What would you like to share with us about the accident? The purpose of the first question was twofold: first, I wanted to know him more as a person, but also I wanted to engage with his embodied Mind. The second question was meant to start a conversation about the accident. The third question was meant to show him I was surrendering control to him, setting aside my agenda and listening to his story.

I waited and listened in patience as Francesco narrated his story, and then after the interviews I revisited his videos and field notes many times to observe his framing and to give this story my own meaning. A consistent theme that appears in our conversation was a sense of betrayal by his subordinates, who he believed had let him down on the day of the accident. In one of the interviews, he told me about the declining levels of training standards in the maritime industry, which he believed was the underlying reason why the bridge team members were not able to detect the rocks as the ship was navigating close to the island. He said:

> I am glad that the industry is organizing many leadership trainings, and I appreciate this. But this is not a matter of leadership, this is the very start of the education of the deck cadet. Even if you know how to share the information, before sharing the information you must have this professional skill to recognise the danger. If you don't recognise the danger, how you can share the information with the others? And which captain doesn't react, if an officer says 'Captain, we are one cable [219 metres] from the rock'? The problem is, I have reason to believe that nobody had the experience to recognise the danger and overestimate the professionalism of the captain and maybe he can have some magician's way out, maybe because the captain is so skilled, he is a good seaman. He has his way to not provoke the accident. We were going ahead, I show you the black box. When I saw the white foam, I don't know how I didn't faint.[10]

During a workshop, upon hearing Francesco's comment, one participant said, 'Instead of reflecting upon what he could have done better to avoid this situation, he is pointing fingers at others. This is unacceptable.' It is likely that you would feel the same frustration. And it is not uncommon for an interviewee being investigated to project their failures on to others. But as a researcher, when the same theme consistently repeats itself, it is imperative that we delve deeper to question the underlying assumptions.

---

[10] White foam is produced when waves hit a solid surface. Its visibility from a ship is a reliable – and urgent – warning that the ship is too close to rocks.

## Three salt tablets

As I listened more to Francesco's version of the accident, a powerful story was waiting to be told. Francesco told me that one afternoon he had visited a jacuzzi on one of the passenger decks, and on finding that it was filled with fresh water instead of sea water, he summoned one of the junior officers to seek an explanation. The captain was told that the seawater pump was not working, and the crew had decided to use fresh water instead. Francesco then asked the officer to get some salt tablets from the ship's hospital to turn the water saline.

The next day the captain returned but found that the jacuzzi water tasted the same. He asked the officer why he had not added the salt to the water. The officer responded, 'But I added three tablets, Captain.' A frustrated Schettino looked into our eyes. '*Three tablets?* Can you believe three salt tablets for a jacuzzi filled with water?'

It shouldn't need a maritime expert to understand Francesco's frustration and the symbolic meaning of this story. In his worldview, an officer whose understanding of a basic principle such as the salinity of sea water was so far from the fact – approximately 35 grams per litre – was a person who could not be trusted as an independent watchkeeping officer at sea. There was no trust between the captain and his subordinates. The basis for the lack of trust was the captain's perception that his officers were not competent to perform their duties.

This brief anecdote became a turning point in the analysis of the narrative, helping me uncover my own assumptions about the accident thus far.

## Thinking beyond the 'power gradient'

When I first heard the captain saying that people don't speak up because they don't know what to say, this felt like a naïve and oversimplified view of the problem: a team of competent people on the bridge of a ship are reluctant to tell the captain that the ship will hit the rocks because they don't recognise the danger? Could it be that the captain is being arrogant about himself?

The industry has traditionally framed this problem as one of 'power gradient'. Many accidents at sea can be explained based on the power gradient myth. It is a familiar narrative of dominant captain and meek subordinates, some of whom are citizens of the 'third world' (Perrow, 1984). The officers struggle to speak up because of the power gradient. The disproportionate use and sometimes abuse of power by those in positions of authority make it difficult for people in lower positions to raise their concerns and share their ideas.[11] If we extend this discussion to other areas of work and life, the issue of power or authority gradient is not new to organisational discourse.

---

[11] A potent and enduring legend in maritime circles is that of a sailor who, having warned Admiral Sir Cloudesley Shovell in 1707 that his homeward fleet was in danger of running onto the rocks of the Scillies, was promptly hanged at the yardarm for inciting mutiny. (Four of the ships, including Shovell's own, did hit the rocks and were lost with all hands, around 2,000 men in all.)

The principles of crew resource management training in the aviation sector, which emerges from the Anglo-Saxon culture, fit naturally with the concept of the 'power gradient'. An overconfident captain and a subservient co-pilot struggling to raise his concerns to the captain is a familiar pattern in the risk and safety discourse, and within maritime history. Perrow (1984) writes:

> the captain of the Medusa, a French frigate that foundered in 1816 with the loss of 152 persons (most of whom were needlessly lost), was drunk most of the voyage and ignored the warnings of his officers about dangerous waters.

Similarly,

> in 1893 the ironclad monster gunboat H.M.S. Victoria, commanded by a brilliant and daring tactician, Sir George Tryon, led a squadron of thirteen ships into Tripoli harbor. By prearrangement the ships were to execute a manuever which his subordinate officers had unsuccessfully questioned, since it would bring the two flagships, the Victoria and the Camperdown, both prides of the English fleet, into a collision (Perrow, 1984).

But even if the captain is being arrogant, falling back to an abstract concept such as 'power' or 'authority' can only take us so far. What is the nature of power, and how does the power gradient manifest in this relationship between the captain and his officers? What is the basis for the captain's arrogance? What hinders his officers from speaking up even when the ship is heading onto the rocks? How well does the power gradient fit with the captain's narrative that his officers lacked the basic competence to detect and report a ship heading onto the rocks? Is this a problem relating to the *Costa Concordia* alone? Is it that simple?

The more I pondered on the story of three salt tablets, the more I became convinced that Francesco's perceptions cannot be disregarded as mere moaning. I decided to take a step back to observe the historical trends in maritime labour and economics.

## A rising tide of tourism

The data from the Cruise Line International Association revealed a different worldview. I started by observing an unprecedented increase in both the demand for and the supply of cruise ships between 2003 and 2013. The global demand for those ships increased by 77 per cent, and within Europe as much as 136 per cent. Similarly, the global supply of cruise ship capacity increased by 84 per cent; in the Mediterranean alone, it surged to 160 per cent.

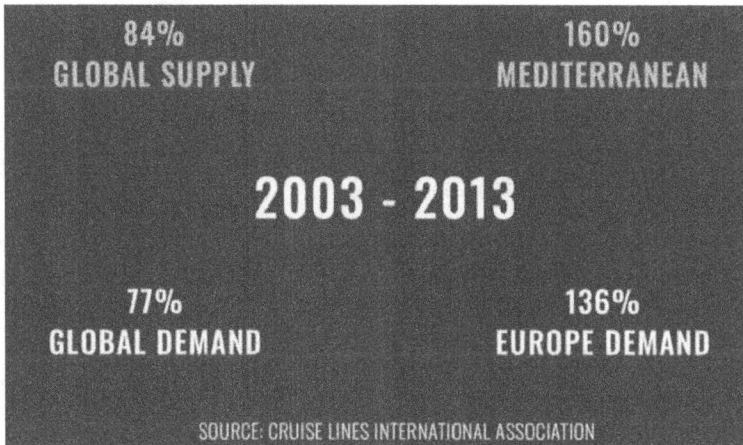

84%
GLOBAL SUPPLY

160%
MEDITERRANEAN

2003 - 2013

77%
GLOBAL DEMAND

136%
EUROPE DEMAND

SOURCE: CRUISE LINES INTERNATIONAL ASSOCIATION

Figure 13.10: Supply and demand of cruise shipping.
(Source: Cruise Line International)

Understandably, the rising tide of tourism in the cruise sector through the increased number of ships translates into a shortage of qualified seafarers. The operators and shipping companies attempt to address this requirement through fast-track training and promotion of seafarers to higher ranks. Under normal circumstances, it takes anything between 12 and 15 years for a cadet to progress through the ranks to become a captain. But when there is an acute shortage of personnel, seafarers are promoted more rapidly, in order to meet the demands of the industry.

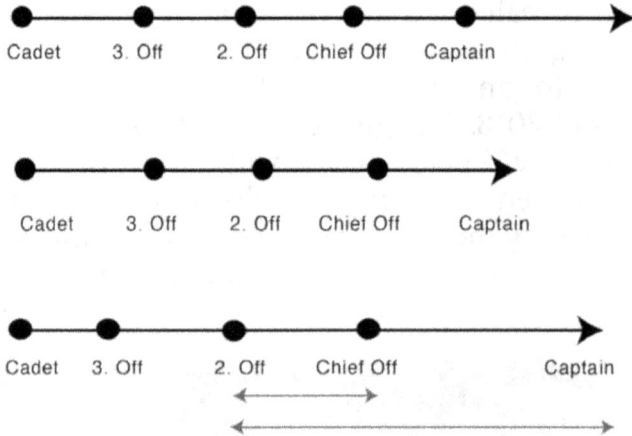

Figure 13.11: Career progression in seafaring.

## Description of ranks

| Rank | Connotation | Level of seniority |
|------|-------------|--------------------|
| Cadet | Cadet | Apprentice |
| 3.Off | Third officer | Junior officer |
| 2.Off | Second officer | Junior officer |
| Chief Off | Chief officer | Senior officer |
| Captain | Master | Senior officer |

It is the cyclical nature of the demand in the maritime industry that the labour markets must learn to respond to, in order to ensure a steady supply of seafarers on ships. An exponential increase in the demand and supply of ships is often addressed by (1) faster promotion of officers through the ranks; and (2) production-line training to bridge the gaps in the training needs of the industry. Both strategies come with often unforeseen implications.

At sea there is a ceiling to progression; once you have been promoted to captain, that's the end of your career development. Add to this a steady supply of junior officers at entrance level. While captains and chief officers continue to grow in experience, they must also be prepared to work with an influx of junior officers entering the profession, in order to meet the demands of the industry.

Things get more complicated. For a myriad reasons (such as socially isolated lifestyle, limited chances to travel the world beyond the port limits, comparable opportunities in shore-based jobs, limited internet connectivity on ships) these young entrants are not driven by the same motivations and aspirations as their older counterparts – a pattern that emerged in my own PhD (Anand, 2011). While on the one hand experience starts to accumulate in senior ranks, on the other a transactional approach to the profession adopted by the new recruits means a dearth of skills and motivation at entry level.

Seafaring has always been characterised by hierarchy, and by rank-based organisation of work, but the emerging patterns of work and skills have given this hierarchy a new form and a different meaning.

The story of the three salt tablets was beginning to make much more sense to me now.

Figure 13.12: The power gradient and the skill gradient. The skill gradient hierarchy (right) is more pronounced and uneven than the traditional power hierarchy.

I refer to this emerging form of hierarchy as the 'skill gradient'. The skill gradient between ranks is when the difference between domain-specific experience becomes significantly large. Typically, this will lead to two subcultures: experts and novices. And as we will discover in the following subsections, when we reframe 'speak up' as an 'expert–novice' issue, it takes on a different meaning.

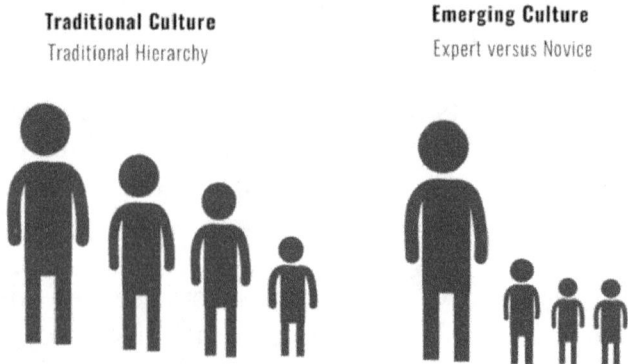

Figure 13.13: Traditional hierarchy as against expert versus novice groups.

## The expert–novice culture

In most high-skilled jobs, work experience has always been a prerequisite. But a single-minded focus on ensuring that captains and chief engineers are adequately experienced in their ranks from both a regulatory and a commercial perspective steepens the skill gradient yet further. When the industry tries to ensure that the senior officers on the ships are adequately experienced and it does not mandate the same requirements for the junior ranks, an imbalance emerges, leading to 'expert–novice' patterns.

On board the *Costa Concordia*, the senior officer on duty at the time of the accident was barely half the age of the captain, and had significantly less relevant experience. Similar crewing patterns have emerged when we examine accidents in other high-risk systems. In the case of the Ethiopian Airlines flight described below, the co-pilot had clocked a mere 200 hours of flying experience, alongside a pilot with 8,000 hours (Premack, 2019).

Figure 13.14: Ethiopian Airlines Flight 302, illustrating an expert–novice culture.

The co-pilot was on his first flight aboard a Boeing 777 as a fully approved pilot, and it was his first assignment without a training pilot overseeing him. Here we see how organisations succumb to cost pressure, struggle to attract the required talent, and find innovative ways to deal with systemic problems. It is in the rare occurrences of catastrophes of this scale that we begin to see how serious issues of this nature are obscured by audit trails, benchmarking standards, assurance reports and training programs that are so distanced from reality. Think how the framing of the problem as 'speaking up' cloaks the seriousness of an industry-wide problem. How can courage and empathy become a replacement for the requisite knowledge and skills?

## When the captain becomes a teacher

The expert–novice relationship complicates the problem of speaking up in more ways than that. In a functional sense, the bridge, flight deck and operating theatre are intended for piloting, navigating and surgery. But in the same space, young novices also receive training from expert staff. How does this impact on their social identity, power perception and relationship? A ship captain becomes a teacher, and a subordinate switches roles to become a trainee. How might they speak up and challenge the authority of a teacher? Where do we draw the line between a teacher and a captain/pilot/surgeon? During the course of a day the boundary is breached on many occasions.

# Is psychological safety a solution to speaking up?

When we reframe speaking up in the context of the expert–novice framework, we arrive at a different understanding of the problem. What does it mean to be assertive? How can juniors raise questions and concerns? How to speak up when in doubt? Let us examine how the construct of 'speak up' translates in practice.

## Closed loop communication

Typically, an example of effective communication is that the captain issues an order and then, to minimise the risk of miscommunication, the officer repeats the order. This is illustrated in Figure 13.15:

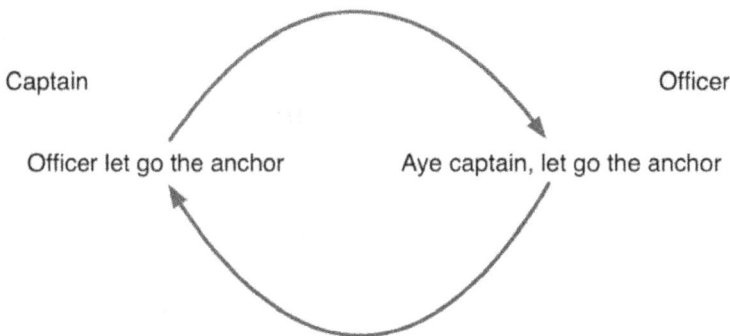

Captain                                                    Officer

Officer let go the anchor          Aye captain, let go the anchor

Figure 13.15: Closed loop communication.

For the communication to be effective, it is imperative that the receiver acknowledges what they have heard and understood from the person giving the message. This is often referred to as closed loop communication. But in an expert–novice culture, effective communication is more than just closing the feedback loop. Depending on the culture, the novice might fear speaking up or being labelled 'wrong'.

**A personal story of closed loop communication**

I recall when I was a cadet, and with a set of binoculars in my hands I was passionately reporting all the navigation hazards to the captain while the ship was transiting the busy sea lanes of Singapore. At one point, the captain politely turned around and said, 'Nippin, I don't need to know about every floating object on the horizon; you're not helping me.'

This recollection from my early sailing days has served as an important reminder of expert–novice interactions. In the middle of the Singapore Straits surrounded by dense traffic, the last thing the captain wants is information overload/psychological flooding. The novice obviously intends to help, but it takes a certain level of expertise to be able to ascertain the correct level of information. And once the captain is annoyed, the novice will think twice before speaking up to the captain again. In this situation, while the printed curriculum may stipulate speaking up, the hidden curriculum tells the novice to remain silent.[12]

While the expert does not see much value in what the novice has to contribute, the novice, on the other hand, is likely to live with a constant fear of being exposed as incompetent. This is not a problem that can be addressed through psychological safety, in

---

[12] https://en.wikipedia.org/wiki/Hidden_curriculum

that even with a high level of psychological safety in the work environment, the expert will not take the word of the novice seriously. In a professional relationship the basis of trust is not psychological safety but the levels of competence.

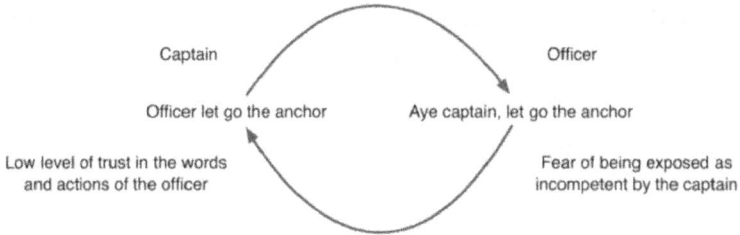

Figure 13.16: Closed loop communication in an expert–novice relationship.

The supply of competent seafarers has not kept up with neoliberalism and the rise in the demand for cruise services. Rather, the systemic issues have been framed as a problem of 'speaking up', 'lack of assertiveness' and 'communication', and presented as a behavioural issue. How can a short course (typically three to five days) in 'non-technical skills' be a substitute for the years of experience and expertise acquired in the profession?

## Cognitive imbalance

Take another example. A typical reaction to the problem of lack of resources in the maritime world is to ensure that in areas of high traffic density the bridge is adequately crewed. But consider once again the expert–novice culture, and we see that a captain surrounded by more junior officers will only lead to a yet more uneven cognitive workload for the captain. All of this can be amplified depending on the levels of stress and distress on the ship. Now the captain has to navigate the ship *and* monitor the actions and movements of the novices, so in an expert–novice work culture more people may not always be an appropriate solution to a lack of resources. On the bridge of the *Costa Concordia* at the time of the accident there were at least three junior officers around the captain.

Increased resources

Figure 13.17: The implications of increased staffing levels in an expert–novice culture; more people may not always be an ideal solution.

## When in doubt speak out

'When in doubt, speak out.' This is the captain's night order to his junior officers before retiring to bed. It is an assurance to the subordinate officer that help is always at hand from the captain should a situation arise. Imagine, however, what this means from a novice's perspective when faced with doubt: 'Do I really want to call the captain and expose my incompetence?' How useful is the construct of psychological safety in an 'expert–novice' work culture?

Figure 13.18: The 'speak up' myth.

## Reframing to arrive at a different worldview

The problem is not one of speaking up but of understanding the tension between two subcultures at play – experts and novices – created by the commercial competition. The problem is both social and relational. To illustrate the relational aspect of this problem, let us go back to One Brain Three Minds.*

Typically, the novice enters the profession in Mind 1 and slowly learns the rules of navigation and ship handling. In the early stages of the novice's career, their decision making is systematic, slow, conscious and inefficient. Like a child observing their parent, the novice watches the captain navigating the ship through difficult situations day in, day out. At this stage it is hard for the novice to determine if and when the captain needs to be alerted. The novice has developed few heuristics and has little understanding of the extensive experience and 'felt' knowledge of the captain. According to Malcolm Gladwell, such knowledge takes 10,000 hours to develop (Gladwell, 2009). What might be all in a day's work for a captain could be a tight safety margin for the novice officer, but knowing that the captain has the power in this relationship, the novice learns to exercise caution in questioning the captain's decisions and expressing his concerns.

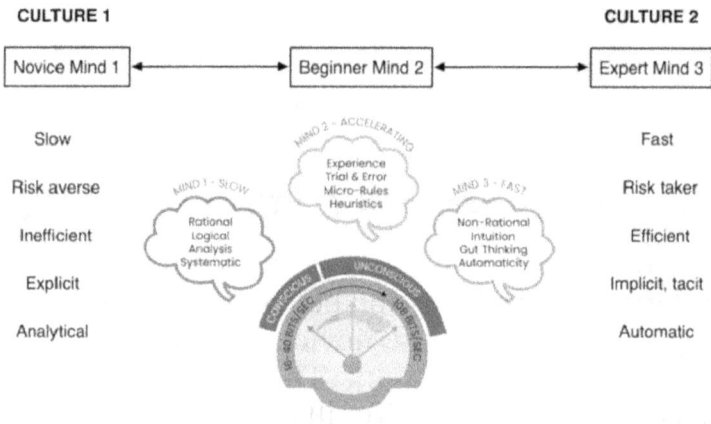

Figure 13.19: 1B3M illustrates the dilemma of expert–novice work patterns.

The captain, on the other hand, is an expert operating in Mind 3. This, as we know, is non-rational, intuitive, automatic, unconscious and superfast. Over the years the captain has learned the skills of the trade, and it is for their efficient, implicit knowledge and work experience that they are rewarded by the ship owner and held in regard by their peers. The decisions made by the captain are embodied and tacit, and therefore not even known to the captain themself. They have been absorbed within their body over their many years in the profession.

Routinely navigating the ship close to the islands adds to the captain's skills, pride and confidence. Perhaps, however, it would not be an exaggeration to say that in the absence of another team member who questions their abilities, the captain can become overconfident. Many accidents at sea (and in many workplaces) are the result of an expert operating in Mind 3 while the novices are still training and learning in Minds 1 and 2. The problem is no longer of speaking up (or down), but how well the experts relate with the novices. **In other words, the problem is not with the individual; it is cultural and relational.**

## The captain is the magician

We return to the point raised at the outset. When the ship sails a few hundred metres from the rock the captain is left frustrated, not understanding why none of his officers has spoken to him about the danger. The rest of us also feel helpless watching the black box, and questioning 'Why the *ell did no one speak up?' Our framing of the problem does not allow us to look beyond managing the fallible humans.

When we reframe the problem of error management and shift our focus onto the embodied Mind, we come to understand a different view of the problem. A frustrated Schettino may not have realised that the answer to his question lay in his own unconscious. With an expert surrounded by novices and beginners, perhaps the captain had turned into a magician – in the eyes of his officers, at least.

If so, no one warned the captain, because no one doubted his mystical powers. When a manoeuvre that requires years of expertise stands far outside the competence of these officers, what choice do they have? When the margins of safety have been eroded and risk becomes embodied in a single expert, what is there left to say? Who should become aware that the ship is heading into a danger? At what point? Why? How?

## Relational problems, relational responses

By reframing the problem, we arrive at a different place. We need a culture where experts can better relate with the novices. It's a relationship where the experts can realise the limits of their expertise and the novices can share their concerns. That is one way to surface what is hidden in the collective unconscious of the organisation. In the words of the renowned organisational psychologist Karl Weick, such initiatives can enrich the expertise of the organisation:

> We prefer the concept of "expertise" to the concept of the "expert" because we want to preserve the crucial point that expertise is relational. Expertise is an assemblage of knowledge, experience, learning, and intuitions that is seldom embodied in a single individual. And even if expertise appears to be confined to a single individual, that expertise

is evoked and becomes meaningful only when a second person requests it, defers to it, modifies it, or rejects it (Weick & Sutcliffe, 2001).

In closing, I'm left with an image in my mind:

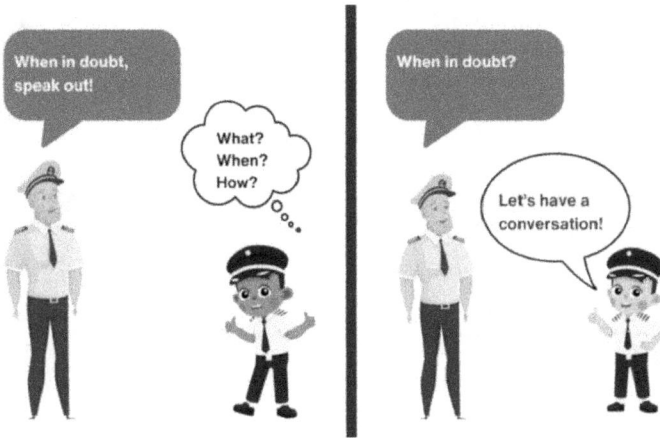

Figure 13:20.

# 14

# Keep Calm and Follow the Plan

⸻

Based on the *Costa Concordia* accident, this chapter will begin with an outline of the emergency response plan for evacuating the ship in a crisis. We will examine the assumptions made in those plans to assess their adequacy in managing and responding to emergencies. We will then turn to the captain to hear his perspective about how the emergency situation was dealt with. The captain's actions and decisions in the crisis will be studied and analysed using Karl Weick's framework of sensemaking. The guiding question of this chapter will be: *What can we learn about human behaviour when faced with an unexpected situation?*

- The 'late' abandonment of the ship by the captain according to the official accident report.
- Understanding the assumptions in the accident report in evaluating the captain's decision to abandon the ship.
- The captain's perspective about the decision to abandon the ship.
- Understanding human decision making in a crisis situation using the framework of 'sensemaking.'
- Understanding the effectiveness of plans and processes in managing the unexpected.
- How predetermined plans and processes can turn accidents into narratives of culpability and crime.

Figure 14.1: A general outline of the chapter.

Captain Francesco Schettino was sentenced to sixteen years and one month in prison – ten years for multiple manslaughter, five for causing the shipwreck and one for abandoning the ship before all the passengers had been evacuated. He was also sentenced to one month for providing false information to the authorities. All the charges were based on the official investigation report published in May 2012 by the Marine Casualties investigative body under the Italian Ministry of Infrastructure and Transport. On 12 May 2017 the highest court of Italy – the Court of Cassation – announced the final decision, reaffirming the charges of the lower court. In the report:

1.  Schettino was wholly responsible for the collision.
2.  He should have given the order to abandon ship much sooner than he did.
3.  He should not have left the Concordia before he had overseen its full evacuation.

Given the eminence assigned to the formal investigation report in the sentencing of the captain, it is crucial that we compare the formal narrative and the captain's view of Item 2 above. (Items 1 and 3 will be discussed more specifically in the next chapter.) In this chapter, we will focus on Item 2. Let us examine the basis for this claim, starting with the Abandon Ship procedure.

## Abandoning the ship

There are three steps to abandoning the ship. First, the captain must decide at what point to abandon ship. Once the decision is made, the next step is to ensure that all the passengers and the crew have been safely evacuated. In other words, the decision to abandon ship should be followed by the evacuation procedure. Finally, the ship is abandoned.

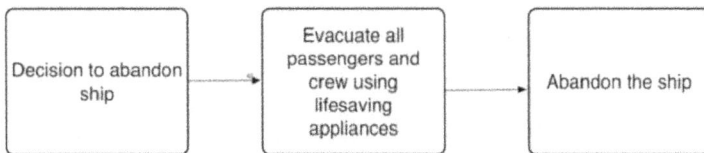

Figure 14.2 The three steps to abandoning the ship.

## Timelines and ship movements

In the discussion of the temporal efficiency of decision making, the relevant timelines and ship movements in the official report may be helpful in establishing whether the decision to abandon ship was given too late.

| | |
|---|---|
| 21:45 | Grounding (contact with the rocks) |
| 21:45 | Master orders closure of watertight doors |
| 21:45 | Ship experiences loss of power |
| 21:46 | Rudder blocked, no directional control |
| 21:48 | Breach confirmed (intake of water into the ship) |
| 21:49 | Master orders lowering of anchors (in preparation, and not letting go) |
| 21:54 | Announcement made to passengers about loss of power |
| 22:07 | First communication between search and rescue coastguard and Costa Concordia |
| 22:12 | Passengers ordered to move to lounges |
| 22:22 | Tugboats requested |
| 22:36 | Passengers ordered to muster stations on deck / Abandon ship announced |

22:50    Lifeboats lowered; Master ordered 'let passengers ashore'

22:55    Ship's list (tilt) exceeds 25 degrees (the maximum list for evacuation systems to function should not exceed 20 degrees)

00:15    Ship listed more than 50 degrees

00:34    Captain left the ship.

Source: (MIT, 2013)

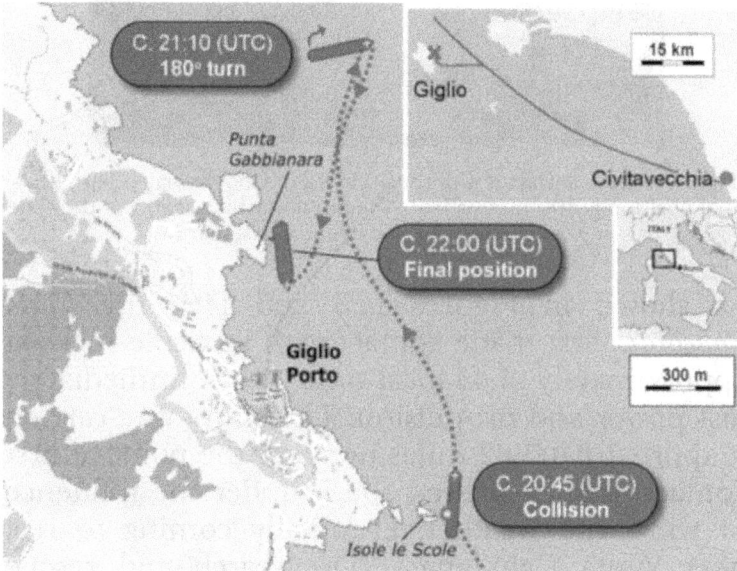

Figure 14.3: An aerial view of the accident taken from the accident report.

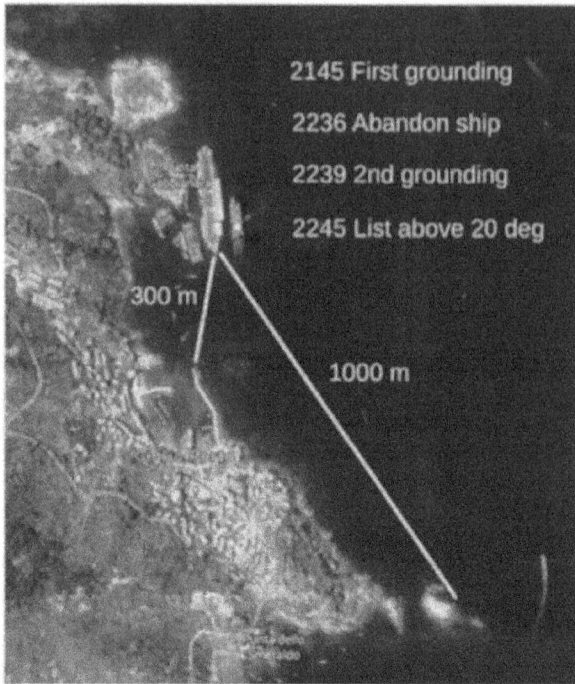

Figure 14.4: An aerial view of the accident in Google maps. The ship's final position is 300 metres from the point at which search and rescue was activated by the Italian Coastguard.

As shown in Figures 14.3 and 14.4, the *Costa Concordia* first made contact with Le Scole rocks at approximately 21:45 local time, and it immediately lost power and propulsion. The ship's way carried it approximately 2 miles north of the point of first contact, then it drifted south under the influence of wind and weather, eventually coming to rest near Punta Gabbianara. The search and rescue services were mobilised from the Port of Giglio, approximately 300 metres from the capsized ship. A total of 2,970 people were evacuated by the ship's crew, and 1,270 by the search and rescue services; 32 people lost their lives in the accident.

## The late abandonment of the ship

Let us first examine the accident narrative about the underlying reasons behind the late abandonment of the ship. The summarising section of the report states:

> The General Emergency Alarm was not activated immediately after the impact. This fact led to a delay in the management of the subsequent phases of the emergency (flooding-abandon ship process).

(MIT, 2013, p. 6)

Further down, the report states:

> In other words, if:

> the general emergency had been launched at 22 03 (a couple of minutes after the first information of three WTC flooded, given to the Master by the Engine staff at 22 01), meanwhile the ship was not listed at all, and persons could move easily;

> and at that stage, the passengers would have gained precious time to reach the muster stations (allowing at this stage even the call by the crew members assigned also for counting), preparing to get embarking in the respective life equipment;

> such as all the lifeboats would be handled for lowering in very manageable condition, with all passengers almost ready on board of those lifeboats, waiting for the abandon ship signal;

> and the abandon ship could be launched 36 minutes after the general emergency signal (matching

the second grounding, which occurred at 22 39), adequate to gather all persons in the capacious and suitable muster stations.

(MIT, 2013, p. 87)

The Abandon Ship process is initiated by a verbal order from the captain followed by an alarm (seven short blasts on the ship's horn and alarm, followed by a long blast). This triggers the evacuation of all passengers and crew, using lifeboats and other means of evacuation. The report suggests in various places that the decision to abandon ship was not made in time, and that the late abandonment of the ship was a contributing factor to the loss of those 32 lives.

# 51
minutes

### 21.45 Grounding

### 21.48 Breach confirmed

### 22.07 Com between CC and SAR

### 22.22 Tugs requested

### 22.36 Abandon ship announced

Figure 14.5: Critical timelines in the grounding and the abandon ship decision by the captain.

Ideally, the decision to abandon ship should allow sufficient time for the passengers and crew to assemble at their muster stations once Abandon Ship has been sounded. In the case of the *Costa Concordia* the captain took 51 minutes (from 21:45 to 22:36) to decide to announce Abandon Ship – which, according to the official report, was considered *too late*.

## Decision support system

Since the decision to abandon the ship was made *too late*, it is worth reviewing the documented plans that set the expectations for how the decisions *should have* been made. The decision support system is extracted from the official accident investigation report. It reads:

> In case of contact-breach, the procedure establishes the following actions (some steps are not reported because these do not influence the analysis of the present casualty):

1. Second Master or the Officer on duty verify the damage;

2. When the breach has been ascertained, the related compartments must be Identified;

3. The occurrence must be notified to the competent MRSC and to the Company (Fleet Crisis Coordinator technical advisor);

4. The situation must be assessed and evaluated with the aid of 'Damage control plan';

5. The SCD (Team in charge to verify the damage) is sent to the zone interested by the contact-breach;

6. All measures according to the event, are activate (such as to isolate the compartments –

to activate the equipments for pumping dry of flooding – to transfer liquids in other tanks) etc;

7. The 'technical advisor' must be informed about the situation developing;

8. If the action taken is not sufficient, the assistance by the on site vessels and MRSC must be requested;

9. The General Emergency signal must be given, thus passengers and crew proceed for the planned gathering;

10. If retaining of persons on board is dangerous, procedures for the abandon ship must be taken, and scenario is monitored till the evacuation of ship is completed.

(MIT, 2013, pp. 70,71)

## Ten steps to abandon the ship

Before we turn to examining the captain's perspective on the 'late abandonment', it is worth reflecting upon the quality of the decision support system (DSS). In a seminal thesis of our times, *Mission Improbable*, Clarke (2001) refers to such systems as 'fantasy documents'. Far from satisfying the functional needs of responding to a crisis, the fantasy documents signify the power of controlling the risk by turning uncertainty into an illusion of certainty.

> As organisations do their planning they transform uncertainty into risk, and the main tool they use in that transformation is a rhetorical one (Clarke, 2001, p. 19).

Such documented plans, according to Clarke, are fantasy documents because the imagination of how a crisis will unfold is so distant from the reality of the situation.

## A review of the decision support system

Before we examine the process in detail, the first question to ask is: What is the meaning of this opening statement in the decision support system?

> Some steps are not reported because these do not influence the analysis of the present casualty.

Why are those steps omitted from the process? Who decides what is relevant and what is not? It is likely that the document contains information that is not within the scope of the emergency. But it is also likely that the decision support system was purchased off the shelf or developed with little input from the ship's crew, the futility of which was exposed only in the aftermath of the crisis. The use of standardised plans and processes purchased from third-party service providers and certified for use by private regulatory bodies is not an uncommon practice in the maritime world. But such an omission is insincere, even unethical to the process of investigation, especially when the official narrative portrays the accident as the crime of one person. When a person is being sentenced to prison for his decision-making abilities, it is imperative that the criterion for the judgement is made transparent in a public document.

Notice also the actions to be taken in the case of emergency. The coherence of the organisational life and the way in which a crisis should be managed is astonishing in the 'Ten Steps to Abandon Ship'. These ten steps give the impression of a cookbook recipe that leaves very little room for ambiguity and uncertainty. It's the same Greek myth at play – Chronos working hard against Chaos, to ensure order. To an outsider reading the ten steps, everything appears simple and straightforward. As far as the organisation is concerned, its interests are protected, and to the regulator facing public scrutiny the risk is managed in those ten steps, at least on paper. The linearity of the processes (from Step 1 to 10) only adds to the simplicity of the documented process.

Now observe the language of the process – 'verify the damage'; 'must be identified'; 'must be notified'; 'must be evaluated and assessed'; 'must be informed'; 'if the action taken is not sufficient'; 'must be requested'; 'must be given'; and 'must be taken'. These are not blueprints and instructions for action; rather it is the rhetorical use of language characterised by certainty and direction in a crisis situation for the following reasons that come to mind:

1. to convince the public that the organisation was equipped with the capacity to deal with the crisis
2. that by creating a simplified process the organisation had carefully thought through the chaos that follows in a crisis (the 'keep it simple' mantra)
3. and that from this point onwards if the risk cannot be managed or controlled it is because those in charge deviated from this defined guide to risk and safety management.

This is evident in the official report:

It is worth to point out, first of all, that the emergency was managed by the Master. Anyway, the related procedure according with the Decision Support System was not followed. More bridge staff members followed duties differently by the established procedures.

(MIT, 2013, p. 82)

In this way, the 'fantasy' documents leave little room for heuristics, experiential knowledge, and the subjective, non-rational, embodied, instinctive and intuitive aspects of decision making of the captain. The symbolic language dominates, overshadows and even curses the sensemaking and decision taking of the captain and his crew in handling the crisis. It should be noted that more than two thirds of the passengers were evacuated by the ship's staff that night, but that is immaterial to the ritual of the investigation that is mostly concerned with scapegoating and witch hunting.

Much more can be said about the nature of discourse used in this ten-step process, but that is not the purpose of this chapter. Instead, let us turn to the captain's view of his decision to order Abandon Ship. Such a comparison will offer an alternative view about human decision making in an uncertain, unpredictable situation.

## The captain's decision to abandon the ship

In this excerpt, the captain explains the situation moments after the ship hit the rocks:

Once I felt the vibration, it was simply vibration because we were not hitting straight inside the rocks because in that case it would have been an impact. It was not an impact, it was like a blade was cutting through butter, just a small vibration. Because I gave a certain sequence of order to the helmsman, I knew in my mind the distance between me and the foam, I thought according to that manoeuvre that I was ordering if we were provoking the damage, and considering the fact there was a very short vibration I thought that we had damaged the left propeller. As a matter of fact, when I reported the damage to the concerned person ashore, I told him that I fucked up, we did a mistake we have a problem but it can be a propeller. And slowly, slowly, once it was the blackout, once it started to build a scenario, it was worse than the expectation.

Even if you are inside a car and you haven't got out of the car and you try to analyse the damage you can't tell if you are inside. I sent the other guy to assess the damage together with the first officer. They went down and slowly, slowly, they were reporting to me the damage. The proper language or terminology in case of a crisis is very vital for a captain to understand which is the extension of the damage that you have provoked. You know that the ship is divided into compartments, the engine compartment we have three diesel generators in one compartment, another three generators in another compartment, another one inside with the electrical motors. In case you realise that we have three compartments flooded you have to report to the bridge: Captain, sorry to inform you that we have three compartments flooded. Instead of reporting these as data they were starting to say diesel electric generator number 1, number 2 and number 3 flooded, that means 1 compartment. I started telling them that there are 3 compartments, but they went on diesel generator, and they said 1, 2 and 3 and now 4, 5, and 6 – that was like they were playing ping pong with this in front of me.

Then I said I just want to make things clear, once they are reporting to you a data and you see that there is confusion then you are forced to ask again. In the meantime, time is passing. Once I realised that the scenario was worse than my expectation, even when the chief engineer told me that we hit a fuel oil compartment on the starboard, then how come it's possible that we have a damage on the left, we have damage on the starboard? And then it was very difficult to imagine that a small vibration was provoking a huge damage. And it took time to build up in my mind according to the information provided to me, sometimes the information was contradictory. Then I asked the guy, 'Take the damage control plan and just mark on the plan the compartment on the chart.' At the end I was asking the officers, 'Guys, can you confirm whether the three compartments were flooded?' And all three of them said, 'Yes, we confirm.' At that moment I said, 'Now we have to abandon the ship.' At the end there were even more.

The NAPA[18] was not working – all the sounding pipe were connected to the NAPA – because it went in the blackout. We had also two double-

---

[18] NAPA is the ship's emergency computer's toolset for risk monitoring, flooding prediction and decision support. As the NAPA system was not connected with the UPS batteries it did not provide continuous monitoring of the ship's stability upon the loss of power.

bottom tanks; they were damaged. And because of these I realised it would have been better to let the ship drift towards the shallow water, and soon the ship would have stopped, to start the evacuation procedure.

## Sensemaking in accidents

Let us go back to Steps 1, 2 and 3 in the decision support system. The notion that when a ship collides with rocks the captain and his crew can (1) determine the location and extent of the damage to the ship, (2) report the occurrence and (3) decide when and how to abandon the ship, goes against the basic principles of decision making in an unexpected situation.

In this section we will examine decision making through the lenses of sensemaking. This can be understood as how we give collective meaning to our experiences in a social context. As Weick suggests, our collective meanings do not have to match an objective reality so long as they resonate with our lived or imagined experiences (Weick, Sensemaking in Organizations, 1995).

Weick (1995) provides the following framework for sensemaking:

1. **Sensemaking starts with examining our own grounding in the situation.** Because we cannot detach ourselves from the situation, it is important to consider our own social identity when we make meaning of the situation: 'What am I assuming?'
2. **Sensemaking is retrospective.** In order to make sense of our experiences and act in anticipation,

we have to look back at what we know so far: 'What is the historical context? What do I know so far?'

3. **Sensemaking is enactive of sensible environments.** What is sensible to enact (act out or achieve) in an environment is based on the individual's abilities to interact with the environment. In other words, what is possible to achieve in an environment through our actions and interpretations and the constraints that the environment places on us. 'What can I practically achieve in this environment?'

4. **Sensemaking is social.** The meanings that we give to our experiences are socially negotiated and consensualised with others: 'How are others influencing my decisions? How am I being influenced by the presence of others?'

5. **Sensemaking is an ongoing process.** No matter how much we understand from the past about a situation, there is always something new to consider when we are moving ahead and making decisions: 'What new cues are emerging that may prove my assumptions wrong?'

6. **Sensemaking is extracting cues.** We can never have complete knowledge of a prospective situation, and so we learn to extract cues and make broad generalisations to move ahead: 'What cues am I relying upon and why? Are there other ways to process information than by relying on the same cues and indications?'

7. **Sensemaking is plausible.** The meaning that we assign to our experiences is not based on some objective truth as long as those experiences seem reasonably aligned with our lived experiences and assumptions. There is always a trade-off between plausibility and accuracy: 'When is the information at hand sufficient to make a decision?'

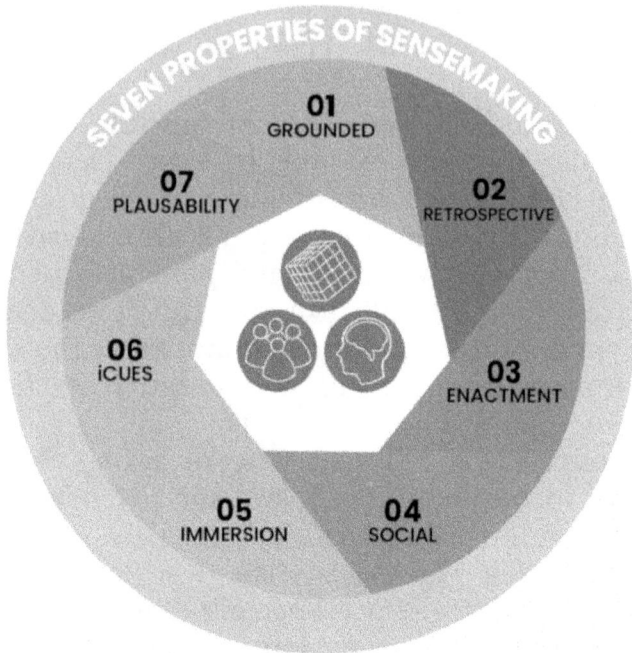

Figure 14.6: The seven properties of sensemaking. (Source: Karl Weick)

|   | Sensemaking | Questions | Examples |
|---|---|---|---|
| 1 | Grounded | What am I assuming ? | Biases, assumptions, prejudice, temperament |
| 2 | Retrospective | What do we know from the past? | Patterns, Trends, History, Timeline |
| 3 | Enactment | "What we possibly achieve? What does the environment allow us to achieve?" | Affordances, possibilities, worldviews, myths, interpretations and constrains. |

| 4 | Social | "How may other influence my decisions? How may I influence others?" | Agency, peer pressure, bystander effect, responsibility diffusion, groupthink, Halo effect, conformity, belonging. |
|---|--------|------|------|
| 5 | Immersion | What new cues are emerging that may prove my assumptions wrong? | Dissonance, mindfulness, awareness, critical thinking, doubt |
| 6 | iCues | "What cues am I relying upon and why? Are there alternative ways to process information than relying on the same cues and indicators?" | Cues, Indicators, Threshold, limits, tolerance parameters, keywords |
| 7 | Plausibility | Is the information at hand sufficient to make decision? | Trade-offs, compromises, bi-products |

Figure 14.7: Sensemaking, questions and examples, based on Weick (1995).

Let us discuss the captain's social sensemaking in examining his decision to order Abandon Ship.

## Sensemaking and retrospection

Foundational to sensemaking is what we know thus far about our social environment. When the ship hit the rocks, the captain felt it as a 'small vibration' akin to a 'blade cutting through butter'. He had given a set of orders to the helmsman which had involved first turning away from the rocks and then, once the ship came closer to the island, turning towards it. As a skilled mariner, his intention behind this manoeuvre was to avoid the stern of the ship sliding sideways into the rocks. (If you are not from the maritime world, imagine how the driver of a long trailer will need to steer away from a bend in the road before turning, in order to avoid the rear wheels hitting the kerb.)

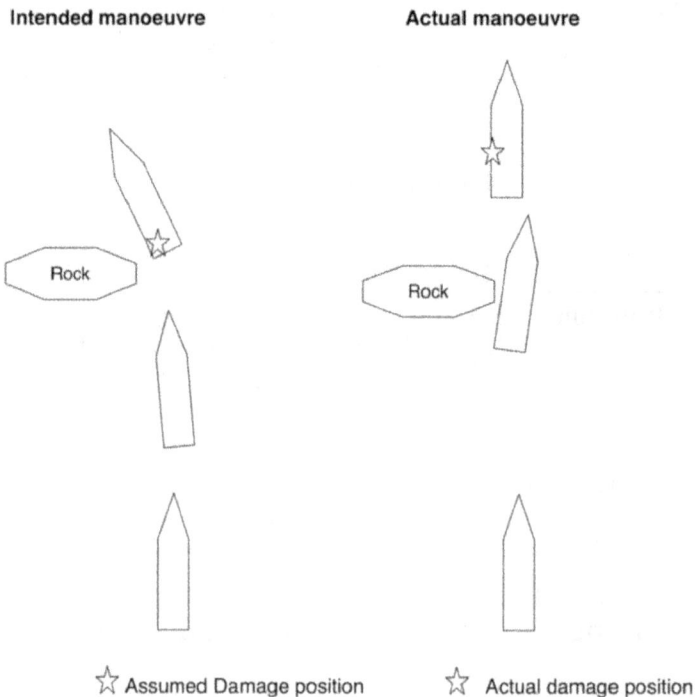

**Intended manoeuvre**          **Actual manoeuvre**

☆ Assumed Damage position     ☆ Actual damage position

Figure 14.8: Intended and actual manoeuvre while closing the rock.

But for reasons that remain unknown in the public domain, the turn towards the rocks was executed with an eight-second delay by the helmsman. The data recorder shows that contrary to the captain's order to turn the ship towards the rocks the helmsman turned it in the opposite direction before he corrected the helm. Francesco was himself never made aware of the incorrect execution of the helm until almost three months after the accident. In his own mind, he was naturally assuming that because he had applied a certain set of helm orders, it was the aft section of the ship that had collided with the rocks. That section of the ship could better withstand damage caused by hitting rocks because in that area there is less longitudinal stress on the ship's structure.

Unfortunately, though, and against the captain's expectations, the rock had penetrated the ship amidships, where all the critical machinery items were located, leading to irretrievable damage and progressive flooding. The official investigation report stated:

> the immediate flooding of five contiguous watertight compartments, where most of the vital equipment of the ship was located, makes the *Costa Concordia* casualty quite a unique event, because the extent of damage is well beyond the survivability standard applicable to the ship according to her keel laying date.

There is a saying in a Chinese proverb which roughly translates as '*Deviate an inch, lose a thousand miles*'. If we think of sensemaking as the basis of what we know from the past (retrospective), the captain's perception of a small amount of vibration, and damage near the propeller, gradually increased the gap between his expectations and the seriousness of the situation.

## Sensemaking and cue extraction

Despite the loss of power immediately after the collision, the non-operative automatic starting of the emergency generator and the power failure on the steering pumps, rendering the two rudders out of control, the captain remained convinced that the damage was caused at the after end of the ship. It was almost as if he was in denial that there was serious and irreversible damage to the ship.

It is understandable that in a crisis we humans want to downplay the risk. Despite all the cues and indications pointing at anomalies, the unexpected and the uncontrollable, the captain's expectations remained anchored in seeking comfort from things being under control. We are guided by what we expect should happen, because doing otherwise causes us enormous discomfort within. But as we start to build up a more accurate picture of the situation about the outside world, we are faced with a challenge within. Our emotions go wild and our feelings betray us, and in such a situation our senses and sensory input are of little value for sensemaking. We believe what we want to believe, and in the process we become selective about the cues we see, hear, smell, touch, taste, extract and ignore. The captain was not prepared to accept that the ship was sinking, so his first reaction was not to understand what was happening but to seek control of his emotions. To do otherwise would be 'to forgo any feeling of control or predictability' (Weick & Sutcliffe, 2001, p. 30) and lose control of the life processes (Damasio, 2021). Being selective about the cues that we are unconsciously drawn towards is more than a psychological reaction; it is a biological need for us, in order to cope with the fear of the unknown.

## Sensemaking and social grounding

Such a strong sense of seeking control also originates from the social identity of a ship captain. Our everyday language says a lot about the symbolic baggage associated with the captain, seas, ships and maritime language in general. The vagaries of Mother Nature – chaos, unpredictability and uncertainty – embodied in a ship pitching and tossing in the high seas are brought into balance by the control and order associated with the archetype of the captain. It used to be said that the old man (captain) was in command of the lady (ship) as she set sail for the high seas. But this delicate command and control relationship, where the captain is in command, has existed only up to the point when there is a ship to be controlled. Once the ship has sunk, the captain is stripped of their power because there is nothing left to for them to control (Dahl, 1957). Hilduberg (2015) describes this succinctly in his master's thesis:

> the shipmaster's power ... and ability to be exercised is only intact until the window of opportunity closed for the abandonment of the ship in an orderly fashion. The shipmaster's ableness (actual power) is limited by the complex nature of the decision-making under uncertainty, his lack of knowledge about the system and the unfolding events that prevents him from mitigating the risks. After a certain tipping point the ship is lost and both the ability (potential power) and ableness (actual power) is lost – the shipmaster is rendered powerless, which challenges the normative

view of the shipmaster. Paradoxically the actual abandoning of the ship is a non-reversible decision to terminate the functioning of the ship, which is both a manifestation of the shipmaster's power, and the abolishment of his power.

(Hilduberg, 2015, p. 90).

During our interview about abandoning ship, Schettino commented, 'No captain would like to believe that his ship is sinking.' Hilduberg's (2015) observation is astute. Although the captain retains the ultimate power to abandon ship, his unconscious knows that the same decision makes him powerless. Such a critical realisation that we are abandoning control of the situation takes courage, especially when it works against our social identity. What good is a captain without control?

## Sensemaking is what is sense-able

Sense-ability is how our perceptions relate with our actions; in other words, what can we possibly imagine that we can and cannot do in a given environment? In this instance, sensemaking was what was sensible to the captain and his crew before and during the crisis situation; and what was sensible (*sense-able*) to them was based on their abilities, limitations, goals, expectations, (past) experiences and environmental constraints. Interestingly, a lot of what people consider sensible is shared tacitly within the group and not always brought to the surface.

The criticism faced by the captain was that he took a long time to decide when to abandon the ship. What was getting in the way of the captain's decision? I believe that understanding decision making through the lenses of sensibility can help.

In the cruise shipping industry two myths are widespread. The first (since the days of the *Titanic*) is that cruise ships are unsinkable, and the second is that in the event of an emergency the ship is its own best lifeboat. The latter means that the captain should keep the passengers on the ship for as long as possible, until sinking becomes imminent.

It is not that the policymakers, design engineers, surveyors and naval architects genuinely believe that the ship is its own best lifeboat. Captain Michael Lloyd wrote that such a myth prevails because

> it avoided the necessary costly changes to the safety equipment, the construction and especially, the watertight integrity issue.

(Lloyd, 2019)

Lloyd further wrote that after the capsize of the *Costa Concordia* the International Maritime Organization (IMO)[14] avoided using the phrase 'the ship is a lifeboat'. When we evaluate the captain's decision to abandon ship as being made *too late*, it is important that we understand the power of such myths in the collective sensibility of the captain and his crew members.

Any ship captain will tell you that the decision to abandon ship in the middle of the night is not a straightforward one. The problem is even more acute on ships carrying thousands of passengers. The

---

[14] The IMO is a UN agency responsible for regulating shipping.

myth that the 'ship is its own best lifeboat' survives because of a certain degree of cynicism about the usefulness of lifesaving appliances in an emergency within the seafaring community; deregulation, quality of inspection services and the design and operation of lifesaving appliances have been an ongoing concern within the maritime industry. Within the seafaring community there is an implicit lack of trust in lifesaving devices. For example, a common adage you will hear from the mariners is 'lifeboats have killed more people than they have saved'. There is often reluctance to deploy lifeboats during emergency drills and emergency exercises on ships, due to the questionable quality and physical integrity of the lifesaving appliances (Seafarers International Research Centre , 2013) (MAIB UK, 2001).

This example illustrates that when technology cannot control the risk, we humans turn towards myths and rituals to ensure symbolic control over an uncertain future. In the risk and safety culture, this is commonly achieved through filling and filing of paperwork and turning 'red' and 'orange' to 'green' in the risk assessments. 'All checked and found ok'; 'tested'; or 'verified' – these are common examples of the slogans used in factory acceptance tests, maintenance management records and technical inspections without revealing the nuanced details of the process of testing and inspections. Myth holds the power to turn the imaginary into real and the uncontrollable into control and order.

The decision to abandon ship was not simply a matter of figuring out the optimum choice in the moment. Rather, it was a matter of sensibility based on how the captain and his crew were *seeing* the 'real' situation. If the captain and his crew tacitly shared the opinion that lifeboats cannot be trusted in an emergency situation, a decision to abandon ship in the middle of the night would be impeded within their sphere of sense-ability. Interestingly, no one will *openly* doubt the lifesaving machinery, yet within their collective unconscious their sensibility will stop them launching the boats.

In the end, the captain's sensibility proved right. When the ship listed to starboard, the lifeboats on the port side were rendered useless. On the starboard side, three of the thirteen lifeboats, with a collective capacity to rescue 450 persons, landed on the embarkation deck because their telescopic davits failed to protrude far enough. The ship's listing was still within the acceptable limits of the regulatory requirements, thus questioning the integrity and functionality of certified lifesaving appliances in an emergency situation.

Figure 14.9: A graphic illustration showing how one of the lifeboats failed to launch during the emergency due to a design fault and the chaos on the embarkation deck.

## The assumptions behind the evacuation of passengers

A second aspect of sensibility was the unrealistic expectation in the emergency management plan of the time it takes to evacuate passengers from the ship in a crisis situation. On numerous occasions the captain suggested that 'it was humanly impossible to evacuate thousands of passengers in the middle of the night'. While Schettino made his own calculations and claims to highlight his concerns, Catino (2023) surfaces those assumptions more succinctly:

> As for the management of the emergency, according to the regulations in force, before giving the order to abandon the ship, the captain should have had the purser carry out a muster call (with megaphones and lists of names) of all the passengers and crew: 4,229 people spread throughout 220 meters at the various meeting points. Doing some basic arithmetic, it would be possible to call, simply by saying the name and surname of each passenger, about 25–30 people per minute. The whole process, then, maintaining the same rhythm and without stopping, would take between two hours and ten minutes and two hours and twenty minutes. If, in addition to calling out the names, it was also necessary to check the passengers' response, in order to ascertain their presence, the time required would be doubled at least. Time would, in any case, have certainly been taken away from managing the emergency. Among other things, investigations revealed that, between the passengers on the list available to the captain and those who were actually on board, there was a difference of over five hundred people. The muster call would

therefore have taken even more time, given that hundreds of people would not have responded and it would have taken a long time to realize the difference between the list and reality. Compliance with this rule would clearly have endangered the lives of passengers. Failure to comply with an absurd rule, instead of being considered an important decision in terms of speeding up emergency operations, was considered a sign of negligence on the part of the captain.

(Catino, 2023)

When we consider the claim about the late abandonment of the ship, it is important to contextualise the sensibility of the captain and his team in their decisions and actions to evacuate the passengers from the ship during the night.

## Sensemaking is social

In any crisis, communication plays an important role. Let us overlay the decision support process with the narratives shared by those at the scene. Notice how the expectations are outlined in the process: verify the damage, inform the authorities, take this action, request this information, almost following the mechanical logic of IFTT (if this, then that). Such is the nature of linear communication that it assumes that people will behave in a predictable and mechanical manner. But in contrast, the official report illustrates several examples of how communication in a crisis environment takes place and how it challenges our understanding of human interactions.

The first engineer, a Bulgarian, testified in court that he could not understand the orders given in Italian during the emergency (interview on 20 March 2012, Enc. 384 cited in MIT (2013)). The radio officer testified that while lowering the lifeboat, the bosun gave instructions both in Italian and in English to the South American crew (testimony on 16 March 2012 – Encl. 383 cited in MIT (2013)). Several passengers from the United States testified in court that during the emergency the crew members were unable to speak in English. The black box data also shows that the Indonesian helmsman did not understand the captain's order on two consecutive occasions, shortly before the ship hit the rocks (MIT, 2013, pp. 75-76).

The official report suggests that despite the presence of 38 nationalities on the ship during the crisis, the official working language on the ship was Italian:

> To have chosen a more widespread, international, known and shared language would have given, of course, concrete advantages for communication between the crew, and between the latter and the passengers, above all in situations where understanding each other is of fundamental importance.

Any attempt to understand why the captain's decision to abandon ship was not made in adequate time should take into account the interpretive nature of communication and the potential for miscommunication and misunderstanding.

## Sensemaking, distress and trauma

Sensemaking is an ongoing process. Moment by moment, as we build a coherent picture of the past by giving meaning to our experiences, we are also faced with a future full of novelties and surprises. In this particular case, as the captain was figuring out the extent and location of the damage to the ship, new information was being brought to his attention by his team – information that was sometimes equivocal or misrepresentative, and on other occasions conflicting, and, indeed, contrary to Francesco's own beliefs and identity as a captain.

Being Mindful (think 1B3M) about how patterns emerge, and how the future unfolds is crucial for sensemaking. By Mindfulness I do not mean a heightened brain-centred situational awareness but the balanced mind–body coordination essential to being immersed in the present. Csikszentmihalyi (2002) calls this a state of *flow experience*:

> They are situations in which attention can be freely invested to achieve a person's goals, because there is no disorder to straighten out, no threat for the self to defend against.

When we work in a high-risk environment, the flow experience is crucial for us to maintain a high level of attention and sensemaking. Our sensory devices work both ways: they connect us with our deeper inner selves, and they gather information from the environment around us. When we experience flow, we are one with our surroundings; sometimes we say 'time flies'.

But when we are in a stressful situation that is not the case. When we are working under stress, every minute becomes an hour, because what we are hearing and seeing starts to conflict with our goals and threatens our identity and existence. When a ship is on fire or sinking, we often use the metaphor *ship in distress*. But, come to think of it, how can machinery experience distress? It's only living beings who can do that.

What happens to us when we are distressed? Our life support systems – nervous, respiratory, endocrine, digestive, skin, and blood circulation – all begin to tell each other that something is not right. Then, when our homoeostasis is out of balance, our emotions are no longer connected with our reasoning abilities. If there is a dog in the vicinity, it will know that you are in distress by sensing the activation of your sweat glands. Our Bodies Keep the Score, and distress turns into a trauma (van der Kolk, 2014).

A trauma, according to the trauma psychologist Peter Levine, is a 'psychic wound that does not allow the person to let go of the past'. Levine calls trauma 'the tyranny of the past' (Levine, 1997). Gabor Mate, in his book *The Myth of Normal*, wrote:

> certain shocks to the organism can alter a person's biological, psychological, and social equilibrium to such a degree that the memory of one particular event comes to taint, and dominate, all other experiences, spoiling an appreciation of the present moment.
>
> (Maté, 2022)

As we attempt to engage with the future, our traumatic experiences pull us back into the past and inhibit our sensemaking.

Various official and media reports illustrate that on the night of the accident the captain was in distress, experiencing trauma:

> After hitting rocks which tore a 70-metre-long hole in the side of the *Costa Concordia*, Schettino rang Roberto Ferrarini, an official manning the company's emergency room. In a recording of the conversation, the court heard him say, 'Captain Palombo told me "Pass by, pass by!" I passed by and hit the bottom with the stern. I am destroyed, I am dead, don't say anything to me.' (Kington, 2013)

> First mate Giovanni Laccarino said that the Captain put his head in his hands and told the officers on the bridge: 'I messed up.'

> During the trial, Mr Laccarino told the court that he was using his Playstation in a crewmate's cabin when the ship hit the rocks. He rushed to the bridge, where instruments showed that the ship had lost propulsion, but was surprised at the captain's calm demeanour.' He was completely lost,' he said. 'He was out of his routine mental state. He was under shock. He wasn't the person I knew.'

> (Winfield & Sportelli, 2013)

> Ms Canessa, the navigator, also said Captain Schettino showed chronic indecision as he contemplated the loss of his ship. 'I was saying to him very insistently that he needed to do something, to give the general emergency signal, but he was telling us to wait,' she told the court, 'even as officers screamed at him to do so', said Canessa. 'He told us to wait, he didn't give us answer,' she said.

> (Kington, 2013)

In an interview with the Naples daily newspaper *Il Mattino*, Gianluca Marino Cosentino, medical officer on board the *Costa Concordia*, also mentions the long delay before abandoning ship and accuses Schettino.

> Everyone was looking for the captain. As a doctor, I thought he appeared upset and no longer rational. He did nothing to coordinate the rescue. Personally, I was very surprised to see Schettino out of uniform on the quayside after midnight.

> (Lloyd, 2019)

You may be aware of the famous phone call between the coastguard and the captain when the former demanded that the captain get back on board 'for fuck's sake'. Now reimagine the same situation, but this time not by framing Schettino as Captain Coward who chose to abandon the passengers and run away from the ship (a topic we will address in the next chapter) but Schettino as a traumatised person.

One newspaper constructed the following narrative:

> Not long after, at 1:46, the angry Coast Guard officer, De Falco, telephoned Schettino once more. The captain was still sitting on his rock, staring glumly at the Concordia. De Falco had heard there was a rope ladder hanging from the bow of the ship. 'Schettino? Listen, Schettino,' he began. 'There are people trapped on board. Now you go with your boat under the prow on the starboard side. There's a rope ladder. You go on board and then you will tell me how many people there are. Is that clear? I'm recording this conversation, Captain Schettino.'

Schettino tried to object, but De Falco wasn't having it. 'You go up that rope ladder, get on that ship, and tell me how many people are still on board, and what they need. Is that clear? I'm going to make sure you get in trouble. I'm going to make you pay for this. Get the fuck on board!'

'Captain, please,' Schettino begged.

'No "please". You get moving and go on board now ... '

'I am here with the rescue boats. I'm here. I'm not going anywhere.'

'What are you doing, Captain?'

'I am here to coordinate the rescue ... '

'What are you coordinating there? Go on board! Are you refusing?'

They bickered another minute. 'But you realise it's dark and we can't see anything,' Schettino pleaded.

'And so what?' De Falco demanded. 'You want to go home, Schettino? It's dark and you want to go home?'

Schettino offered more excuses. De Falco cut him off one last time. 'Go! Immediately!'

Later, I asked De Falco's boss, Cosma Scaramella, whether he thought the captain was in shock. 'I don't know,' Scaramella told me. 'He didn't seem very lucid.'

A half-hour or so after his last call from the Coast Guard, a rescue boat plucked Schettino from his rock and ferried him to the harbor. He talked to the police for a bit, then found a priest, who later said the captain, in a daze, cried for a very long time.

(Burrough & Mckenna, 2012)

I find this narrative inhumane, lacking both rigour and the ethics of journalism. Everything in this narrative and what we have known so far in the public domain indicates that the captain was in a state of trauma. How, then, do we expect a traumatised person to think logically and behave rationally (in Mind 1)? Granted that this should not mean the captain should be absolved from his duties – but can we think of an alternative framework to understand this situation?

A question that comes to mind is that despite all the evidence suggesting that the captain was suffering from trauma and knowing that decision making is severely impeded in a trauma, neither the public media nor the official report makes reference to the captain's state of mind during the crisis. In fact, as I sift through many other examples of maritime accidents, trauma and distress are rarely acknowledged in accident investigations. Why is that so?

Perhaps because a society seduced by the myth of individualism and superheroism finds solace in scapegoating a professional rather than attempting to understand a person's psyche.

A narrative that depicts a captain in distress looking for another person – perhaps a priest or a chaplain

– to help them cope with their situation does not sound like a superhero myth. Our individualist society expects the image of a captain as a superhero in uniform and in the foreground of control panels and joysticks, working out the optimum move in the midst of a crisis. Our Hollywood culture expects everyone around the captain to be in a rational state of mind doing exactly what the superhero expects – verify the damage, inform the authorities, take this action, request this information, do this and only do that which ultimately leads us to salvation. Captain Francesco Schettino absorbed all the sins of our society – cheap design, questionable regulations, a race-to-the-bottom approach to operating standards, material consumption habits – but in doing so, he failed to fulfil the hedonistic expectations of our society for a cheaper, better, safer cruise holiday. Instead of being a superhero who could go yet another step farther to absorb all the flaws of shipbuilding and operations, he allowed distress and trauma to take over his decision making. In an investigation framed as a quest for heroes and anti-heroes, such a narrative is not plausible.

Captain Michael Lloyd (2019) wrote further about the traumatised state of the captain:

> The evidence overwhelmingly suggests that Captain Schettino was suffering from traumatic shock syndrome and was in a mental state of denial therefore obviously incapable of taking any decisive action. This was supported by video evidence of the chaos on the bridge. As this was recognised by two officers on the bridge, then this should also have been recognised by the Staff Captain who was also present. It was therefore his duty to

assume command while the Captain was in this state. The question must be then why didn't he?

This is a fair question, and one that begs for a deeper understanding of the nature of organisation in a crisis. The staff captain is the second in command, and by default a deputy for the captain. Again, effective organisation in a crisis is the ability to delegate duties and responsibilities in the event of collapse of formal structures. But this is nowhere to be seen as part of the official investigation, perhaps because of the limitations of an expert–novice culture (see Chapter 13) and the cognitive imbalance between ranks that makes it difficult for the deputy to carry out substitute activities in an emergency. When an official investigation report claims that the delay in abandoning the ship led to a loss of lives and when sloppy decision making becomes a pivotal accusation used against the captain in the court of law, it is imperative that we question the basis for such claims.

I am left with more questions than I have answers. For example, where was the team for the captain? Where was the pastoral support for him? Where were the structures to help him in trauma? What culture had been cultivated on the bridge? Why are leaders expected to be superhuman in a crisis? What kind of culture has been created such that captains can't listen to others below them in the hierarchy?

## Why resilience comes through relationships

Businesses and policymakers recognise the importance of enhancing technical and operational redundancies to ensure business continuity and operational resilience. But what do we do when people responsible for overseeing critical operations are overcome by distress and trauma?

On the night of the accident, the captain was traumatised. He needed someone to recognise his trauma, but everyone around him was judging him and perhaps expecting a miracle from a superhero. I accept wholeheartedly that in making any such claim we should also be aware that everyone around the captain may well have been in the same state of mind. As Van der Kolk writes:

> The critical issue is reciprocity: being truly heard and seen by the people around us, feeling that we are held in someone else's mind and heart. For our physiology to calm down, heal, and grow we need a visceral feeling of safety. No doctor can write a prescription for friendship and love: These are complex and hard- earned capacities. You don't need a history of trauma to feel self-conscious and even panicked at a party with strangers—but trauma can turn the whole world into a gathering of aliens. Many traumatized people find themselves chronically out of sync with the people around them.

(van der Kolk, 2014, p. 92)

What comes to mind is a crowded city of individuals in a crisis, each one trying to cope with their own situation and preserve their own social identity. We can design the best emergency procedures and contingency plans, but without empathy, vulnerability, humility and wisdom there can be no resilience in a team.

Unfortunately, many of our training initiatives and wellbeing programmes focus excessively on the cognitive capacity of our brain. I once attended a resilience workshop where the emphasis was on taking frequent breaks at work and going out for long walks to avoid burnout. But in this discourse I think we are missing something important: the problem is not one of individual capacity, but one that arises from a lack of emotional, embodied and holistic engagement with a traumatised person. In those moments when the captain was experiencing trauma, what was needed was a 'critical friend' who could earn his trust, engage in a conversation, listen to him and question his assumptions. Unfortunately, a 'lean and mean' crewing structure underpinned by the expert–novice culture does not create the conditions to draw from the collective wisdom of a team of professionals; it only weakens the team resilience and makes the crisis situation more vulnerable.

*The captain was too late in ordering Abandon Ship. If he had made a decision in good time, the accident might not have resulted in the loss of so many lives.* This is the claim that we discussed in this chapter, first by examining the basis for the assertion in the official narrative, and ultimately by applying this question to the captain himself. We have analysed the captain's perspective within the framework of sensemaking and examined what it means to make decisions in a crisis. As I researched and wrote this chapter, memories kept bringing me back to my own experiences at sea. Perhaps I will write an entire book on trauma and resilience as a future project.

It is not my job to convince you that the captain was justified in what he did that night. But I think it is important to understand the gap between what our society expects from professionals, and what it means to experience and live through a crisis. If you are left with some questions about the adequacy of emergency response plans, I have achieved my purpose in writing this chapter.

In closing, an image comes to mind. **The futility of plans and processes serves not only as what Clark (2001) would refer to as 'fantasy documents' but also shows how those documented fantasies become the basis for turning accident narratives into stories of culpability and crime.**

Figure 14.10: An illustration of the adequacy of emergency response plans.

# 15

# The 'No-Blame' Culture Myth

On 12 May 2017 the highest court of Italy – the Court of Cassation – announced the charges against the captain of the *Costa Concordia*. In the report:

1. Schettino was wholly responsible for the collision.
2. He should have given the order to abandon ship much sooner than he did.
3. He should not have left the Concordia before he had overseen its full evacuation.

In the official accident investigation report, the captain was considered the 'main cause' of the accident. Subsequently, he was sentenced to sixteen years in the prison. The sentence included ten years for manslaughter, five for causing the shipwreck, one for abandoning the ship before passengers and crew were clear, and one month for lying to the authorities afterwards. The captain was nicknamed 'Captain Coward' by the media, after the coastguard released recordings of him in a lifeboat resisting orders to return to the stricken vessel.

It is against the background of the charges laid out and the media reports that we will seek to understand the captain's perspective. The guiding question of this chapter – *Can we really do without blaming?*

---

- Captain as the scapegoat in the accident.
- The captain's perspective about why he became a scapegoat.
- Understanding how scapegoating works.
- Can 'science' rid us of scapegoating?
- The hidden powers in the ritual of scapegoating.
- Can there be a 'no-blame' culture?
- Are we learning from accidents?

Figure 15.1: A general outline of the chapter.

## The captain's perspective

Historically, ship captains are known to go down with the ship. It does not matter what is stipulated in the merchant shipping conventions; myth has it that the captain should be the last person to evacuate. The maritime industry and society at large are critical and unforgiving of Francesco's decision to leave the ship when several passengers were still trapped on board.

But speaking with the captain gave me a different perspective of this narrative. In Francesco's view the circumstances in which he evacuated the ship have been grossly misunderstood, and distorted in the public discourse. In a letter from prison dated 19 August 2017, approximately five months after being sentenced, he wrote to me:

> 4 days after the incident, I reported to the Judge that I slipped and fell due to the fact that the ship tilted over her side, I added as well and that I had not anymore the soil under my feet.
>
> Actually I was describing exactly what happened and mainly the feeling that I experienced when affected by the gravity.
>
> I explained as well that the last lifeboat was trapped under the extended arms of the crane and that due to the relentless capsizing of the ship, the lifeboat was in the process to be carried under the surface together with all the occupancies. According the depositions during the trial the Chief Nurse stated that there were several passengers inside.
>
> The useless phone call has prevailed over any logical explanation and evidences emerged during the trial. Once that we clarify the abandon ship, then we will remove the psychological prevention to analyze the incident and your investigation will be deserved value.

Several interviews, records, statements and a book co-authored by the captain (in Italian) along with a journalist indicate that Francesco had decided to leave only when the ship had capsized (Abate, 2015). It would be impossible to hang onto the ship without 'soil under my feet', he had said. In fact, he had the presence of mind to jump on top of a lifeboat trapped under the ship and being sunk by its own davits on the ship, which would have crushed and killed all its passengers and crew. After landing on the boat, Francesco opened the hatch and told the coxswain to release the throttle on the engine, which was constantly pushing the boat into the ship.

UBICAZIONE          81

COGNOME E NOME      SCHETTINO FRANCESCO

Data di NASCITA     14/11/60

DA INVIARE SUB MAIL   NiPPiN.ANAND@NiPPiNANAND.com

Dear Nippin,
                                SLiPPED
4 days after the incident, I reported to the Judge that I slept and fell due to the fact that the ship tilted over her side, I added as well and that I had not anymore the soil under my feet. Actually I was describing exactly what happened and mainly the feeling that I experienced when affected by the gravity.

I explained as well that the lost lifeboat was trapped under the extended arms of the crane and that due to the relentless capsizing of the ship, the lifeboat was in the process to be carried under the surface together with all the occupancies. According the depositions during the trial the Chief Nurse stated that there were several passengers inside.

The useless phone call has prevailed over any logical explanation and evidences emerged during the trial. Once that we clarify the abandon ship, then we will remove the psychological prevention to analyze the incident and your investigation will be deserved value.
                                HAVE THE
I do not have the opportunity to translate the book, here I do not have even a pc. I will try to arrange something for the future. In the mean time, please translate the 3 video that I suggested to you. I believe that at the university there is some someone able to speak Italian, step by step they can translate the video in real time. YOU WILL UNDERSTAND MORE

Please also have a look to the SURFCRUISE on face book. My will be presented at Genova the international boat show. Please have a look on the web side, you have been the first one to see the prototype

Keep in touch and let me know if I can help in clarifying any other detail

DATA 19/08/2017     FIRMA

Figure 15.2: Francesco's letter from prison, dated 19 August 2017.

Professor Maurizio Catino (2023) wrote:

> As emerged from the evidence, in the last few moments, as the ship rotated on itself and collapsed onto one side, the surface of the bridge was gradually transformed into a slide and then into a vertical wall. For this reason, the second in command had thrown himself into the sea. It is in this specific context that the captain had no alternative but to move away as quickly as possible from the ship, together with the last passengers left on that side, and only after having helped to disengage the last lifeboat, which otherwise risked being left unused after the ship had keeled over. The investigative unit of the Carabinieri of Grosseto also confirmed that the captain abandoned the ship at precisely that moment of extremity. Not only was staying aboard on that side of the ship practically impossible, given the inclination of almost ninety degrees, it was also certain that the captain would have died had he not left the ship just then, given the position the vessel was in. This is a point worth repeating: the only other behavior possible in this situation was to die. Yet this evidence was never communicated correctly by the media. (Catino, 2023)

Figure 15.3: The conditions in which the captain landed on a lifeboat full of people. The risk was that the boat would be sunk by its own davits.

What should otherwise be regarded as an act of professionalism to save a boat full of people in distress turned into a story of cowardice, garnering hate and public anger. Francesco believes that this was a deliberate attempt to project the systemic problems of an entire industry onto a single person.

> The real news is not the news they [company] have given. They have preferred to build up a character, because maybe this was good for the business, for them to build up the story that the captain was escaping from the ship because maybe we sell more newspapers maybe I don't know. Maybe someone was driving this kind of information because all the attention went on the captain that is abandoning his ship. The people were not focusing that the ship was capsizing on one side because this is not good publicity, this is not good advertising. Because if you buy a cruise ship ticket and you think a ship like this can capsize like that, it is bad to imprint this in the mind of the people.

Interview with Francesco Schettino

To understand why and how a single individual became the burden-bearer of a systemic accident, let's start with an overview of the mimetic theory. This theory, its name originally coined by the French philosopher René Girard, helps us to understand the psychosocial mechanism that leads to scapegoating in four distinct steps. (1) Our desires are mimetic (we desire what others desire); (2) mimetic desire can turn into mimetic rivalries; (3) the ritual of scapegoating is essentially deployed to put an end to mimetic rivalry; and (4) the story that emerges from scapegoating (in our case, accident investigations) serves to ensure political and social order. Let us examine the mimetic theory and its application to the *Costa Concordia* accident in practice.

## Our desires are mimetic

Human beings, according to Girard, are creatures of desire. Once our basic survival *needs* are met, we turn towards *desire*. But desire is not an individual-instinctual need, it is imitative in nature (Girard, 1976) (Girard, 2013). We know what we desire when we look to others for what they desire, and often our *wants* converge on the same object. The problem is compounded when the object of our desire is scarce: several men eyeing one woman (or the other way about); a highly sought-after property in a posh suburb; the limited release of a new model of car; a one-time offer on a cruise ship, or even something as simple as positive feedback from a customer in a competitive work environment.

I grew up watching a famous TV commercial that transformed the entire approach to selling televisions in India by exploiting the mimetic nature of human desire. The television brand Onida used the slogan *Neighbour's envy, Owner's pride*. The Dutch philosopher Thorstein Veblen viewed this as the power of conspicuous consumption to reach the masses (Veblen, 2006). As Veblen suggests, and the sales initiatives on today's social media reveal, much of what we consume is a matter of display and a desire to imitate the ruling classes, although on the latter, Veblen and Girard took to diverging thoughts.

As I studied the economics of the cruise industry, I noticed the same pattern of mimetic desire at work:

an exponential increase in both the demand and the supply of cruise shipping in the years preceding the accident. For Girard, all this sets the path towards a 'cruise culture' in which cruising has become a product for mass consumption. This is succinctly captured on a website that monitors the market growth in the cruise shipping:

> The market talks to each other, influences each other. So progress gets amplified. The more people who have ocean cruised, the more who will tell others, the more who will want to take an ocean cruise too.[15]

The question for us is how this rapid increase in the demand for cruise services is managed not just at the operator level but also at the regulatory level. In our investigation of this accident we came across several instances of shortfalls in regulatory controls, including: design issues in shipbuilding; ambiguous rules and standards, which work in favour of ship owners; privatisation of regulation by appointing classification societies and recognised organisations to act on behalf of the flag states; access to cheap labour; an expedient approach to the education and training of seafarers; and the questionable quality of the lifesaving equipment and systems.

Despite all the shortcomings in ship design and operation, both the accident report and the public opinion turned on the captain as 'the main cause of the accident'. Within just 48 hours of the accident, when the company CEO released his press

---

[15]  https://cruisemarketwatch.com/growth/

statement, the captain's fate had been sealed. Was this a deliberate move?

## From mimetic desire to mimetic crisis

Francesco was convinced that he had been framed as the cause of the accident. But framed by whom? In the midst of a crisis unfolding, who has the power to distort the truth in their favour? The shipping company, do you think, or the coastguard? The answer to this problem is not, as I see it, a deliberate strategy crafted to vilify the captain's character, but once again a need to understand the power of mimesis in a crisis. In good times a neighbour's envy is the owner's pride, but in bad times – famine, disaster, drought – the same envy can turn into jealousy, looting, wrath, misery and violence. Human beings are known to imitate violence more than they mimic desire. This is true of all human conflict – playground quarrels, wars, riots, street fighting and massacres, even bar brawls.

For Girard, violence lies at the heart of all human culture, and it is the fear of violence that holds the social fabric of our society together. In a crisis, one group will turn against another and many will turn against many. It is a feature of human beings that we have learned to reciprocate like few, if any, other living creatures on this planet. If you extend your arm to me for a handshake, I will reciprocate with the same gesture. If I don't return the handshake, you would probably feel offended. Or if I were to look at you with vengeance in mind you might reciprocate with an escalated form of anger. I know of no other animal that has learned to reciprocate in the way humans do.

Anyone who participates in social media brawls is likely to find that in those conflicts the cause is often forgotten. What remains is a feeling of vengeance and an urge to reciprocate – flaming, trolling ... Mahatma Gandhi understood this all too well: 'an eye for an eye makes the whole world blind'.

As groups argue and clash over a capsized ship, the social, ethical and political order of the country is disrupted. If the conflict continues for too long, it has the power to destabilise an entire nation. The timing plays an important role in turning this accident into a national crisis.

> The disaster took place at time when Italy's economy had deteriorated amid the eurozone crisis. As the cost of its huge public borrowings soared to near-unsustainable levels, images of the stricken liner were widely presented as symbolic of national failure. (Hooper, 2014)

Human culture has through the ages worked out a way to tame violence and restore social and political order: turning the clashing of many against many into many against one. Girard sees in the mimetic crisis the emergence of a scapegoat that can bring the conflict to a resolution.

## Scapegoating as a universal mechanism

Before we discuss the forming of a scapegoat in the *Costa Concordia* accident, let us attempt to understand how scapegoating as a ritual has evolved since prehistoric times. Burgis (2022) takes us back to ancient Israel in his book *Wanting*:

> The Torah contains an account of a strange ritual in ancient Israel. Once a year, on the feast of Yom Kippur, or the Day of Atonement, two male goats were brought to the Temple in Jerusalem. Lots were drawn to determine which goat would be sacrificed to God and which one would be sent away to Azazel, an evil spirit or demon believed to reside in remote regions of the desert. The high priest would lay his hands on the head of the goat that was bound for Azazel. As he did so, the priest would confess all the sins of the Israelites, symbolically transferring them onto the animal. After the priest had said the appropriate prayers, the people would drive the goat out into the desert, to Azazel, expelling their sins along with it. This goat came to be called, in English, the scapegoat. (Burgis, 2022)

Historically, the ritual of scapegoating has extended to include almost all human cultures. The scapegoat kings of Africa, the dismembered Greek god Dionysus, the cannibals of Tupinambá, the prisoners, slaves, and virgins sacrificed on the altar of the Sun in ancient Mexico, and the children consumed in the fiery furnaces of Moloch in north Africa and the Middle East. The Ainu and the Greeks turned to sacrificing animals instead of humans, and that was their version of scapegoating.

In modern times, the ritual of scapegoating can be observed in terrorist attacks, political assassinations, corporate failures and all forms of social unrest. The news about the blood-testing company Theranos, after it was found that the company's $10 billion valuation was turned to zero overnight because the company's claims about its technology were false, is another classic example of how the CEO Elizabeth Holmes became the scapegoat of a corporate-wide scandal.

Beyond such extreme examples, the human tendency to find a scapegoat also exists in everyday life. Our tabloid culture routinely serves up stories of scapegoating, ranging from famous celebrities, politicians and sportspeople to people living in slums and on street corners. In countries such as India, the collective unconscious of an entire country instinctively points fingers at the neighbouring country for everything from internal political conflicts to losing a cricket match with it. In Jungian analytical psychology, as we have discovered earlier, finger pointing allows the unconscious projection of our day-to-day frustrations and unfulfilled desires onto those who absorb the sins of the society i.e. the scapegoats.

## Can 'science' rid us of scapegoating?

There is a growing trend towards questioning the efficacy of the ritual of scapegoating in our modern society. Driven by science, technology, logic and reasoning, modern humans tend to distinguish themselves from their prehistoric ancestors. The Scottish social anthropologist James Frazer admonished those who use the term 'scapegoat' in relation to innocent people (Frazer, 2009). What Frazer wanted, and what the risk and safety world is attempting to do, is to break away from the cycle of mimesis and scapegoating as a universal psychosocial mechanism of daily life, and make it appear to be a wasteful human trait that impedes learning; scapegoating is a ritual that has no place in the modern society; it belongs to the uncivilised savages of the past. And we do this by shifting our metaphors from mimetic desire, scapegoating, rituals, sacrifice, violence and social order towards a no-blame culture, Just Culture, accountability, process improvement, redundancy, capacity building and fail-safe systems.

But shifting the language does not create a change without a shift in our disposition. Our imagination remains anchored in the worldview in which blame is what keeps us from learning, and blame is the necessary evil, to set against efficiency and profitability. And invariably, all our efforts are directed towards avoiding blame. We should no longer be subsumed by the superstitions of religious rituals, because we are progressive and infinitely superior to our ancestors. It is a noble thought of our so-called civilised societies and reminiscent of Victorian anthropology, but one that runs counter to what it means to be a human being when faced with suffering.

When an accident leads to death, injury, bloodshed, commercial losses, environmental catastrophe or any form of suffering, the organisation, and indeed society, are not interested in learning. Not immediately, and certainly not as an admission of weakness. Our quest for meaning in suffering is still the same as that of our hunter-gatherer ancestors – non-rational, inward, subjective and existential. It is no surprise that even though many organisations invest heavily in modern 'scientific' approaches to risk and safety management, their understanding of failures of the consequences remains embedded in the ritual of scapegoating.

You might wonder what has really changed by shifting focus from safety to work. Can we now say that by focusing on work we have become more tolerant of human fallibility? In my view, quite the opposite. When we invest in 'work', 'safety of work', or 'fail-safe systems', accidents and failures frustrate us even more because we have not really understood and accepted our fallible being. Instead, lost in numbers and focused on business gains, we dread our investments in those fail-safe systems because we have not come to terms with the core of existence. We reject failures because we do not want to be reminded of our mortality and fallibility.

Hidden in the dogma of science, the process of accident investigation follows the same pattern as those in ancient Israel. We gather as a learning team, investigate, search for process improvements, write reports, recommend changes, lay our hands on the person(s) we don't like, thank them for their services, walk them to the exit door, close the door, and gather once again over coffee and cookies to celebrate our uncompromising values about safety, work and business.

The ritual of accident investigation, whether it follows orthodox or contemporary thinking, has the same structure as that of our ancestors, except that our modern enactment is masked in the ideology of science (scientism) and superiority, and a denial of superstition, religion and mortality. We fail to ask ourselves a simple question: Why does scapegoating appeal to us so much? As John Sanford points out, when familiar patterns such as these emerge in a story, it must have an archetypal quality, i.e. it must speak to a place in us that is universal.

# The hidden powers in the ritual of scapegoating

These days we hear the usual scoff against scapegoating: 'We operate a no-blame culture.' But the power of this ritual is often underestimated. In this section, we will discuss the hidden powers in the ritual of scapegoating.

## The scapegoat gives meaning to human sufferings

Have you ever wondered where would we be as a species without the ritual of scapegoating? How would we react in the face of an existential upheaval? Where would you go for meaning, causation and a sense of being in the wake of a catastrophe, calamity, or social injustice? Given our violent nature, as Girard points out, the entire human species would be wiped out in just one crisis. For this, we must thank our ancestors who came up with the ritual of scapegoating.

Francesco was surprised that despite his innocent and heroic act to save the lives of those trapped in the lifeboat, he became the scapegoat in the accident, but for Girard this is a recognisable pattern in a mimetic crisis, and the foundation of all human culture. Herein lies the first paradox of scapegoating: to have a scapegoat is to believe that we don't have one. That by sentencing the captain – or for that matter a doctor, entrepreneur, firefighter, pilot or any other professional – there is no moral wrongdoing in our act. In fact, we are doing a service to humanity by keeping the criminals at bay. The act of scapegoating is unconscious and therefore unintentional. We do not realise, as a society, when we have created one.

The second and a more powerful paradox is that the scapegoat is both the poison and the cure for society. The Greeks even had a word for it, *pharmakós*, related to the English word 'pharmacy'. Burgis describes the *pharmakós* as 'a person at the margins of society—usually a castoff, criminal, slave, or someone thought to be excessively ugly or deformed'. (Burgis, 2022, pp. 154-54). Francesco was none of these, but the mimetic crisis and the ritual of scapegoating found a way to make him one, based on his *Italian* demeanour.

## Scapegoating does not seek reasoning and thinking

The presence of a Moldovan entertainer alongside the captain on the bridge at the time of the accident became a popular myth after the accident, to defame the captain's character. One glance at the Instagram account of this person tells us that it does not take a lot of convincing and thinking for humans to herd in masses and turn violent once we believe we've found the moral monster responsible for our sufferings. It is a myth that seduces an entire population, and once we see the hostility towards the captain as a myth everything starts to make sense. **Such is the power and energy in this myth that an entire industry is convinced that the captain left** the ship too soon, even when no one cared to listen to his story.

**Never argue against a myth!**

> When my daughter was three years old, I told her to eat broccoli because it is good for health. She refused. I said, 'If you eat broccoli Santa will bring you a nice present.' She agreed to give it a try.

As parents, we learn not to reason with children; no amount of convincing and reasoning will help – in fact, the opposite – so we may take refuge in myths. Francesco tried hard to disprove the allegations against him through counter-reasoning but none of this worked. It is a mistake to debate against a myth. A myth is not untrue; it forms the belief pattern for all those who belong to the culture. So what is the point in arguing against a belief?

This brings me to another question. It is possible that the captain is making up his story to rescue his image? In my view, once again it is pointless to go into rational discussions at this point, a suggestion I made to Captain Francesco Schettino before I left his hometown. Roland Barthes (1957) makes a crucial point here; when a myth becomes so deeply embedded that it becomes our 'normal', no amount of reasoning or counter-reasoning is helpful. Remember, reasoning works when we operate with a shared worldview. I don't see the point in debating with you that an apple a day is good for your health when your image of an apple is an addictive gadget whereas mine is a fibre-filled crunchy fruit.

Moreover, who am I to demystify a 'myth' to someone anchored to their worldview and who has no time to engage in critical thinking? Here is one more personal story to share.

> In June 2023, we were in the Canary Islands out for dinner with family when an Italian waiter named Francesco came to serve at our table. Out of curiosity, I asked him if he knew Captain Francesco Schettino. He rolled his eyes. 'Stupid man,' he said in a calm, disinterested tone, and then asked us if we were ready to place our order.

As an anthropologist, I find that it is the mundane and the ordinary that intrigue me every time I sense the attitude of the mob about this accident. When the world has embodied the myth of 'Captain Coward', there is nothing more to discuss. I could try and explain to this waiter that the story of the captain leaving the ship is simply not true – it is fake tabloid news. But that wouldn't move him an inch. The myth that the captain abandoned the ship and ran away allows the common person to get back to cruising. To expose society to the systemic problems of neoliberalisation, the rapid growth of the cruise sector and questionable safety standards lands people in dissonance. Thinking is hard: judgement is far easier. The idea of expecting people to engage in a critical enquiry and the pain that comes from the mental gymnastics of dissonance is quite frankly, naïve and futile.

## Scapegoating restores social and political order

A popular myth in the cruise industry since the *Titanic* is that these luxurious floating hotels are designed to be unsinkable. After a sinking, then, should everyone in the cruise industry accept that those ships are not seaworthy after all? Or should they believe that the disaster was the result of the actions of a self-destructive captain? The latter is a practical reconciliation for us humans to locate meaning, seek closure, and move forward after the disaster. If we as a society did not accept the narrative of 'Captain Coward', the cruise culture might well have come to a sticky end on the night of the accident. In this sacrifice of Francesco Schettino there is both the crucifixion of the victim and the redemption of the cruise industry. In other words, we've had an accident, and thank god we've found the cause. Back to the (highly profitable) business of cruising again!

Figure 15.4: The hidden power in the 'Captain Coward' myth.

# Can scapegoating be avoided in accident investigations?

From the *Hoegh Osaka* and *El Faro* through to the *Costa Concordia*, a consistent pattern that repeats in accident investigation reports is the inevitable search for scapegoats in bringing closure to the case. Of course, the *Costa Concordia* case is an extreme example, but that is because of the dire consequences of the accident. The ritual of accident investigations is about acknowledging the violent nature of human beings, finding ways to tame violence and striving to maintain social and political order in society. Accident investigations are therefore not about learning or change (not, at least, as a priority) but a cultural retelling of the events to maintain societal order. Once we understand the prime purpose of accident investigations, we are at peace with ourselves and we can rethink our expectations and resources more wisely.

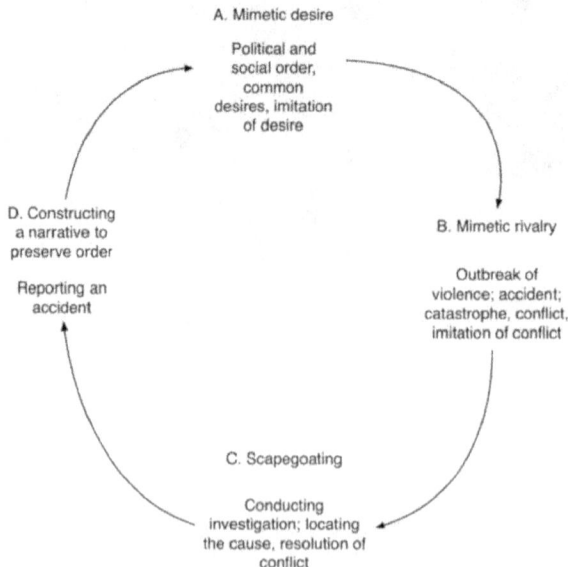

A. Mimetic desire

Political and social order, common desires, imitation of desire

D. Constructing a narrative to preserve order

Reporting an accident

B. Mimetic rivalry

Outbreak of violence; accident; catastrophe, conflict, imitation of conflict

C. Scapegoating

Conducting investigation; locating the cause, resolution of conflict

Figure 15.5: The application of mimetic theory to accident investigations.

Back to our original question: Can there be a no-blame culture? **In my view, there cannot be a no-blame culture. When misfortune strikes, we must accept that blaming is our first instinct because violence is in our being. We must learn to appreciate the hidden power of scapegoating in accident investigations, and seek to create alternative rituals for learning and change.**

## Can we stop blaming and start learning?

The humans of the 21st century have learned to set a binary divide between learning and blaming. To learn something, we must avoid the temptation to blame. Blaming, which impedes human progress, is the antithesis of learning.

In my view, learning does not stand in opposition to blaming or scapegoating. In fact, there is no such binary divide. Learning begins by accepting that our being is fallible and violent and that when faced with suffering our first instinct is always to blame. When we acknowledge our being, we open doorways to learning and a transformation within. The power of learning is not in denial but in the humble acceptance that it is not easy to avoid blaming.

## Are we not learning from accidents?

A final thought. Where suffering is involved – death, injury, socio-economic loss, environmental catastrophe at scale – it is difficult for accident investigations to lead to meaningful learning and change. A counterargument to that assertion that I often hear, however, is: if you say there is no learning in accidents, how did we reach the advancement in technology, operations, policy reforms, and education and training standards? If we examine the conventions and codes in the maritime world, such as the SOLAS, MARPOL, the ISM Code and so on, most of these are the result of major accidents. That is true in every accident and across industries. Although my learning is not so much focused on the outer world, it is worth pondering on this question. The burgeoning regulations, the extent of bureaucracy and procedures and the psychosocial harm that we face today in our pursuit of the management of safety and the measurement of safety performance – are these indications of improvement? It is difficult to imagine any 'improvements' when the outcome of an inspection is to seek more control and to objectify people. It is also difficult to imagine improvement when the thought of an inspection or an audit makes people sick and leaves them in a state of anxiety and insecurity. If 'improvement' means managing and controlling the number of slips, trips, falls, and broken ribs or shoulders, it is a myopic view of safety, and one that comes with hidden motives and agendas. Often, the hidden agendas will surface when we come to realise the futility of our dashboards and databases on the day of the accident.

But here we are not discussing the change in the outer world. What I am concerned about is the change in our inner world; in other words, embodied learning. The change that impels us to see the world differently, and brings our biases and assumptions to the surface so that we start to become critical and conscious of our language, rituals, habits, heuristics, gestures, metaphors, symbols, and myths, and then expand the limits of our cognition and perception.

Sustained change begins from within us, at the individual level and gradually permeates through our unconscious and embodiment. If your worldview is not challenged when you investigate, there cannot be any learning or change. If your imagination, language, metaphors, and the framing of your questions remain the same, there cannot be any learning or change.

The insights that Francesco offered about everything from the heuristics of everyday work, the contrast between the theory and practice of crew resource management, the emergency preparedness, and how predetermined plans and processes actually pan out when the 'rubber hits the road' and a variety of themes discussed in this book – those insights come from a simple but challenging philosophy of life i.e. **existence is fallible; we cannot manage or control fallibility; and we must learn to embrace fallibility and the fallible person with our whole being.**

It was never my intention to find out what went wrong, how the captain ended up with his boat on the rocks or why he evacuated the ship so late. Instead, I travelled to Sorrento to get to know him as a person. As he began to speak, I saw in him a captain who felt that he had made mistakes about which he was deeply regretful. But beyond his regret, I saw in him an accident victim who wanted to be heard, a father who was concerned about his daughter's future, a caring husband, a proud son, a respected member of the local community who, through his social influence, had helped many young boys find recruitment at sea, a pet owner, a funny guy who laughed and joked with us, and a kind-hearted host who gave us his attention, time and the gift of his unconscious mind to help create this book. I did not need to ask many questions, and most of what Francesco offered me was unexpected.

This book is not about Francesco's story or the accident narrative, but it is about what I took away, reflected on and now feel is worth sharing with the world. It is not to be read as an objective truth, but as my own story within that of Captain Francesco Schettino, laden with my own subjectivities and assumptions. I have since realised the power of paying attention, observing, and listening to all forms of interaction. We are visual and verbal creatures, but at the same time there are limits to our consciousness. As this book has taught me, the unconscious is mysterious and non-knowable, and learning is to a significant degree a matter of making the unconscious conscious.

In order not to leave you wondering about what a learning-oriented accident investigation should look like, we will turn to the final chapter of this book.

# 16

# A Practical Method of Learning from Accidents

How can we truly learn from accidents? This chapter is intended to provide an example of a learning-oriented accident investigation. In this example, we will apply the iCue method based on the Social Psychology of Risk (SPoR) framework.

The iCue method is a visual tool which involves mapping human decisions and learning from the hidden assumptions and biases in our decisions. The chief purpose of the iCue method is to surface the unconscious in a conversation. The term 'iCue' means the ability to extract intelligent cues (iCue) by asking open-ended questions and relinquishing control (the traits of a leader and a skilled facilitator).

Figure 16.1: An illustration of the iCue method.

- The iCue method in practice.
- An example of an accident investigation report.
- The iCue method.
- The iCue engagement and mapping process.
- Investigation questions and analysis.
- The learning outcome of the iCue engagement process.
- Summary of the book.

Figure 16.2: A general outline of the chapter.

We will take as an example an accident case on board a merchant ship, and examine how we can learn from accidents using the iCue method. The example is drawn from the Transport Safety Investigation Bureau (TSIB) Singapore, an independent investigation authority responsible for the investigation of air, marine and land transport accidents and incidents in Singapore. The aim of this exercise is to demonstrate how we can achieve an improved learning outcome using the iCue method in comparison with traditional approaches. An improved learning experience, as we will discover in this chapter, comes from a consistent philosophy, methods and tools to understand fallible humans, instead of managing and controlling errors. An improved learning outcome also comes from the ability to ask questions that would acknowledge the non-conscious and unconscious nature of human decision making.[16]

The chapter begins with the narrative of the official report, followed by the main conclusions drawn from that report. I will then outline the foundational method used in the report, i.e. iCue and the visual process of mapping a conversation. Next, we will apply the iCue method to the accident narrative to identify the hidden unconscious (beliefs, assumptions, myths and biases) in the report. The hidden unconscious will then be explored in detail by asking questions that were not raised as part of the accident report. The chapter will end by summarising the main message of this book.

## A limitation of this chapter

Since we do not have access to the accident data beyond what is stated in the report, our responses to the questions raised will rely on past accidents of a similar nature, on interviews with other seafarers, and on my own experience.

---

[16] Motivations, perceptions, emotions, feelings, instincts and intutions that cannot be understood at the conscious level.

It is my view that in any investigation the questions are always more important than the answers. This is because although the answers may change with time – and even with the same person in a different situation – the questions endure. It is the quality of the questions that helps the reader decide whether the investigation was conducted with an ethic of learning, change and fairness to those involved. The strength of the iCue method (and of this specific example) lie in illustrating an ethical method of enquiry for understanding fallible humans.[17]

I will begin by presenting the narrative of the accident taken from the official accident report (TSIB, 2022). This narrative will be used as the basis for iCue mapping. The next section of the chapter is largely drawn from the report, with a few edits to clarify the message for my non-maritime readers. The detailed report is available for free download, and also appendixed in the book.[18]

# A death in an enclosed space on board a merchant ship

On 19 March 2022, a bulk carrier ship 'Nozomi' arrived and anchored at the Tanjung Api-Api (TAA) anchorage, South Sumatera, Indonesia, for loading coal cargo. Upon completion of cargo work, the ship

---

[17] There is a video library of iCue examples on our YouTube channel with examples of risk assessments, incident investigations, management of change, strategic decision making and even general stories.

[18] https://www.mot.gov.sg/docs/default-source/default-document-library/bulk-carrier-nozomi-(imo-9558701)-fatality-of-crew-onboard-in-bangka-strait-indonesia-1-april-2022-final-report.pdf

was scheduled to depart the anchorage at noon time on 1 April 2022. Two hours prior to the departure, as the ship was awaiting cargo clearance documents, the head of the crew (bosun) requested the three able seamen on deck (ASD 1, ASD 2 and ASD 3) to assist him in carrying out maintenance work (greasing) of the shipboard cargo cranes on the main deck. When the group arrived near the crane, bosun was doubtful if the grease that they were using was appropriate for use. The bosun then spoke with his supervisor i.e. the chief officer and the two decided to abort the planned maintenance on the crane and rather switch to the greasing of the dog handles[19] on the booby hatch covers[20] (see figure 1).

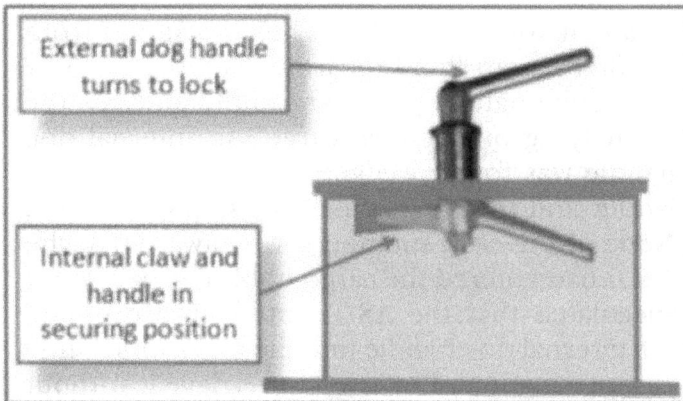

Figure 16.3: A set of dog handles securing a booby hatch (illustration from the accident investigation).

[19] A lever commonly used on board ships to wedge against typical watertight or weathertight access doors and hatches for isolating adjoining compartments or external access against fire, smoke, and water ingress.

[20] Also known as Access Lids. A raised or hooded form to access a ladder from the weather deck to the cargo hold or other hatches.

The Bosun and the three ASDs then transferred the grease and tools to the forward booby hatch. While turning the external dog handles to open the booby hatch cover, two out of the four were found to be seized. The deck crew used a short pipe to slot into the external dog handles and managed to turn them so they could lift open the booby hatch cover. To free up the seized dog handles for greasing, the Bosun continued using the short pipe, assisted by the ASD2. At the same time, with the booby hatch cover in open position, the ASD1 used a hammer to strike the internal dog handle of the other set of seized-up dog handles. After a few strikes, the external dog handle dropped onto the main deck and was picked up by the ASD3.

At about 1030H, the ASD2 heard a sound from another cargo hold nearby. He looked over the booby hatch of the cargo hold and saw the ASD1 lying on the coal cargo. An internal dog handle was found wedged between the vertical ladder and the side stringer of ship's structure. None of the crew members were aware that the ASD1 had entered the cargo hold. The deck crew speculated that the ASD1 could have dropped the internal dog handle into the cargo hold while hammering it and he tried to retrieve it without informing anyone.

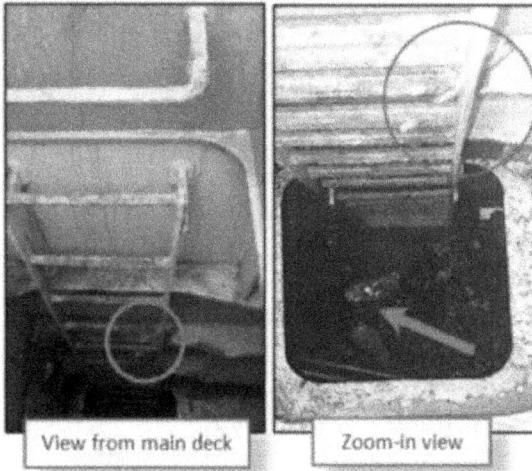

Figure 16.4: The picture on the left indicating the dog handle and the picture to the right indicating the safety shoes of ASD1 inside the cargo hold in relation with the handle (for illustration only, taken from the official accident report).

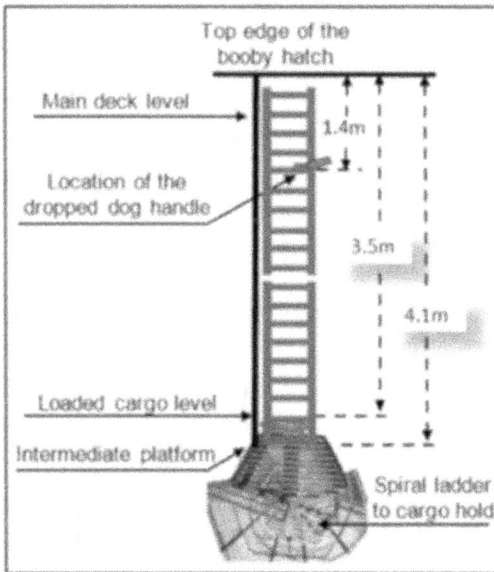

Figure 16.5: The various height levels inside the cargo hold (illustration from the official accident report).

337

The Bosun shouted to the ASD1 but did not receive any response. The Bosun then ran towards the accommodation to get safety harness and ropes while shouting to attract the attention of other crew members. The ASD2, at about the same time, reported the incident on the walkie-talkie to the Third Officer (3O), who was the duty officer keeping anchor watch on the bridge. At the time of the accident, both the Master and Second Officer (2O) were on the bridge liaising with ship's local agent in preparation for departure clearance.

Upon hearing the report by the ASD2, the Master instructed the 2O to activate the ship's general alarm and made an announcement for rescue operation in cargo hold. The 3O ran down to the main deck. On the way to the main deck, while grabbing two EEBDs,[21] the 3O called the Bosun on the walkie-talkie and asked him to take the stretcher and the self- contained breathing apparatus (SCBA) with the rescue ropes and safety harness from the ship's locker.

After the 3O left the bridge, the Master instructed the 2O to remain on the bridge to attend to the incident site. The Master noticed that the ASD1 was motionless lying on the coal cargo and recalled seeing some crew arriving at the site with the EEBD, stretcher, safety harness and some other equipment. The CO and other crew members also arrived at the booby hatch and noticed some engine crew rigging and pulling

---

[21] Emergency Escape Breathing Device, to be carried on board cargo ships under the Fire Safety Systems Code, Chapter 3. It is a personnel protection device used for escaping from a compartment that has a hazardous atmosphere, and not be used for fighting fires, entering oxygen-deficient voids or tanks, or worn by fire-fighters. Its usage duration is about 10 mins.

two air hoses into the booby hatch. When the 3O arrived at the booby hatch, he put on the EEBD (see Figure 16.6) hood and entered the cargo hold through the vertical ladder while the two air hoses were being connected to the air supply. But the 3O came out of the booby hatch, reporting that it was difficult to breath [*sic*] and it was hot inside the cargo hold.

Figure 16.6: The EEBD set used by the 3O (taken from the investigation report).

At this point, the Chief Cook (CCK) took the two air hoses, safety harness and ropes and climbed into the cargo hold to rescue the ASD1. He managed to secure the safety harness below the arms of ASD1 and the crew pulled the ASD1 out of the cargo hold. The crew assessed that the ASD1 was not breathing and there was no heartbeat or pulse. They took turns to perform CPR[22] on the ASD1. A self contained breathing apparatus (SCBA) was brought to the site after the CCK had entered the cargo hold.

Subsequently, the Master called the local agent and the local port authorities for assistance. By

---

[22] Cardiopulmonary resuscitation.

about 1200H, the local port health officials came on board with a medical team and examined the ASD1 before conveying the ASD1 to a local hospital. The Master was later informed by the agent that the ASD1 had passed away. Nozomi departed TAA anchorage on 5 April 2022 and sailed for the next port of call, Singapore.

The investigation concluded (taken from the report):

- The ASD1 had likely entered the No.5 cargo hold without the knowledge of the other crew members to retrieve a dog handle. The cargo hold had low concentrations of oxygen due to the cargo of coal. The ASD1 collapsed while climbing out of the cargo hold.

- The maintenance of the booby hatch was an unplanned task and did not require entering of cargo hold. The dropping of parts into the cargo hold was not anticipated for this maintenance. The risks associated with working in the vicinity of a hazardous environment (cargo hold loaded with coal) had not been identified, a risk assessment was not carried out.

- The hazards associated with the coal cargo had been overlooked when the maintenance of booby hatch was being carried out.

- There was a misconception on board the ship that EEBD could be used for rescue operation and the crew used inappropriate equipment to rescue the ASD1. The crew also did not follow the assigned duties as per the muster list.

- There were no signages to warn the crew to treat cargo hold as enclosed space when it has been sealed for some time.

The detailed investigation report can be found in the appendix.

Let us now turn to the iCue method and how it works in practice.

## The foundational model of the iCue method

When learning about the Social Psychology of Risk (SPoR) there are several foundational concepts/ models that govern practice. Two of these used in the iCue method are:

- One Brain Three Minds (1B3M),
- Layers of Risk in our language: Workspace, Head-space, Groupspace (WS, HS, GS).

The social aspect of SPoR is critical. When risk is considered as a social experience, all that follows from that is based on the ways we engage, meet and interact with others. For a more comprehensive discussion on SPoR methods read *SPoR and Semiotics* by Thorne and Long (2023); it's a free download.

## The embodied Mind for tackling risk

Many of the ways we seek to deal with risk draw upon only one mode of decision making: the (slow) rational mind, which we loosely refer to as the brain. Whilst we know so much about the brain, we know so little about the Mind (as described in Chapter

5: the embodied Mind of the whole person). The embodied Mind takes decisions and actions in three distinct ways – head, heart and gut – and this has been embedded within many cultures and societies for thousands of years. An understanding of the three distinct modes of decision making has significant implications for how we can assess, tackle and manage risk.

# Why 1B3M is important for understanding human decision making

SPoR is founded on a methodology of dialectic,[23] the i-thou dialogue. But unlike the Hegelian dialectic that finds synthesis and stability in a search for *the* truth, in SPoR we accept that learning is not about finding an absolute, objective truth. In other words, my truth and your truth will differ and what we discover through our dialogues and discussions will hold true to the context alone, and will remain incomplete. That is the basis for learning, and why our learning and understanding of the world will always remain imperfect. The imperfect nature of truth will make us curious and humble about ourselves and others.

In SPoR, we also acknowledge the embodied Mind as the basis for human decision making. We know that when we get stressed and anxious our heart races, when we feel overwhelmed fearful or guilty we get butterflies in our stomach, and when we feel emotionally sick we get an ache in the gut. It is not

---

[23] The art of using dialogue and discussions to widen our perspectives.

uncommon for people who are not coping emotionally to rush to the toilet, to cry uncontrollably or have high blood pressure. These sensations may come partly from the brain, yet they are triggered and communicated independently by the body's endocrine, nervous and immune systems. Under acute stress, the body shuts down – and, most importantly, the sensations are felt in the heart and the gut, meaning we cannot think, act and learn from our actions and decisions.

The first model to be reviewed is based on the concept of One Brain Three Minds (1B3M).

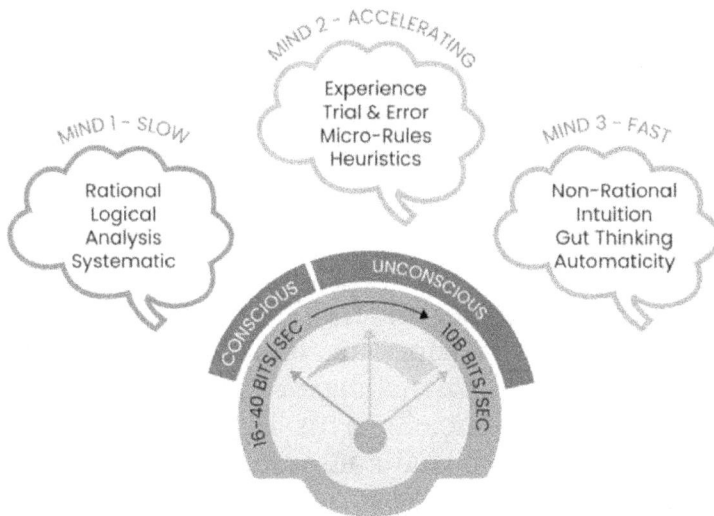

Figure 16.7: One Brain Three Minds.*

In order to represent the embodied nature of learning and decision making, we use three brain images as Minds in the semiotic of a speedometer. Inasmuch as every model has flaws and weaknesses, this model provides an understanding of how the human embodied Mind 'thinks'. This triarchic model seeks to explain both automatic human decision making and the slow, rational mode of decision making and thinking. This model is expressed semiotically in Figure 16.7, One Brain Three Minds, and Three Centres of Being.

To remind you of the model explained in Chapter 5, we are summarising it here:

## Mind 1

In Mind 1 we make slow rational decisions, as when completing a checklist or form. (If we do a 'tick and flick' on the same checklist, then we're doing that in Mind 2 or Mind 3.)

Mind 1 encompasses methodical, systematic and rational thinking.

## Mind 2

Mind 2 is about heuristic thinking i.e. thinking that relies on learned shortcuts and practised habits. This kind of decision making is essential for humans to be fast and efficient. This is decision making based on patterns, trial and error, and habits that, having become infused into our thinking through experience, are triggered by perception, experience or memory. Much of this type of decision making doesn't involve rational choice or analytical thinking.

## Mind 3

Mind 3 thinking is about total automaticity, what Damasio states as non-conscious decision making. In this state, we are unaware of the processes of deciding, thinking and rational processing. This is often referred to as intuitional thinking, but commonly understood as autopilot or gut thinking.

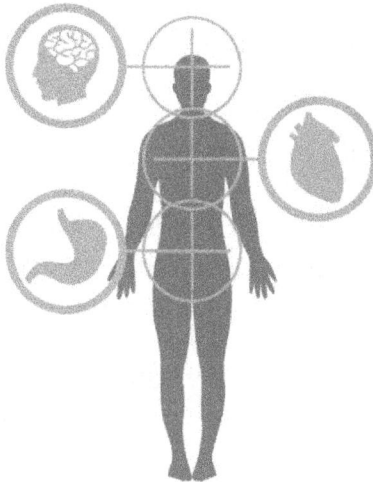

Whole Person Whole Mind

Figure 16.8: One Brain Three Minds* Embodied person.*

# Workspace, Headspace, Groupspace

The second foundational model considers the language that we use in managing risk. Much of our language in risk management evolves from Workspace (WS). We call this the physical or 'primary' dimension of risk. This is easy to administer and regulate, because what is required is visible, measurable and accountable through the use of checklists and metrics matched to regulations. Most walks and observations at work are physical (primary) in focus. Walking around and observing what is physically not in compliance with rules is relatively easy.

The language in Headspace (HS) reflects the state of mind of the person, their feelings and their emotions. When people use the expressions 'confused', 'depressed', 'happy', 'sad', 'angry', 'positive', 'overwhelmed' and so on, this gives us an opportunity to understand what is going on in their mind.

Similarly, words or phrases in Groupspace (GS) will represent the cultural and social attributes of a group. Language in this space can include the metaphors, slogans, mantras, habitual responses, symbols and myths that are common to a group. Listening to words in HS and GS can be challenging to begin with, but as you learn to pay careful attention to words in WS, HS and GS you will become *intelligent* about extracting the cues in a conversation (hence the term iCue).

## Balancing our language for tackling risk

Understanding, observing and influencing WS (Physical), HS (Psychological) and GS (Cultural) is foundational to the Social Psychology of Risk. In the risk and safety industry, much of our focus on listening and observing remains in the physical space (WS). For instance, observation walks and cards often take the form of pedantic repetition cycles. This repetition may take the form of nagging and/or threatening people about personal protective equipment and clothing, trip hazards, tags, tickets, barricades, traffic, exclusion zones etc.

In contrast, if we look beyond the WS and consider HS and GS as well, we will develop a sense of maturity in tackling risk.

- We can go on as many walks and observations as we like, but if we only engage with the primary/ physical dimension, we will be ignoring the psychological and cultural layers of risk.
- We must understand and learn to engage with not only WS but also HS and GS, and with the interactions between all three dimensions. We must know how to question, engage and influence the physical (primary), psychological (secondary) and cultural (tertiary) dimensions of risk.
- WS, HS and GS are represented as icons in Figure 16.9: WS, HS, GS.

These two foundational concepts – 1B3M and WS, HS, GS – enable us to map all forms of conversations, including accident investigations, and surface the hidden biases of the embodied Mind to improve learning.

## WS, HS, GS characters

It is from the basic WS, HS, GS icons that the characters in the next section are developed for use in an Engagement Board or Concept Mapping process. The meaning of each icon character is explained here, and the method will be explained subsequently.

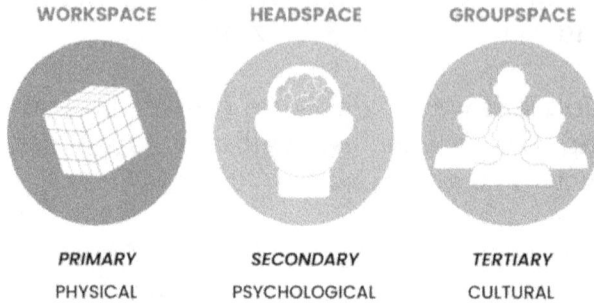

Figure 16.9: Workspace, Headspace and Groupspace icons.*

Both 1B3M and WS, HS, GS must be understood semiotically (visually). Together, the two models form the basis of the iCue method. The iCue method can only be truly learned after we have moved beyond the standard, deductive form of thinking and reasoning. When iCue is undertaken effectively by a skilled SPoR facilitator, it is an essentially intuitive process.

# The iCue engagement board

The iCue Engagement Board Process is a format for open conversation with a group, mapped collectively on a whiteboard, usually with a nominated facilitator and a scribe. The process can be used as a format for short conversations, risk assessment, management of change, risk method, work method or process method, to capture how people think about a task. In this instance, we will use an engagement board to capture the narrative of the accident report.

# The Five Steps of the Basic iCue Method

1.  **Capture** the sequence and flow on the iCue Matrix template (see Figure 16.10). The first step is to listen to the flow of the conversation and identify the sequence without interrupting it. Since this is an exercise based on a document review, we will identify the discrete sequence of events in the narrative and lay them out on the board.

    WS, HS GS Mapping

    If the language is about a WS, practical physical positive (or neutral) (+), it goes in the top left square.

    If it's about a practical physical negative (-) (for example, a case of physical injury or a non-compliance with rules), it goes in the top right square.

    If it's about a HS (psychological) matter, it goes in the bottom left square.

    If it's about a GS (cultural) matter, it goes in the bottom right square.

2.  **Mapping** involves linking words and phrases across the quadrants in the iCue Matrix template. This step can be undertaken concurrently with Step 1, but new relationships may also emerge when the story is mapped on the board.
3.  **Coding** is an exercise involving analysing the text, when the emerging themes are given a shared meaning by the participants (through dialogue and discussions) undertaking the iCue exercise.

Unlike forms and checklists with predetermined 'causes' in drop-down boxes, coding is meant to be a creative and collaborative exercise. Collaborating during the iCue engagement saves us time, and avoids misunderstanding and surprises when the report is produced.

4. **Trade-offs and by-products:** In the next step, we identify the trade-offs and by-products of decision making. Identifying the tensions (denoted by a line with two arrows pulling in opposite directions) helps us understand when people are caught up in trade-offs in making decisions. Trade-offs can reveal how decisions are made with incomplete information, excess information, conflicting goals, pressure of time and so on. By-products are similar to trade-offs, except that they force us to question the (unintended) consequences of decision making that we don't tend to consider in the traditional risk and safety models.

5. **Gifts:** You will notice in the coding below a capital G beside several comments in a coded iCue listening reflection. This denotes a gift i.e. someone telling you something that you had not asked for. Often people unconsciously test us with these gifts, to work out if we are truly listening. But as most interviewers (and in this case, investigators) do not realise they are being trusted with something significant that has special meaning to the speaker, these gifts often fly over the listener's head and are lost to the conversation. In addition, when the listener is busy thinking about what to say next, or they have not suspended their own agenda, or they want to control the conversation or give a solution, they never hear that the speaker has just given

them an unconscious gift. In all iCue listening, however, we learn to hear gifts, and follow them up with the question: 'Can you tell me more?'

1. LISTEN AND SCRIBE
Workspace, Headspace, Groupspace

2. CONCEPT MAPPING
Establish relationships

3. CODING
Metaphors, clarification, repetition

4. CHASE THE GIFT
What was given but not asked for

5. TRADE-OFFS AND BI-PRODUCTS
Doubt, confusion, workarounds

6. BALANCED CONVERSATIONS
Positive, negative, neutral; 25% rule

WORKSPACE POSITIVES | WORKSPACE NEGATIVES

HEADSPACE QUESTIONS | GROUPSPACE QUESTIONS

Figure 16.10: The iCue Engagement Process.*

These skills and coding are considered basic to the enactment of iCue. There are also advanced skills, beyond these basics, that enable a more intuitive and nuanced enabling of dialogue. For details about mapping using the iCue method, please refer to the iCue manual.[24]

## The iCue mapping process

In the mapping process, you will find words and phrases placed in WS, HS and GS. Each step reflects a sequence of events and actions.

Steps 1 to 7 involves capturing and mapping the various sequences of events in the narrative. Step 8 illustrates the process of coding; Step 9 involves identifying the trade-offs; and Step 10 is a discovery of gifts that were received in the process.

---

[24] https://safetyrisk.net/icue-listening-engagement-manual/

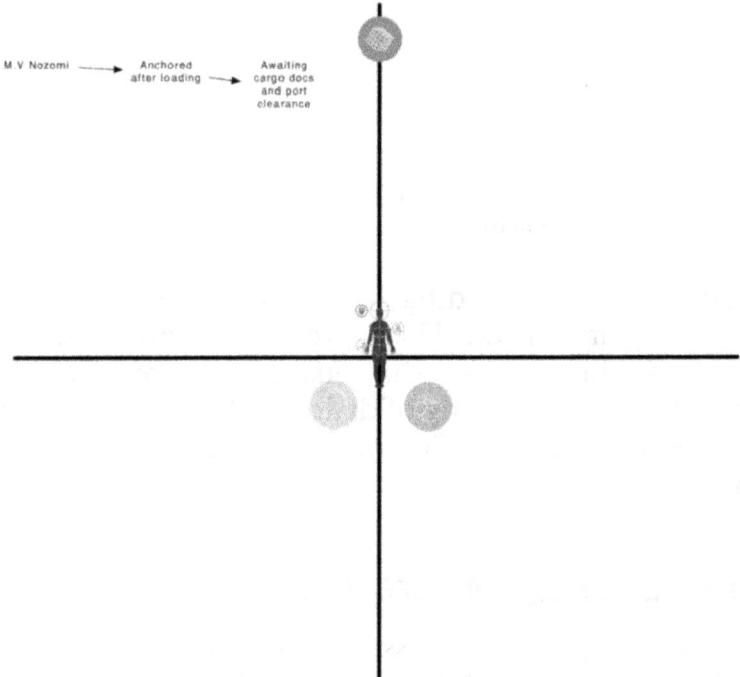

M V Nozomi ⟶ Anchored after loading ⟶ Awaiting cargo docs and port clearance

Step 1 of iCue mapping

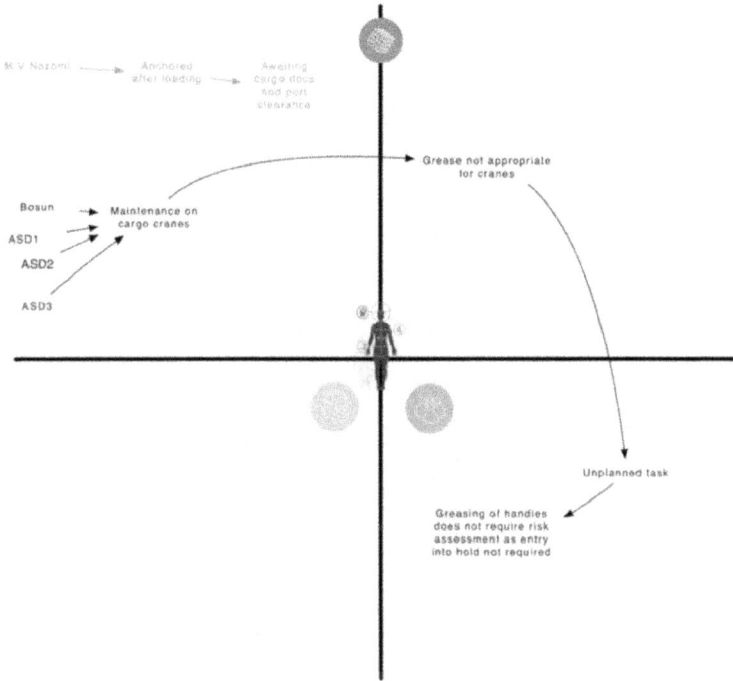

Step 2: Explanatory note - The term 'unplanned task' is mapped in the GS because the term 'unplanned' can mean different things to different groups of people. Similarly, the expression 'greasing of handles does not require risk assessment as entry into hold not required' is a heuristic worked out by the ship's crew, hence it is a GS expression reflecting the gap between documented processes (WS) and the collective behaviour of crew members (GS)

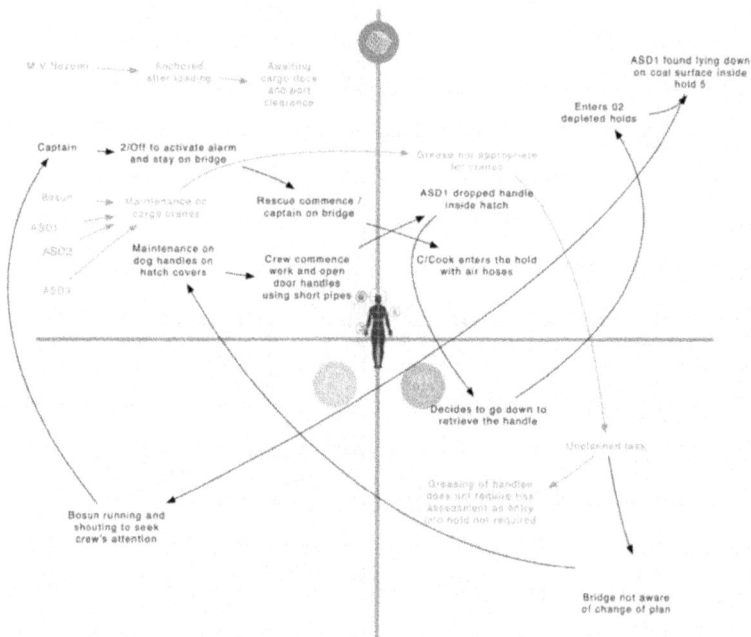

Step 3: Explanatory note – The expression 'Bosun running and shouting to seek crew's attention' reflects the state of mind of an individual, hence is placed in the headspace quadrant.

# A Practical Method of Learning from Accidents

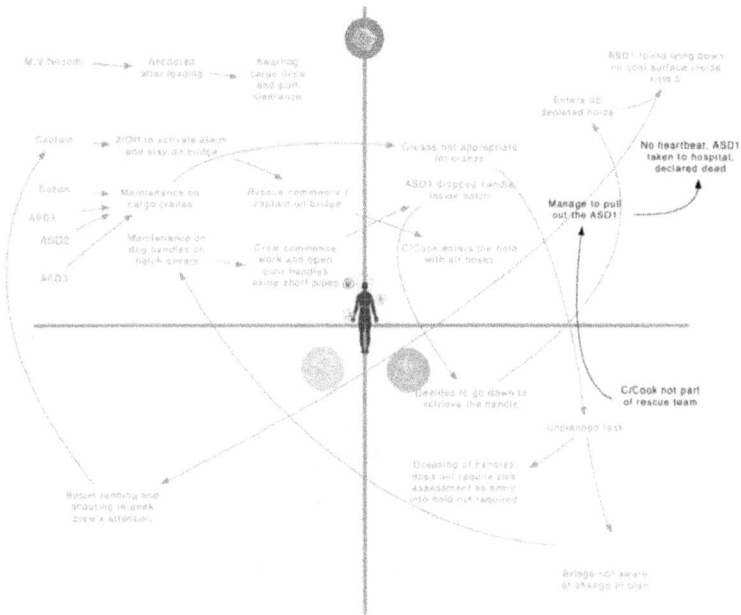

Step 4

# A Practical Method of Learning from Accidents

Step 5

# A Practical Method of Learning from Accidents

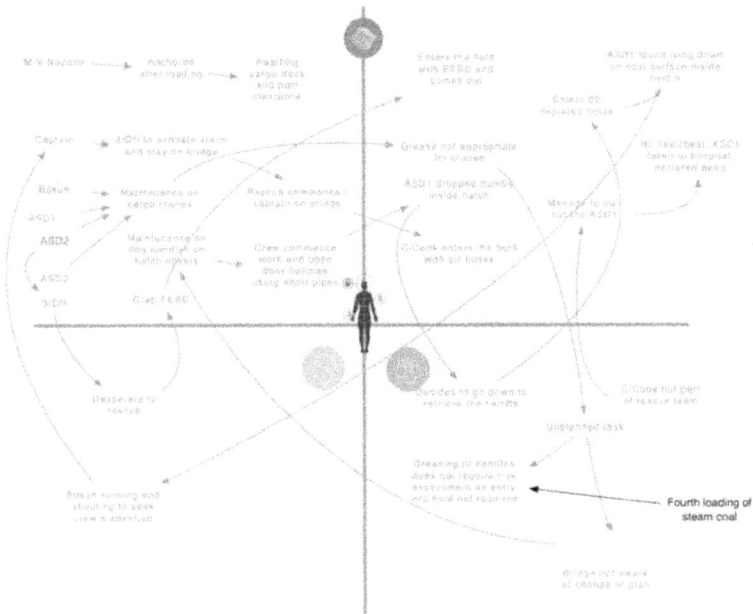

Step 6

357

Step 7

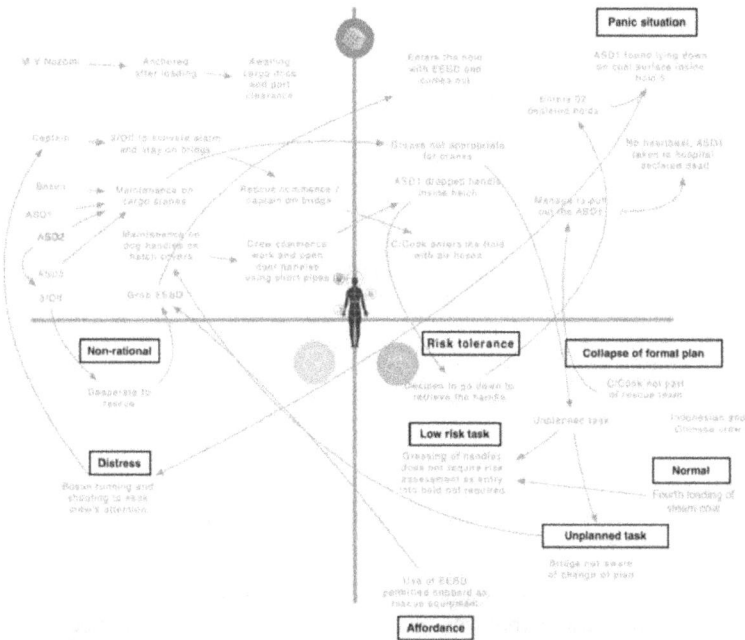

Step 8: Coding the narrative with meanings and validations in boxes. Our own meanings should not be mixed with the words from the other person, so boxes are necessary to maintain the separation.

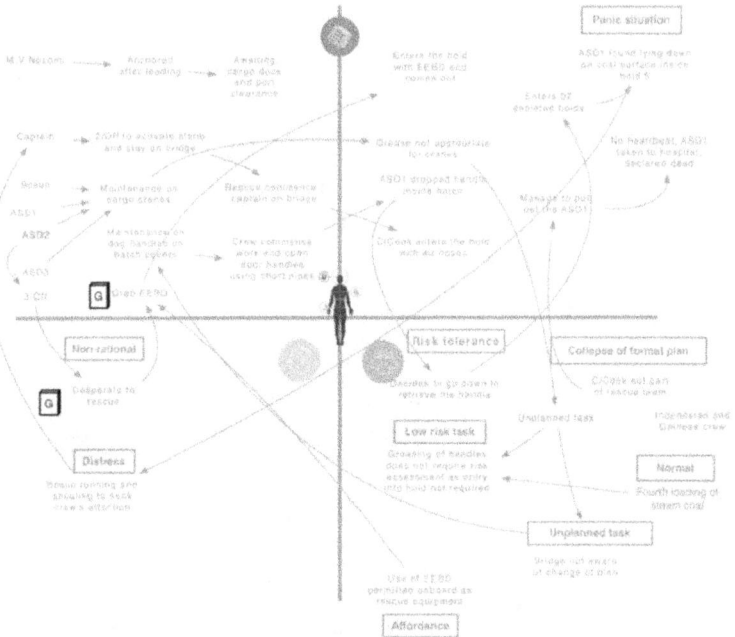

Step 9: Explanatory note - Gifts (G in the boxes) represent strong words or phrases that were given or discovered but not expected. Typically, in investigations focused on facts and evidence, we do not pay attention to such words. But consider the term 'desperate'. What does this word mean? Where does this word come from? Who used this word, and why? Following this line of enquiry often reveals our hidden biases and assumptions.

# A Practical Method of Learning from Accidents

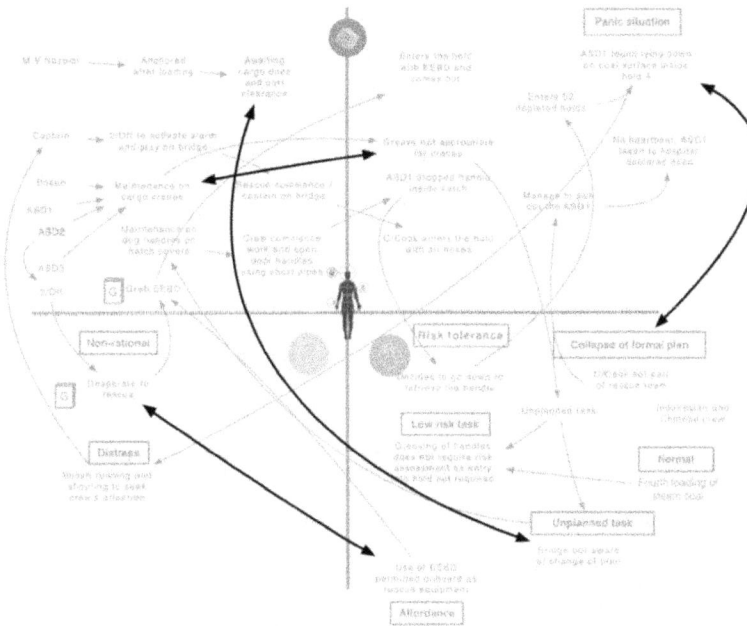

Step 10: Trade-offs and by-products are denoted by lines with arrows pointing in opposite directions. Trade-offs and by-products are rarely discussed in traditional accident investigation reports because in those documents decision making is characterised by the rational, deductive, evidence-based and systematic reasoning, in Mind 1.

All the above figures (from step 1-10) can be downloaded as images using this link: https://bit.ly/4cIvQuE

Notice how trade-offs and by-products are identified in the iCue mapping process. For instance, if someone is 'desperate' to rescue another person they might well use an EEBD to do that even though this item of equipment is not designed for rescue work. Similarly, although the chief cook was not part of the rescue team, when he found another person lying on the surface of the cargo hold he went against the process. Such connections can only surface in visual mapping, and often through a creative exercise that allows for imagination. A form, a checklist or a regimented process will not be able to capture such nuances and subtleties of human behaviour.

# A holistic view of the accident narrative

Once we have mapped the conversation (in this case the investigation), we are able to generate discussions, because it is now a verbal exchange set out visibly on a board. So in the iCue method the participants can actually see what you mean, unlike in traditional approaches that hide our assumptions and methods of enquiry in forms and checklists. The transparency inherent within iCue enables trust, listening and ethical relations to be normalised. Once a more holistic view emerges, we are in position to grasp the rounded view of this accident; in other words, what we want to write about, and what questions we seek to answer. It is important to understand that the seeking for and framing of questions is not determined at the start, but results from thorough engagement with the holistic view of the accident narrative following the iCue exercise.

The benefit of this exercise is that it makes the process of analysis and report writing a lot more focused and effective, thus saving the time and effort needed to go back and forth in search of the coherence and validity of the data gathered.

## The questions

Below are the three questions that I intend to ask relating to this accident report. My choice of questions came from familiarising myself with the content of the report and organising the text on the iCue engagement board. Notice the framing of the questions. They are intended to enable the understanding of behaviours, motivations, perceptions, emotions and intuitions originating from the unconscious mind. In other words, the questions are consistent with the philosophy of embodied Mind and more specifically, One Brain Three Minds.

The purpose of this exercise is to find honest, ethical and relational means to access the unconscious Mind, in this case the hidden unconscious in the investigation process.

1. What explains the crew member's motivation to enter an oxygen-deficient enclosed space?
2. What explains the behaviour of the crew members in a crisis situation?
3. What can we learn from the crew's perception of the use of EEBD as rescue equipment?

As stated earlier, I did not have a chance to interview the crew members on the ship. The response to the questions above are based on interviews with seafarers, a historical review of similar accidents in enclosed spaces in the maritime sector, and my own experiences both as a seafarer and as a researcher.

# What explains the crew member's motivation to enter an oxygen-deficient enclosed space?

The crew members turned up to grease the ship's crane. Upon discovering that the grease provided was not suitable for the crane wires, the head of the crew (bosun) agreed with the chief officer that they would instead grease the hatch handles. As the ship was at anchor waiting to depart, this was an opportunity to carry out routine maintenance work.

The greasing of the hatch cover handles was considered a low-risk activity, which explains why there was no real need for a risk assessment. In addition, the carriage of steam coal was not a new activity; this was the fourth time the ship had carried coal in its holds. The crew did not expect to enter the holds as part of their job scope, and perhaps the thought that a hatch cover handle might fall inside the hatch and the possibility of toxic gases present inside the hatch was not something they imagined.

To assert that one should consider all worst-case scenarios prior to starting a job does not make practical sense, as it assumes that all risks can be imagined and managed prior to starting any activity; but that is not how humans make decisions. Instead, we learn to satisfice i.e. pursue actions with minimum effort to achieve our goals in the face of an uncertain future (see Herbert Simon on *Bounded Rationality*).

As the work proceeded, one of the crew members found himself working alone on one of the hatch covers. As part of greasing, the removal of hatch handles required improvised tools, plus hammering and pounding, and in the process one of the handles fell inside the hatch and stuck on the ladder, a little way down. It is my speculation that the crew member would have faced a dilemma: either get hold of a fellow crew member and discuss his concerns before entering the space, or step into the space on his own. Given that it was only a matter of climbing a couple of metres down the ladder, the instinct to get the job done would have taken over; he might have thought, 'I'll be okay.' Besides, in that group of four people, only that crewmember and the bosun were Chinese; the other two were Indonesian, so it was hard for him to communicate with them.

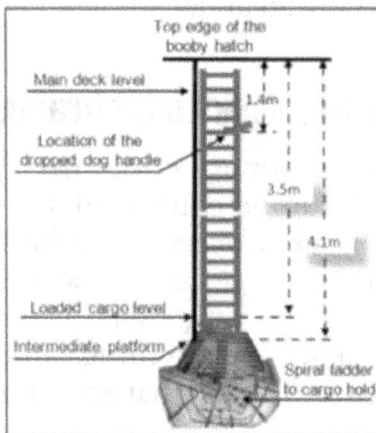

Figure 16.11: Various heights in the cargo hold (Source: accident report). The hatch cover handle was stuck about 1.4 metres below the main deck level.

Some were new to the company while others had been there some time. It is worth exploring the interpersonal factors at play in this small group. Too much is at stake: saving face, peer pressure, pride in profession, risk perception, risk tolerance, language barriers, cultural differences, rank seniority, time served in the company etc. It would have been seen as far easier to drop down a couple of metres to pick up a handle than engage in a risky conversation with another person. Between the physical hazard of momentarily entering an oxygen-deficient space and the emotional and psychological risk of engaging with a peer, the unconscious mind may have opted for the former. If we were to have disciplined this crew member (if he had survived) for not speaking up or not raising a 'stop card' in this situation, it would have been like disciplining a two-year-old for not calling their mother before soiling their nappy. The mind needs a reference to turn emotions into feelings and to articulate feelings in verbal language. Neither the toddler nor the deceased crew member would have been consciously aware that they were stepping into a no-go area.

## From controlling risk to embracing error

The investigation report omits the crucial point that not all risk can be controlled and managed at the outset. As work proceeds, previously unknown risks will always emerge, and crew members learn to tackle those risks with their heuristics, habits, intuitions and skills. If everything can be taken into consideration in advance, what good is seamanship?

The purpose of risk assessment is not to control the risk but to help people be mindful, considered and focused. That the future holds surprises should instigate within us what the Danish philosopher Søren Kierkegaard calls 'fear and trembling'. And it is that fear and trembling – and doubt – that makes us humble and mindful, and keeps us safe in a high-risk environment.

Conversely, the language of managing and controlling all the risks before the start of an activity induces desensitisation, hubris, overconfidence and mindlessness. In an uncertain world, the concept of risk should be about being prepared to tackle the unknown, and not managing and controlling what lies ahead. This is not to say that we should leave everything for the individual to tackle on the go, and not conduct a risk assessment at the start, but we should instead view a risk assessment as a ritual of mindfulness, thinking and caring for oneself and others. In that case, the crew need less reminding and less requirement to follow and comply with instructions, and more dialogue, discussions and conversations. The act of telling, yelling and reminding instils fear. The unconscious does not manifest from receiving more reminders – on the contrary, reminders create suppression deeper down. As investigators and risk managers, what we need to do is ask open questions, and conduct conversations and dialogue with others that help us all realise the limits of our consciousness, senses, perception, imagination and biases.

## What explains the behaviour of the crew members in a crisis situation?

According to the muster list, the Emergency Squad comprised the CO,[25] the bosun, two ASDs[26] and two ordinary seamen, and at the incident site their role was first to assess the situation and then to respond accordingly. The Emergency Squad was to be assisted by the Support Squad, led by the 2O.[27] The Master was in charge overall, in the Command Squad.

The chief cook was assigned to the First Aid Squad, together with the steward, led by the 3O. The roles of the First Aid Squad were to provide medical aid to the injured in an emergency, mobilise a stretcher, convey the casualty to a safer place for first aid treatment and other duties, as directed by the Master.

As we noticed from the report, the formal structure of the Emergency Squad collapsed in the emergency. It was in fact the chief cook and the third officer from the First Aid Squad who entered the space, instead of the designated team. The accident investigation team could not establish the reason for the change of plan. This is understandable, because our accident models and methods are not equipped to understand non-conscious, non-rational decision making.

Understanding the collapse of the formal structure in an emergency requires an appreciation of the

---

[25] Chief officer
[26] Able seamen on deck
[27] Second officer

embodied Mind. In an emergency it is difficult for anyone to think logically and make rational decisions. Decision making is characterised by satisficing i.e. optimising decisions, with limited information, conflicting goals and an unknown future. Second, when panic kicks in, research shows that people experience stress, distress, de-stress and eustress to varying degrees, depending on their temperament.

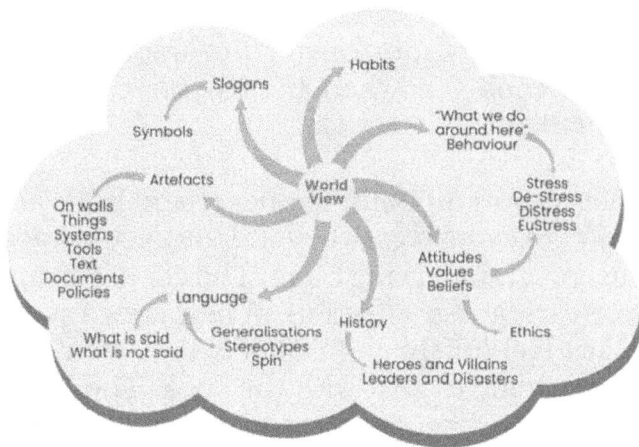

Figure 16.12: Culture Cloud.* This illustrates behaviour under stress – stress, de-stress, distress and eustress. While experiencing stress can be healthy and constructive, de-stress is the opposite, meaning that we are unaffected by the incident; nothing bothers us. Eustress is positive stress, meaning that we perform well under excitement. Distress is the opposite, in that we go into the shadow side of our personality.

A person who is usually calm and composed may when under stress become anxious and fear-driven. Seeing the bosun running and shouting would have put the chief cook and third officer into distress. Perhaps the formal structure collapsed because the two could not think and act in accordance with the predetermined plan that they had followed without problem during emergency drills, as shown by the investigation report.

In those moments, the chief cook, otherwise not part of the rescue team, would be overcome by stress, and instead of following the First Aid Team procedure, he might have assumed the role of rescuing the ASD1 regardless of the captain's presence on the scene. Interestingly, the chief cook is a Chinese national and therefore had more in common with the deceased ASD1 than the other crew members. Did the investigation team try to understand how the chief cook felt when he saw his countryman lying on the coal?

Another important point to understand is the archetype of 'cook', which goes beyond the duty of cooking for the crew, and serving them. The cook is an archetype of caring and affection. When crew members on board feel lonely and isolated, they would often go to the galley to chat with the cook. The irregular patterns of work on ships mean that the cook would even store food for crew members who didn't turn up to eat at mealtimes. So as well as being a fellow countryman to the ASD1, the cook felt like a mother and guardian to him, as one of the crew. The cook's instinct to rescue that crew member echoes what a mother would do on seeing her child lying unconscious in an oxygen-deficient space.

The third officer also went against his formal role, and entered the space to rescue the man, because he felt the same stress. These were not deliberate and conscious decisions to breach the rules; the two men were overwhelmed by their emotions. A history of maritime accidents involving seafarers' deaths in enclosed spaces is a testimony of the instinctive nature of humans to rescue another human person in a crisis, even if this means going against the rules. Deep inside we are the same as all sentient beings.

## What explains the crew's perception of the use of EEBD as rescue equipment?

While the company had stated, in accordance with regulatory requirements, that the EEBD was not to be used in an emergency rescue, the crew members and the captain apparently believed otherwise. This is a powerful insight that begs for an understanding of the mismatch between the investigator's worldview and that of those under investigation. Here is a possible explanation of this gap.

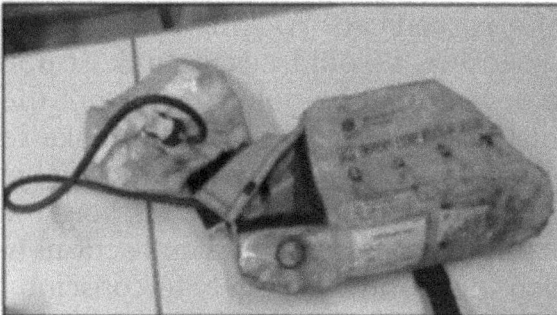

Figure 16.13: Emergency Escape Breathing Device (EEBD) used by the officer on the ship (source: accident report).

There are at least two instances in this report where the investigators use the term 'desperate'. On another occasion, the investigator wrote 'grabbing the EEBD' and crew members 'running down'. Seeing a crew member suffocating must have made the third officer feel desperate. In a desperate situation, with time running out and rational thought impossible, the EEBD offered an optimum solution to get into that hot and confined space to help an unconscious shipmate. While donning the SCBA would have been time-consuming, the EEBD only required 'grabbing on the way from the main deck'. For you to understand the criticality of this statement, you need to become familiar with the concept of 'affordance'.

## Affordance

Our senses do not give us an objective view of the external environment. Instead, how we perceive the world around is locked in what actions are unconsciously 'afforded' to us. A chair affords sitting, a saucepan affords cooking, to a baby a breast affords sucking milk, a lamp affords switching on and off, and a driveway affords playing basketball (in the absence of a parked car). Walking by a pole or a tree on the roadside, I would never think of uprooting the tree or bending the pole. Such is not the affordance of those objects. We learn to make sense of objects around us in the way that those objects afford manipulation and meaning. As we grow older, those manipulations, meanings and actions become embodied in us, and it is largely unconscious.

People on board ship have unconsciously worked out that SCBA sets are not very helpful for rescue in an emergency. It takes time to don one, and furthermore, its design makes entering a confined space challenging. While the investigation gave us a glimpse into the difficulty of breathing and the hot temperature in the space, it never really developed the analysis further. An EEBD, on the other hand, is readily available. In the words of the investigator (twice), it can be *grabbed* from the main deck, hence affords a swift and practical solution to a problem that has persisted in the maritime industry for many years. It is a cultural belief amongst the seafarers that the EEBD can be used in such situation, although as a regulatory requirement and from the company's viewpoint this behaviour is strictly non-compliant. But what do you do when people share an unconscious belief which manifests so strongly during an emergency? We can either discard this as an act of rule violation, or attempt to understand human behaviour in stressful situations, and improve the design of rescue equipment at sea.

Figure 16.14: A comparison between the use of EEBD and SCBA whilst entering an enclosed space. (Picture sources: https://www.labour.gov.hk/eng/public/os/D/Safe_Work_in_Confined_Spaces.pdf https://bulkcarrierguide.com/personal-protective-equipment.html)

## More signs, fewer signs, proper signs – or learning to interpret signs?

As a sidenote, the terms 'reminders' and 'instructions' appear at least 16 times in the 29-page report. Against the backdrop of rules, regulations and processes, the role of the investigator and ship managers is clearly, then, to constantly remind and instruct the crew to follow the rules that are meant to ensure their safety. We seek standardisation in signs and symbols so that instructions and reminders are followed without misunderstandings. Such a worldview assumes that the artefacts of communication are neutral and objective, and that if we try hard with reminders and instructions, error-prone people will eventually get the message. The underlying assumption is that human beings are mechanical beings and that the brain works like a computer: if correct information is fed to the brain, it will perform accordingly – the classic adage 'Your analysis is only as good as the data you feed in.'

But this is not how the embodied Mind makes decisions. If the investigation team had spent time listening to the ways various crew members interpreted the meanings of, for instance, 'KEEP CLOSE AT SEA' or 'CHECK BEFORE ENTRY' (and for that matter any other signage on the ship) the team might have discovered that the same signage had different meanings for different people. Risk is subjective, and symbols are interpretive. When we understand the subjective and interpretive nature of being a human person and the hermeneutics of communication, we can spend less time reminding people, and more time listening to them.

When we realise that risk is subjective, that our worldview is biased and limited, and that our conversations with others can improve our chances to survive and flourish, the same signs and symbols can open up possibilities for discussions, reflection, discovery and learning. By having open conversations, we improve our relationships with others, and through those relationships, we uncover what is hidden in our unconscious. All this means fewer misunderstandings and improved quality of decisions. I am reminded of the saying 'You cannot organise me, and I cannot become a part of your organisation, if you don't take the time to understand me.'

When will we stop issuing reminders, and start listening and understanding, to learn from accidents?

## A comparison of the iCue method and the traditional models of accident investigation

|  | Orthodox view | iCue method |
|---|---|---|
| How are humans viewed | Human beings are aware of their actions and decisions. | Human beings are largely unconscious and therefore mostly unaware of what drives their decisions and actions. |
| What is the purpose of the investigation | To identify, manage and control errors and failures through training, procedures and barriers. | To begin with an understanding of how human beings make decisions by surfacing the assumptions and biases. |
| Who needs to learn | Those involved in the accident should learn from the investigation. | Everyone (including the investigation team) should learn from the investigation. |

| | | |
|---|---|---|
| How we understand risk | Risk can be made objective and therefore it can be determined, eliminated or mitigated through corrective actions. | Risk is subjective and therefore can only be perceived and felt through experience. This also means that in can only be tackled as it is experienced. In tackling the risk, we become mindful that our actions and inactions may have (unintended) implications. |
| What is expected | Saving lives. | Making people mindful and doubtful so that they remain humble and take ownership of their actions and decisions. |
| What counts as success | Minimised (quantified) risk; Zero harm; measuring injury and incident data. | Due diligence; ALARP; healing traumatised people is part of learning initiatives. |
| Culture | Safety Culture. | Learning Culture. |
| Learning outcome | The deceased person entered an oxygen-deficient space without informing his colleagues. | The deceased person may have been caught between sharing his concerns with his colleagues and the physical risks involved in the activity (which became visible only during the process of the investigation). Much of the conflict between what we ought to be doing and what we end up doing happens internally and below the conscious level. |

| | | |
|---|---|---|
| Learning outcome | The crew members did not conduct a thorough risk assessment prior to commencing the 'unplanned maintenance' work. | The crew could not possibly imagine the dropping of a handle in the cargo space. An unplanned activity and the associated risks requires discussions, conversations and sharing of experiences and not necessarily more paperwork. |
| Learning outcome | The hazards related with carriage of coal were not considered prior to opening the hatch cover. | The hazards related with carriage of coal had not been experienced before by the crew members. The risk assessment, in its current form and shape, does not encourage imagination and active conversations. |
| Learning outcome | The EEBD device should not be used for the purpose of rescuing people from the enclosed spaces. | The EEBD offers a practical solution for rescuing people in what is otherwise a poorly designed workplace. The crew has worked this out in an unconscious manner. |
| Learning outcome | There are not enough signs to remind the crew of the risk of entering enclosed spaces. | There is no attempt made to understand what the crew thinks of the signs and symbols. |
| Action | More posters and safety messages. | Engaging with seafarers on regular basis to understand their views on safety signs and messages. |

| Action | Crew members to be made more aware. | Conversations, reflections and action-oriented exercises with all crew members. |
|--------|-------------------------------------|-------------------------------------------------------------------------------|
| Action | Emergency drills with proper scenarios. | Drills and emergencies to recognise the experiential nature of learning. Briefing and debriefing to be used to surface the unconscious (habits, heuristics, assumptions, biases, and language in use) to enrich shared experiences. |
| Action | Improved relationship between officers and crew. | Relationships improve when we (as investigators and managers) care to understand another person's worldview and not impose ours on to them. |

## Learning from accidents

Our modern society claims to liberate itself from the dogmas of the past by taking a 'scientific approach' to truth, and putting an end to human sufferings through science. I have no problems with science *per se*; the issue I take, as I have outlined consistently in this book, is with the *ideology* of science. If science were truly intended as a medium of progress, we would not be living in a world where half of the population is on the trajectory to become overweight in just over a decade (World Obesity Atlas, 2023), climate change has reached a point of no return (in the foreseeable future, at least), and 'some

10 per cent of the world's population owns 76 per cent of the wealth, takes in 52 per cent of income, and accounts for 48 per cent of global carbon emissions' (Stanley, 2022) – a rise in social inequality, healthcare disparities and ecological imbalance on a scale that a couple of decades ago was unimaginable. What more evidence do we need to show that science has been manipulated by hidden motives and political agendas?

We may scoff at primitive humans for being mythical and irrational, and for lacking the sophistication of science and scientific methods, but when we dig into our own rituals and narratives we observe the same superstitions and dogmas in our science. At least the primitive humans believed in their myths and practised their rituals whole-heartedly, but we seem to have uncritically embraced our myths as *the* word of science. When misfortune strikes us, we go through a rigorous process that we call an accident investigation – but we end up in precisely the same place as the Azande of Sudan, the Aztecs of Mexico, the Zulus of South Africa or the Aboriginals of Australia.

What, then, is a 'scientific enquiry'? In search for an objective truth, our narratives and rituals are anchored to the same myths of certainty, control and comfort as those of the primitive humans. True science rejects certainty; in contrast, it acknowledges that our search for answers will always remain incomplete. To claim that accident methods and models are scientific would make sense if accident investigation reports reflected humility and subjectivity, and invited the possibility for competing narratives

379

– and, more importantly, brought the narratives of the powerless and the marginalised to the forefront.

## The embodied Mind and learning

This book is an attempt to illustrate that sustained learning is achieved by adopting a philosophy and a method to understand fallible humans. Learning, unlearning and understanding how humans make decisions requires an appreciation of the embodied Mind.

The metaphor of One Brain Three Minds should not be taken literally; it is a figurative representation of how the whole body is involved in the process of thinking, enacting and decision making, and why understanding the mutual interplay of the mind–body relationship is essential to learning. I have observed many arguments in favour of Kahneman's System 1 and System 2 thinking to make a case for the two modes of the brain – fast and intuitive along with slow and rational.

But this brain-centric model is not congruent with how the human mind actually functions; I concur with Mervin and Kay in that Kahneman's dualistic distinction is intended to simplify human decision making, rather than provide a descriptive understanding of it. The evidence for our body's involvement in decision making is overwhelming, from religion, to mythology, anthropology, social psychology, evolutionary sciences, biology, and on through to new research in neurobiology, neuroscience, and neuropsychology (Libet, Gleason,

& Wright, 1983) (Kruglanski & Gigerenzer, 2011) (Mercier & Sperber, 2017).

A crew member died because his habits, heuristics, rituals, gestures and his 'normal' reflected that he genuinely did not imagine the need to 'risk assess' before getting into that enclosed space. Who are we to judge his actions as right or wrong? Whether or not a cargo hold should be considered an enclosed space, or what safety signage is appropriate to the context from an investigator's perspective, are immaterial if the deceased person and his fellows do not see their decisions as risky. How interesting that the marvels of evolution, the mysteries of the unconscious, the wisdom of ages and sages, and an abundance of leading research that validates embodiment and the non-conscious nature of life are all silenced in the accident discourse in favour of a rational, mechanistic, brain-centric, and simplistic view of how human beings learn and live. One hears every now and then the admonition to *Keep it simple* within the risk and safety industry, despite the fact that accidents such as these are so common in the maritime world. Unfortunately, simplicity is not a solution once it proves chronically weak when applied in practice. We must learn to become critical of our methods and models.

**We are human beings, not human doings. In other words, our being will always precede doing and action. But in standard investigations we are trying to solve the problems of our being[28] by using rational methods and calculative tools. The**

---

[28] Automaticity, reflexes, instincts, emotions, intuitions, learned short cuts, heuristics and habits.

problem is that when learnt behaviours have found their way into our bodies and the unconscious mind, focusing on the brain is not helpful. Trying to solve the problems of Minds 2 and 3 using the methods and tools of Mind 1 is not a sustainable strategy for learning and change. Successful and sustainable change is achieved by helping others become aware of their unconscious, not by telling and controlling those others.

One only needs to look at the cautionary signs and images on a cigarette packet to realise that only a few human beings learn from warnings, reminders, statistics and facts. I stopped smoking about two decades ago because I heard a radio announcer saying, 'It's a crazy world where we take care of our cars more than our bodies.' That catchphrase gave me more incentive to quit smoking than all the research of medical science. I could tell you there are currently hundreds of people dying in Ukraine or Gaza each day, but what movement will that create in you? We are not an evidence-seeking but a meaning-making species, and our meaning is embodied in the myths, rituals and metaphors that we live by. For any organisation to contemplate sustainable learning and change, the embodied nature of the human Mind should be taken seriously at the foundational level and become part of learning strategy.

## Learning is a personal journey

What I chose to learn and share from my meeting with Francesco has been articulated in this book. I can choose what I want to learn, and I would expect the same of you. In this case, I have focused on questioning: the construct of 'normal work' seen through cultural lenses; how psychological safety masks some of the deeper, systematic problems in the cruise shipping industry; how human beings behave in a crisis as against how we document and formulate our plans and processes; and why as a species we cannot avoid the ritual of blaming when faced with misfortune.

I could have asked a different set of questions. That choice is your decision, and that is what makes learning deliberate, strategic and a personal journey. In whatever we choose to learn, we should be mindful about our metaphors, how we frame our narratives and how our words can create and limit our worldviews.

## Learning is embracing fallibility

One cannot ignore the dialectic between the Mind and body that continues from birth to the grave. Our consciousness is always in tension with our unconscious being, and our decisions are largely driven by unconscious.[29] All this makes us frail, vulnerable, and susceptible to fallibility. We are fallible because existence itself is fallible. That brings me back to where I was when I started writing this book.

The thirty seconds of my life when I met with a near collision changed the entire ship crew's perception

---

[29] That is, the automaticity, reflexes, desires, motivations, temptations, habits, impulses, instincts, intuitions and bodily necessities over which we have so little control.

of me. In all these years, I have come to realise that a single mistake can turn expertise into error and pride into shame; in some people's eyes, once you have made a serious mistake you cannot be trusted, you are not worthy of receiving love; a fallible person is less than a human. Is it not strange that as investigators we reach out to passengers, entertainers, voyage records and black boxes on the ship to collect 'data' about the accident, but we rarely have conversations with those directly involved? The *Nozomi, Hoegh Osaka, Costa Concordia, El Faro, Sewol, Wakashio, Ever Given* ... the list is endless. Once fallibility is established, people cannot be trusted, only interrogated, communicated with, disciplined, controlled – and even the dead cannot escape the curse of error. Spinoza was right in that our species has not learned to understand a fallible person. Our models, methods, languages and worldviews have not matured to understand fallibility – only to deny, control, mock and fix it.

My attempt throughout this book has been to outline a coherent philosophy, a methodology, and practical methods and tools to engage with fallible humans. If this book has encouraged you to meet another fallible person with an open heart and mind, I have achieved my purpose. My research, however, will continue.

I am **listening** when:

I **suspend** my agenda
I **submit** control
I **attend** to the other

Figure 16.15: A conversation with a fallible person requires us to suspend our agenda, to submit control and to pay attention to the other.

# Reflections and realisations

We live by our myths.

Life is not lived above the shoulder.

Human beings are mostly non-conscious.

Learning takes surfacing the mysteries of the unconscious.

Human Mind is embodied.

It takes two whole persons to meet.

Listening takes suspending our agenda, surrendering control and attending to the other.

Listening is an orientation towards the other.

Learning is an embodied movement.

Learning is a movement towards the other.

Understanding takes standing under.

Science provides insights; myth gives us meaning.

Wisdom takes the ability to hold doubt ... a little longer than what we are used to.

Words matter because words create worldviews.

Humankind would wipe itself out if we did not practise the ritual of scapegoating.

Truth is temporal, unstable and incomplete.

Truth is what resonates with our belief.

Risk is subjective.

Learning takes patience, wisdom and discernment.

Science is a humble and ongoing enquiry into the unknown.

The world needs more science and less scientism.

At its heart, human culture is a denial of our mortality and fallibility.

As we go deeper, there are few cultural differences.

A true friend is like a mirror helping us recognise our biases.

Learning is in the dialectic between knowing and being.

A conversation is where we experience a soul-to-soul connection.

Existence is fallible.

Suffering is integral to learning.

Learning is embracing fallibility.

The purpose of all learning is to spread love and enhance the flourishing of life.

# Appendix: *Nozomi* Accident Report

⎯⎯⎯⎯⎯ ⊷⊶⊷ ⎯⎯⎯⎯⎯

## Final Report

## FATALITY OF CREW ON BOARD NOZOMI

## IN BANGKA STRAIT, INDONESIA
## 1 APRIL 2022

TIB/MAI/CAS.122

Transport Safety Investigation Bureau
Ministry of Transport
Singapore

30 November 2022

# The Transport Safety Investigation Bureau of Singapore

The Transport Safety Investigation Bureau (TSIB) is the air, marine and rail accidents and incidents investigation authority in Singapore. Its mission is to promote transport safety through the conduct of independent investigations into air, marine and rail accidents and incidents.

TSIB conducts marine safety investigations in accordance with the Casualty Investigation Code under SOLAS Regulation XI-1/6 adopted by the International Maritime Organization (IMO) Resolution MSC 255(84).

The sole objective of TSIB's marine safety investigations is the prevention of marine accidents and incidents. The safety investigations do not seek to apportion blame or liability. Accordingly, TSIB reports should not be used to assign blame or determine liability.

# TABLE OF CONTENTS

## SYNOPSIS

On 1 April 2022, after completing the loading of coal cargo, the Singapore registered bulk carrier, Nozomi, was anchored at the Tanjung Api-Api anchorage, South Sumatera, Indonesia.

While waiting for cargo export documents and scheduled pilot to embark, four crew members were tasked to grease the booby hatch dog handles for the No.5 cargo hold. During the greasing process, one of the four crew members, an Able Seafarer Deck (ASD), was discovered lying inside the cargo hold on top of the coal cargo. An emergency rescue was initiated but could not save the ASD.

The Transport Safety Investigation Bureau classified the occurrence as a very serious marine casualty.

The investigation revealed that the ASD had entered the cargo hold to retrieve a dropped dog handle and had likely succumbed to the oxygen deficient atmosphere while exiting the cargo hold. The investigation also determined that the greasing task was unplanned, and the hazards associated with the coal cargo were overlooked.

The investigation also revealed that there was no proper signage to warn the crew to treat the cargo hold as an enclosed space.

# DETAILS OF VESSEL

| Name | NOZOMI |
|---|---|
| IMO Number | 9558701 |
| Flag registry | Singapore |
| Classification society | Nippon Kaiji Kyokai (Class NK), Lloyd's Register (LR)[30] |
| Ship type | Bulk carrier |
| Hull | Steel |
| Delivery | 14 September 2011 |
| Owner/ ISM Manager[31] | Golden Galaxie Maritime Pte Ltd / Glory Ship Management Pte Ltd |
| Gross tonnage | 33338 |
| Length overall | 190.00m |
| Moulded breadth | 32.26m |
| Moulded depth | 18.50m |
| Summer draft | 13.02m |

Nozomi

---

[30] ClassNK and LR are the Recognised Organisation (RO) for carrying out ISM audit and issuance of ISM related certificates. Statutory survey and issuance of certificates were by LR.
[31] As per the International management code for the safe operation of ships and for pollution prevention – ISM Code. The "ISM Manager" is referred to as the Company in this investigation report.

# 1 FACTUAL INFORMATION[32]

All times used in this report are Western Indonesian Time unless otherwise stated. Indonesian Local Time is seven hours ahead of Coordinated Universal Time (UTC+7).

## 1.1 Sequence of events

1.1.1 On 19 March 2022, Nozomi arrived and anchored[33] at the Tanjung Api-Api (TAA) anchorage, South Sumatera, Indonesia, for loading coal cargo, which took place between 22 and 26 March 2022.

1.1.2 On 1 April 2022, Nozomi waited at the anchorage for cargo export documents, and the departing pilot to embark at about 1200H. At about 1000H, the Bosun asked three ASD's (ASD1, ASD2 and ASD3) to assist him in carrying out maintenance work (greasing) of the shipboard cargo cranes on the main deck. When the group arrived at No. 4 crane at about 1010H, the Bosun was doubtful whether the grease available on board was appropriate for the moving parts of the cranes. The Bosun informed the Chief Officer (CO) via walkie-talkie

---

[32] Gathered by interviewing relevant crew members, information collected on board and provided by the Company such as photographs of the incident location and Safety Management System (SMS) requirements.

[33] Approximate location at latitude 02° 08.3'S, longitude 104° 59.3'E. Her last port of call was Chittagong, Bangladesh for discharging cargo in aggregates and arrived this location in ballast condition for loading coal.

of the matter and requested the CO to go to the main deck for confirmation.

1.1.3 The CO, who was resting in his cabin, went to the main deck and met up with the group. After discussing with the Bosun, the CO mentioned that he would inform the Company to supply the correct grease for the cranes at the next available port. The Bosun told the CO that the grease was however suitable for lubricating the dog handles[34] (see **figure 1**) of the booby hatch[35] accessing cargo holds, and that the crew could grease these dog handles instead. Each booby hatch cover is secured by four sets of internal and external dog handles. Each set of the dog handles has a claw to secure the booby hatch cover internally. The CO agreed with the Bosun's suggestion and thereafter the CO went back to the ship's accommodation to rest.

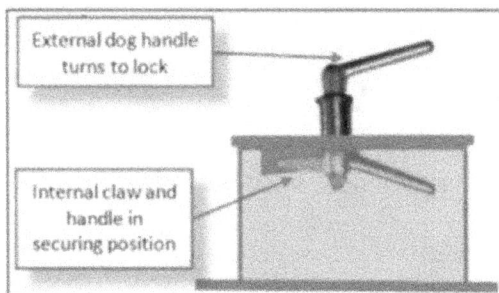

---

[34] Comprises a lever which is commonly used on board ships to wedge against typical watertight or weathertight access doors and hatches for isolating adjoining compartments or external access against fire, smoke, and water ingress.

[35] Also known as Access Lids. A raised or hooded form to access a ladder from the weather-deck to the cargo hold or other hatches.

Figure 1 - Illustration of a set of dog handles securing
a booby hatch (not to scale)

1.1.4    The Bosun and the three ASDs transferred the grease and tools to the forward booby hatch (for accessing No.5 cargo hold, see **figure 2**). While turning the external dog handles to open the booby hatch cover, two out of the four were found to be seized. The deck crew used a short pipe to slot into the external dog handles and managed to turn them, and thereafter were able to lift open the booby hatch cover.

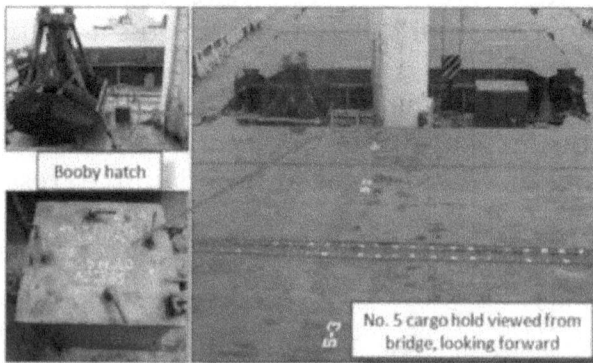

Booby hatch

No. 5 cargo hold viewed from
bridge, looking forward

Figure 2 - No.5 cargo hold forward booby hatch -
*Source*: the Company (Annotated by the TSIB)

1.1.5    To free up the seized dog handles for greasing, the Bosun continued using the short pipe, assisted by the ASD2. At the same time, with the booby hatch cover in open position, the ASD1 used a hammer to strike the internal dog handle of the other set of seized-up dog handles. After a few strikes, the external dog

handle dropped onto the main deck and was
~~picked up by the ASD2. Figure 3 shows the~~

Figure 3 - Enactment of the positions of the deck crew (*Source*: the
TSIB)

1.1.6   At about 1030H, the ASD2 heard a sound from
No. 5 cargo hold, he looked over the booby
hatch and saw the ASD1 lying on the coal cargo.
An internal dog handle[36] was found wedged
between the vertical ladder and the side stringer
of ship's structure (see **figure 4**). No one was
aware that the ASD1 had entered the cargo
hold. The deck crew assessed that the ASD1
could have dropped the internal dog handle
into the cargo hold while hammering it and
tried to retrieve it without informing anyone.

---

[36] This internal dog handle was found to be the other part of the
external dog handle picked up by the ASD3.

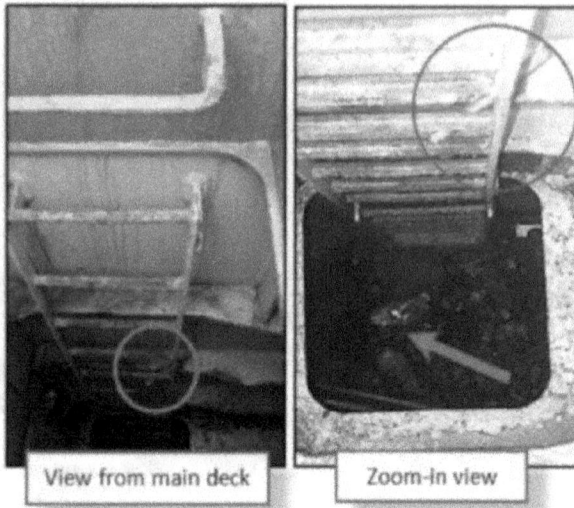

Figure 4 - Red-coloured circles indicating the dog handle
and the arrow points to the safety shoes of ASD1 inside the cargo hold
(*Source*: The TSIB)

1.1.7 The Bosun shouted to the ASD1 but did not receive any response. The Bosun ran towards the accommodation to get safety harness and ropes while shouting to attract the attention of other crew members. The ASD2, at about the same time, reported the incident on the walkie-talkie to the Third Officer (3O), who was the duty officer keeping anchor watch on the bridge. The Master and Second Officer (2O) were also on the bridge liaising with ship's local agent in preparation for departure clearance.

1.1.8 Upon hearing the report by the ASD2, the Master instructed the 2O to activate the ship's general alarm and made an announcement for rescue operation in cargo hold. Shortly after, the 3O ran down to the main deck.

1.1.9　On the way to the main deck, while grabbing two EEBD[37]s, the 3O called the Bosun on the walkie-talkie and asked him to take the stretcher[38] and the self- contained breathing apparatus (SCBA) with the rescue ropes and safety harness[39].

1.1.10　A short while later after the 3O left the bridge, the Master instructed the 2O to remain on the bridge and thereafter the Master went to the incident site. The Master noticed that the ASD1 was motionless lying on the coal cargo and recalled seeing some crew arriving at the site with the EEBD, stretcher, safety harness and some other equipment. There was no SCBA brought to the site. The CO and other crew members arrived at the booby hatch separately and noticed some engine crew rigging and pulling two air hoses into the booby hatch.

1.1.11　When the 3O arrived at the booby hatch, he put on the EEBD (see **figure 5**) hood and entered the cargo hold through the vertical ladder while the two air hoses were being

---

[37] Emergency Escape Breathing Device, to be carried on board cargo ships under the Fire Safety Systems Code, Chapter 3. It is a personnel protection device used for escaping from a compartment that has a hazardous atmosphere, and not be used for fighting fires, entering oxygen deficient voids or tanks, or worn by fire-fighters. Its usage duration is about 10mins.
[38] Neil Robertson stretcher which was stored in the infirmary.
[39] SCBA, rescue ropes and harnesses were stored in the fire locker.

connected to the air supply. The investigation team gathered that the 3O subsequently came out of the booby hatch, citing that it was difficult to breath and hot in the cargo hold.

Figure 5 - EEBD set used by the 3O

1.1.12 The Chief Cook (CCK), on his own accord, took the two air hoses, safety harness and ropes climbed into the cargo hold to rescue the ASD1.

1.1.13 After about 3-5 minutes, the CCK managed to secure the safety harness below the arms of ASD1 and the crew on the main deck pulled the ASD1 out. The CCK climbed out of the cargo hold soon after by himself. The crew assessed that the ASD1 was not breathing and there was no heartbeat or pulse. They took turns to perform CPR[40] on the ASD1. According to the Master, the SCBA was brought to the site after the CCK had entered the cargo hold. Subsequently, the Master called the local agent and the local port authorities for assistance.

---

[40] Cardiopulmonary resuscitation.

1.1.14 By about 1200H, the local port health officials came on board with a medical team and examined the ASD1[41] before conveying the ASD1 to a local hospital. The Master was later informed by the agent that the ASD1 had passed away, as assessed by the hospital on arrival. Nozomi departed TAA anchorage on 5 April 2022 and sailed for the next port of call, Singapore.

## 1.2 The ship and her past voyages

1.2.1 Nozomi is a Handymax size[42] bulk carrier, with four cargo cranes mounted on deck along the centreline for loading / discharging of cargo from its five cargo holds. She was in tramp service and capable of carrying many types of bulk cargo.

1.2.2 At the time of occurrence, Nozomi was carrying about 57,000MT of non-coking type of Indonesian steam coal in all cargo holds, as per the cargo manifest provided to the Master, and drawing a draught of 13.3m. According to the ship's voyage records, since December 2020, this was the fourth loading of steam coal at the TAA anchorage and a total of nine voyages had been on coal carriage consignments out of the 15 voyages in the same period. The most recent consignment of coal was loaded

---

[41] Confirming no visual external injuries nor bleeding.
[42] A way of categorising bulk carriers basing on ship's capacity, a Handymax sized ship is typically about 35000-59000 deadweight (DWT).

on 24 October 2021 and discharged on 11 November 2021.

## 1.3 The crew

1.3.1 There were 24 crew of four nationalities on board Nozomi. All of them held valid STCW[43] competency certificates required for their respective positions on board, and the working language was English.

1.3.2 The qualification and experience of the Master, relevant officers and crew are tabulated below.

| Designation on board | Nationality | Age | Qualification | Duration onboard (month) | In rank service (Year) | Service in Company (Year) | Working schedule on board |
|---|---|---|---|---|---|---|---|
| Master | South Korean | 64 | COC – Master / STCW II/2, IV/2 | 4.6 | 15 | 8 | N/A |
| Chief Officer | South Korean | 60 | COC – Master / STCW II/2, IV/2 | 9.9 | 13 | 0.8 | Day worker |
| Third Officer | Indonesian | 26 | COC – OOW / STCW II/1, IV/2 | 10 | 4 | 0.8 | 0800-1200 2000 - 0000 |

---

[43] The International Convention on Standards of Training, Certification and Watch keeping for Seafarers (or STCW), 1978 sets qualification standards for masters, officers and watch personnel on seagoing merchant ships.

| | | | | | | | |
|---|---|---|---|---|---|---|---|
| Bosun | Chinese | 53 | Deck/Catering Rating per STCW II/5 | 12 | 23 | 29 | Day worker |
| ASD1 | Chinese | 48 | | 12.2 | 26 | 26 | 0800-1200 2000 - 0000 |
| ASD2 | Indonesian | 58 | | 10 | 34 | 26 | 0800-1200 2000 - 0000 |
| ASD3 | Indonesian | 53 | | 0.2 | 30 | 27 | Day worker |
| Chief Cook | Chinese | 50 | | 12 | 22 | 22 | Day worker |

1.3.3 Both the CO and the 3O were first time with the Company and joined Nozomi in June 2021. The others listed in the table had served with the Company for many years. All the crew received their familiarisation[44] training after joining ship as per the Company's training requirements. In addition, the CO and the 3O had received a briefing at the shore office before joining the ship.

1.3.4 The 3O had six years of sailing experience on bulk carriers including on ship carrying coal cargo. Prior to the incident, he was not aware of the booby hatch maintenance work while keeping watch on the bridge.

1.3.5 The ASD1 was declared medically fit for service at sea dated 15 March 2021 in accordance with

---

[44] A template form named as "The record of onboard familiarisation". Once completed, the original copy of the form was to be kept in the Company, with one copy for the individual crew and another to retain on board.

the STCW Code[45], by an international travel health care centre which was authorised by the China Maritime Safety Administration for seafarers' medical check-up. The medical certificate was valid for two years, without any limitations or restrictions on fitness. According to the medical certificate, the ASD1 was about 1.70m in height and weighed about 70 Kg.

1.3.6 According to Nozomi's work / rest hour records, in the past 24-hour prior to the occurrence, the ASD1 had 16 hours of rest and in the last 7-day period, he had 107 hours of rest, indicating compliance with the STCW and MLC Convention's requirements concerning the hours of work and rest[46], as documented.

## 1.4 The booby hatch

1.4.1 The booby hatch structure typically has a coaming height of about 0.8m above the main deck. All booby hatches on board Nozomi are of the same design, having four sets of dog handles to lock the four sides of the hatch for watertightness. As shown in **figure 2**, the booby hatch that was open for maintenance

---

[45] STCW Code, A-1/9 which defines the standards of medical fitness for seafarers.
[46] STCW Chapter VIII and MLC, Reg 2.3 with regards to rest hour - Minimum hours of rest shall not be less than i) ten hours in any 24-hour period; and ii) 77 hours in any seven-day period. Hours of rest may be divided into no more than two periods, one of which shall be at least six hours in length, and the interval between consecutive periods of rest shall not exceed 14 hours.

at the time was located at the forward of No.5 cargo hold.

1.4.2   The outer side of the booby hatch was marked "KEEP CLOSE AT SEA" and "NO.5 HOLD AC-CESS" (see **figure 2**). On the inner side, a red metal plate on the hatch marked the number of the cargo hold for access together with "CHECK SAFETY BEFORE ENTRY" (see **figure 6**). These markings were a part of the ship's original design from the shipyard. There was no other sign or notice in the vicinity indicating that the cargo hold was an enclosed space or that the cargo hold was carrying coal at the material time.

Figure 6 – The booby hatch cover for No.5 cargo hold (*Source*: The Company, annotated by the TSIB)

1.4.3   Access to the cargo hold from the booby hatch is via two connecting vertical ladders which end at an intermediate platform (with a grating) and from there, via a spiral ladder. The internal dog handle was wedged at about 1.4m from the booby hatch cover on the upper vertical ladder. The top of coal cargo was about 3.5m from the hatch cover, where the ASD1 was seen lying. The intermediate platform is about 4.1m from the hatch (see **figure 7**).

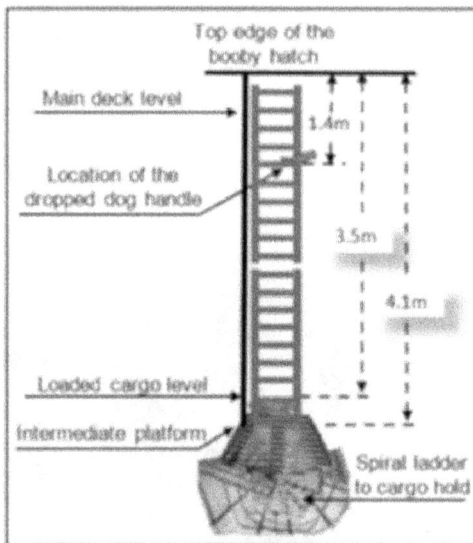

Figure 7 – Illustration of various heights (not to scale)

## 1.5 SMS on enclosed space entry and booby hatch maintenance

1.5.1 The Company managed three types of ships, i.e. bulk carrier, oil and chemical tanker. A full-term Document of Compliance certificate was issued to the Company by ClassNK on 19 October 2017 based on the audit completed on the same date and it was valid until 22 October

2022. The last verification audit for this issuance was carried out on 20 October 2021.

1.5.2 A full-term Safety Management certificate was issued by LR for Nozomi on 2 July 2018, based on the audit completed on the same date and was valid until 8 September 2023. The last intermediate verification was conducted on 21 April 2021.

1.5.3 The last Port State Control inspection was carried out on 14 April 2021. Six deficiencies were raised, but none of them were related to safety procedures on board. The last Flag State Control inspection was conducted on 17 April 2019. Four deficiencies were issued, which were also not related to safety procedures and were rectified subsequently.

1.5.4 The Company's SMS procedures in English has a section of "enclosed space entry procedures" which describes the characteristics of an enclosed space as - *limited opening for entry and exit, inadequate ventilation and not designed for continuous work occupancy, **such as cargo space, fuel tank, void space, etc.*** The procedures state that these spaces would be hazardous and could result in rapid death from harmful gases and/or lack of oxygen and should never assume a cargo hold or tank is safe.

1.5.5 The SMS procedures also state that *any cargo hold which had been sealed*[47] *must be assumed to*

---

[47] Openings to cargo hold are closed, such as hatch covers and booby hatches.

*have a dangerous atmosphere and consequently be deemed unsafe for entry* without the protection of breathing apparatus. Unprotected entry should not be attempted until a competent person[48] has made an assessment and taken the appropriate measures to ensure the space is safe for entry.

1.5.6 The SMS procedures further highlight that the Master is responsible to identify hazardous spaces and establish procedures for safe entry. According to the SMS, the Master or the CO must ensure that an enclosed space is safe for entry by identifying potential hazards, ensuring the space is ventilated, the atmosphere is tested at different levels for oxygen deficiency and enclosed procedures (according to the SMS) are instituted before and after entry. An enclosed space entry checklist is required to be completed prior to the entry.

1.5.7 The same procedures also require crew members with enclosed space entry or rescue responsibilities to participate in enclosed space and rescue drills[49] held on board the ship at least every two months. The scope of the drills includes checking and using of gas measuring instrument, donning of PPE[50], coordinating with other squad teams,

---

[48] A person, referred to the Master and the CO having sufficient theoretical knowledge and practical experience to make an informed assessment of the likelihood of a dangerous atmosphere being present or subsequently arising in the space.
[49] SOLAS, Chapter III, Regulation 19, Emergency training and drills.
[50] Personal protective equipment.

demonstrating the use of rescue equipment[51] as well as identifying hazards and recognising signs and symptoms caused by exposure to hazards during enclosed space entry.

1.5.8 In the event of an emergency, and after the ship's general alarm is raised, under no circumstances should the attending crew member enter the enclosed space before help arrives and the situation has been evaluated to ensure the safety of those entering the enclosed space to undertake rescue operations. Personnel performing rescue operations in enclosed spaces should be trained and equipped.

1.5.9 The records on board Nozomi obtained by the investigating team indicate that both the ASD1 and the 3O acknowledged reading the related SMS procedures and had attended familiarisation training within the same month after joining the ship. The records also indicate that the ASD1 and the CCK had participated in at least six enclosed space entry and rescue drills, and the 3O had participated in four such drills.

1.5.10 The Company has in place a Deck Maintenance Inspection and Record system. The system includes the general inspection of booby hatch. The investigation team could not establish whether any maintenance had been done on the booby hatch of dog handles

---

[51] Such as SCBA, Neil Robertson stretcher and rescue rope and harness.

411

in the past. The investigation team noted that there were no spare dog handles carried on board the vessel for replacement.

## 1.6 Carriage of coal and related procedures

1.6.1 According to the ship's cargo stowage plan, there was 11,700MT of coal loaded in No.5 cargo hold. The significant hazards information contained in the Material Safety Data Sheet (MSDS) for this type of the cargo is as follow:
- Dust irritates the respiratory tract and chronic inhalation may lead to decreased pulmonary function;
- Wear appropriate mask to avoid direct in-halation of content (when in physical con-tact with the coal); and
- Cargo is black in appearance and odourless.

1.6.2 Section 3 of the IMSBC[52] - The Safety of Personnel and Ship, highlights that some solid bulk cargoes are susceptible to oxidation, which may result in oxygen depletion, emission of toxic gases or fumes and self-heating. Many solid bulk cargoes are liable to cause oxygen depletion in a cargo space such as coal cargoes.

1.6.3 The Appendix in the IMSBC re-emphasised that the properties and characteristics of coal may be subject to oxidation, leading to

---

[52] International Maritime Solid Bulk Cargoes Code – facilitating the safe stowage and shipment of solid bulk cargoes by providing information on the risks associated with its shipment and procedures to be adopted for carriage.

depletion of oxygen and an increase in carbon dioxide or carbon monoxide concentrations in the cargo space. Carbon monoxide is an odourless gas, slightly lighter than air and is toxic by inhalation, with an affinity for blood haemoglobin over 200 times that of oxygen.

1.6.4   In accordance with the IMSBC, the coal cargo carried on board Nozomi was declared[53] under group B which possesses a chemical hazard and could give rise to a dangerous situation on a ship such as fire, release of toxic gas and corrosion. This cargo is also not considered liable to emit significant[54] quantity of methane as checked in the shipper's declaration.

1.6.5   One of the requirements of the IMSBC is for the Master of a ship or his representative to be provided with information about the cargo, such as toxicity, corrosiveness, and propensity for oxygen depletion (if applicable). In this case, the Master of Nozomi was made aware of the propensity for oxygen depletion of coal cargo loaded on board.

1.6.6   The same section also highlights appropriate procedures prior to entry into an enclosed space on board should be followed. Personnel shall not be permitted to enter the cargo space unless the space has been ventilated, the atmosphere tested and to be gas-free to have sufficient oxygen to support life.

---

[53] Shipper's declaration.
[54] There was no explanation on how much is quantified as significant.

1.6.7 An emergency entry into the cargo space may be permitted without ventilation, or testing the atmosphere, provided that the entry into the cargo space is undertaken only by trained personnel wearing SCBA with protective clothing, under the supervision of a responsible officer.

1.6.8 The COSWP[55] was incorporated into the Company's SMS procedures and was carried on board its fleet of ships, including Nozomi. Chapter 15 of COSWP highlights that dangerous space may not necessarily be enclosed on all sides, e.g. ships' holds may have open tops, but the nature of the cargo makes the atmosphere in the lower hold dangerous. The atmosphere of such spaces may become dangerous because of a change in the condition inside or in the degree of enclosure or confinement, which may occur intermittently. Personnel need to exercise caution before entering any space on board a ship that has not been open for some time.

1.6.9 The same Chapter also highlights that for entrances to all unattended dangerous spaces aboard a ship should be kept locked or secured against entry. Any hatches readily accessible

---

[55] Though not a mandatory publication for carriage on Singapore registered ships, the Company's SMS had incorporated the Code of Safe Working Practices for Merchant Seafarers (COSWP) as the part of procedures for reference. The COSWP, edition 2015, published by the UK Maritime and Coastguard Agency (MCA), provides best practice guidance for improving health and safety on board ships. A copy of COSWP was on board at the time of the accident.

to enclosed spaces should be marked as the entrance to a dangerous space. When the space is open for work to be carried out, an attendant should be posted, or a barrier and warning sign put in place. As far as possible, work should be arranged in such a way that no one has to enter the space.

1.6.10 An IMO Resolution A.1050(27)[56] highlights the Company's responsibilities under the safety management for entry into enclosed space. One of them is to ensure that a risk assessment is conducted to identify all enclosed spaces on board its ships. This risk assessment should be periodically revisited to ensure its continued validity. The Resolution also emphasised that no person should open or enter an enclosed space unless authorised by the master or the nominated responsible person **and** unless the appropriate safety procedures laid down for the particular ship have been followed. Entry into enclosed spaces should be planned and the use of an entry permit system, such as the use of a checklist.

1.6.11 The investigation team gathered that there is no standardisation of signage for enclosed spaces at the time of occurrence. The Implementation of IMO Instruments (III) Sub-Com-

---

[56] The International Maritime Organization (IMO) Resolution A.1050(27) - Revised Recommendations for Entering Enclosed Spaces Aboard Ships. The same Resolution was addressed under Shipping Circular No.4 of 2012 of the Maritime and Port Authority of Singapore (the Flag Administration of Nozomi) to inform its shipping community.

mittee[57] invited the CCC Sub-Committee[58] to consider a review of Res. A.1050(27) in 2022 involving entering enclosed spaces aboard, regarding the standardisation of signage for enclosed spaces.

1.6.12 According to the information obtained by the investigation team, there was no list of enclosed spaces on board the Company's fleet of ships. A reminder to not to open any hatch including booby hatch of a cargo hold carrying coal was given by the Master when he first joined the ship, which was confirmed by the CO. There was no evidence to confirm whether any notices were placed, or reminders given to the ship's crew when this cargo of coal was loaded for this voyage, from 22 March 2022 to the day of occurrence.

## 1.7  Post incident information

## Oxygen level in the No.5 cargo hold

1.7.1 The oxygen level for all the five cargo holds was measured by the CO on 4 April 2022 (three days after this occurrence). The sampling tube was extended down from the booby hatches (forward and aft) at about 2-3m and the two

---

[57] Brings together flag, port and coastal States to consider IMO instruments implementation issues and deals in casualty analysis and issuing lessons learned from marine accidents.
[58] The Sub-Committee on Carriage of Cargoes and Containers deals with the carriage of packaged dangerous goods, solid bulk cargoes, bulk gas cargoes and containers. The Sub-Committee keeps updated the IMSBC and reviews other Codes.

readings taken: first reading at the opening of booby hatch and second reading after 10mins, were recorded in the table below:

| | No.1 | No.2 | No.3 | No.4 | No.5 | Remarks |
|---|---|---|---|---|---|---|
| % of oxygen (1) | Forward - 7.7 Aft - 20.1 | Forward - 6.9 Aft - 6.3 | Forward - 6.2 Aft - 6.1 | Forward - 9.6 Aft - 6.9 | Forward - 6.8 Aft - 7.5 | First open |
| % of oxygen (2) | Forward - 13.1 Aft - 20.1 | Forward - 6.9 Aft - 6.3 | Forward - 8.2 Aft - 8.1 | Forward - 12.7 Aft - 13.6 | Forward - 8.3 Aft - 15.2 | After 10mins |

## Enclosed space entry and rescue drills

1.7.2 According to the records obtained by the investigation team, a physical enclosed space entry drill was conducted at the duct keel on 10 October 2021, where the pre-entry checks and risk assessment were carried out, the SCBA, stretcher and other equipment (See **figure 7**) were deployed, the rescuing operation was simulated, and the outcome of the drill was documented as satisfactory. All the crew listed in the table (paragraph 1.3.2) participated in that drill.

Figure 7 – Deployment of the SCBA, stretcher, rope and harness for the rescue drill (simulated at ship's duct keel) (*Source:* photographs 1&2 from the Company, 3&4 from the TSIB)

1.7.3   The ship's records also indicated that the last two enclosed space entry and rescue drills (in the form of tabletop), prior to the occurrence, were conducted at a void space tank and one of water ballast tanks on 23 November[59] 2021 and 18 February 2022, respectively. The two tabletop drills did not include demonstration of wearing of the SCBA for entering the enclosed spaces or the use of a Neil Robertson[60] stretcher for rescuing a casualty out from the enclosed spaces.

## Additional information regarding the rescue operation

1.7.4   When asked by the investigation team on the rationale of using an EEBD, the 3O recalled that the EEBD was one of the listed equipment to be used for enclosed space rescue operation, and it was used for all the enclosed space entry and rescue drills on board, which was confirmed by the Master. Both the ASD2 and the ASD3 also had the same understanding that using the EEBD for rescue operation in enclosed space was permitted on board Nozomi.

1.7.5   The 3O informed the investigation team of his understanding that the EEBD has a duration of 10mins usage and cited in desperation to

---

[59] It was scheduled to be in December, the Master brought it forward few days due to the anticipated voyage.
[60] This type of stretcher is used for moving a casualty safely from a difficult place where the ordinary stretcher with stiff poles would be useless. It can be bent slightly in turning sharp corners in narrow passages, as when being hoisted up the ladder ways from engine rooms or through the hatches of cargo tanks.

save his fellow shipmate, resorted to the use of the EEBD.

1.7.6 In an emergency involving enclosed space, according to the muster list, the Emergency Squad, comprising the CO, Bosun, two ASDs and two ordinary seamen, is to assess the situation first and respond accordingly at the incident site. The Emergency Squad is to be assisted by the Support Squad led by the 2O. The Master is the overall in-charge under the Command Squad.

1.7.7 The CCK is assigned to the First Aid Squad, together with the Steward, led by the 3O. The roles of the First Aid Squad are to provide first aid to casualties in an emergency, mobilise a stretcher, convey the casualty to a safer place for first aid treatment and other duties directed by the Master.

1.7.8 The Company confirmed that as per the SMS, the EEBD was not listed as a rescue device for enclosed spaces, and that the SCBA would be used instead. The training and physical drill for enclosed space conducted on 10 October 2021 did not record EEBD as part of the rescue equipment. The reasons for the misperception of the crew of Nozomi, for the use of EEBD in drills, or how long had it been so, could not be established.

## Understanding of the greasing work

1.7.9 The maintenance work (greasing of the booby hatch dog handles) was an unplanned activity.

Neither the Master nor the 3O, as the officer of the watch, was aware of the booby hatch maintenance work (possibility of opening the booby hatch) on deck while both were on the bridge waiting for the pilot to board.

1.7.10　According to the CO, the task of greasing the dog handles did not require entering the cargo hold. As such, the CO did not remind the deck crew not to enter the cargo hold or to seek his permission if there was a need to enter the cargo hold. The Bosun had similar thoughts as the CO's, i.e. greasing of the booby hatch dog handles did not require entering the cargo hold. The ASD2 and ASD3 did not object the opening of the booby hatch by the Bosun for greasing the dog handles.

## Cause of death

1.7.11　The body of ASD1 did not undergo an autopsy examination, a death certificate was issued on 1 April 2022 by the Bhayangkara Mohamad Hasan Hospital, Palembang, Indonesia. The exact cause of death of the ASD1 could not be confirmed.

## 1.8　Environmental condition

1.8.1　At the time of occurrence, Nozomi's logbooks indicated that there was southerly gentle breeze of about 7-10 knots (Beaufort wind force 3), the sea condition was slight about half to one metre. The sky was cloudy but good visibility. The ambient air temperature was at about 30 degrees Celsius.

# 2 ANALYSIS

## 2.1 The likely cause of death

2.1.1 The ASD1 was found motionless on the coal cargo and there were no bodily injuries as observed by the crew. The exact cause of death of the ASD1 could not be determined as the body did not undergo an autopsy examination.

2.1.2 Based on available evidence, the ASD1 was medically fit without limitations or restrictions for servicing at sea and had 16 hours of rest in the past 24-hours. He had not performed any strenuous activity since the morning and was last known to be working in freeing up the internal dog handle of the booby hatch's securing mechanism.

2.1.3 The investigation team considered the possibility of the ASD1 accidentally falling into the cargo hold. Correlating the build (height) of the ASD1, the position where the ASD1 before being discovered and the coaming height (0.8m) of the booby hatch, it is probably unlikely that the ASD1 accidentally fell into the cargo hold. An accidental fall would have caught the attention of the other crew members as well as resulted in some injuries sustained by the ASD1, which was not the case.

2.1.4    Nozomi was carrying coal, of which 11,700MT was loaded in No.5 cargo hold. The cargo hold had been sealed (closed) for five days after loading. As seen in paragraphs 1.6.2 and 1.6.3, coal may be subject to oxidation (leading to depletion of oxygen), resulting in an increase in concentrations of carbon dioxide or carbon monoxide, which can be lethal. The oxygen readings taken after the occurrence (three days later) were at 6.8% and 8.3%, lower than what is needed for supporting human life (minimum acceptable level at 19.5%[61]). Having been sealed for more than three days (cargo operation ended on 26 March 2022) prior to the opening on 1 April 2022 for booby hatch's securing mechanism maintenance, it is likely that the oxygen content inside No.5 cargo hold would have been lower than those taken post occurrence.

2.1.5    The investigation team considered the probability that the internal dog handle had dropped into the cargo hold when the ASD1 was attempting to free it. The ASD1 then entered the cargo hold to retrieve it without informing the other crew. When the ASD1 had retrieved the internal dog handle and was climbing up the ladder, due to the depleted oxygen condition in the cargo hold, he lost consciousness and

---

[61] IMO Resolution A.1050(27), steady readings of 21% oxygen by volume by oxygen content meter for enclosed space entry purposes.

fell, leaving the dog handle wedged between the ladder and the stringer.

2.1.6 This hypothesis is further corroborated by the height of the ASD1 and the location where the dog handle was found. From the location where the dog handle was found to the coal level, it is about 2.1m (see **figure 7**). When a person climbs up a vertical ladder, both hands are extended to hold the sides of the ladder. With the height of 1.70m and the arms' length of about 0.5m, it is likely that the ASD1 was either about to climb up the ladder or making the first couple of steps on the ladder, before losing consciousness. The fall was from a low height which explains the reason for no visible injuries sustained by the ASD1. The investigation team opined that the ASD1 might have deemed the cargo hold to be safe for entry and that retrieving the dog handle was a simple task which could be done quickly.

2.1.7 The occurrence serves as a reminder that a cargo hold can have a dangerous atmosphere and should not be assumed to be safe for entry. An assessment should be performed, and appropriate measures implemented before any entry is made.

## 2.2 Unplanned maintenance on booby hatch and risk assessment

2.2.1 The greasing of booby hatch dog handles was an impromptu task while Nozomi was waiting for departure. According to the CO and the Bosun, the task was expected to be straightforward and did not require entering the cargo hold. As such, there was no risk assessment done for entering enclosed space as per the SMS procedures.

2.2.2   The last maintenance (greasing) of the booby hatch dog handles was unknown. While the nature of the task understandably did not require entering the cargo hold, the task required opening of the booby hatch to grease the dog handles, which increased the risk of crew working in the vicinity. In addition, the risks associated with the greasing of the dog handles, such as the dropping of the dog handle into the cargo hold, was not anticipated by the crew. It would have been prudent for the crew to conduct the risk assessment for the task, more so when the cargo carried in the cargo hold was hazardous, and to anticipate the worst-case scenario of the need to enter the cargo hold.

2.2.3   Had a risk assessment for enclosed space been done, the ASD1's reactions may have been different.

## 2.3   Awareness of cargo hazards

2.3.1   The Master had reportedly reminded all the crew on board not to open any hatch including booby hatch of a cargo hold carrying coal after he joined ship. In the Master's opinion, all the crew had a clear understanding of his instructions.

2.3.2    The CO had agreed for the deck crew to grease the dog handles and the booby hatch cover had been opened to facilitate the greasing. There was no evidence that reminders had been given to the crew about the hazards of the coal inside the cargo hold when the booby hatch cover was opened.

2.3.3    While the crew may be expected to remember or recognise the hazards associated with the cargo carried on board, the occurrence had proven that such important aspect could be overlooked. For the crew's safety, it is important to remind them of the hazards of the cargo carried.

## 2.4    Rescue operation

2.4.1    The SMS procedures document that in an emergency, personnel performing the rescue operation in enclosed space, i.e. the Emergency Squad, should be trained and equipped with SCBA. Based on the muster list, the personnel for the Emergency Squad were supposed to be the CO, Bosun and two ASDs. Instead of these persons performing the rescue operation, the 3O entered the cargo hold with an EEBD out of desperation, and subsequently the CCK entered the cargo hold with two air hoses, to rescue the ASD1.

2.4.2 It could not be established why the trained Emergency Squad did not undertake the rescue operation as per the muster list.

2.4.3 While the attempts by the 3O and the CCK to rescue a workmate were understandable, they could put themselves in danger and fallen victims themselves when performing the rescue operation using inappropriate equipment.

2.4.4 The Master was aware of the risk associated with the carriage of the coal cargo. Despite being the overall in-charge under the Command Squad (expected to provide direction for the rescue operation), the Master did not intervene when the CCK entered the enclosed space with air hoses.

2.4.5 It is fortunate that no further injuries resulted from the rescue attempt which was conducted by personnel who were not assigned to conduct the rescue. While it is understandable that crew would want to rescue their fellow workmate unless exceptional circumstances required, it is important that crew follow the assigned roles. In addition, appropriate equipment should be used for conducting the rescue.

## 2.5 Enclosed space signage

2.5.1 The investigation team recognises that a cargo hold may not be considered as an enclosed space all the time, especially when its hatch covers are open for loading or discharging of cargo, or its cargo spaces have been adequately ventilated throughout the voyage. However, if a cargo hold carries dangerous goods (such as coal or other cargo that emit harmful gases) and has been sealed (without ventilation), it would pose a risk to the safety of personnel entering or working in the vicinity.

2.5.2 The booby hatch of the No.5 cargo hold was marked "KEEP CLOSE AT SEA" on the outside, to remind the crew to ensure the watertight integrity of the cargo space. The inside booby hatch was marked "CHECK SAFETY BEFORE ENTRY" which was meant to serve as a reminder to the crew who intend to enter the cargo hold. While such a reminder can prompt an individual to carry out some checks, it does not highlight the risks associated with enclosed spaces entry.

2.5.3 It is thus desirable that proper signage be placed to warn the crew that cargo hold should be treated as enclosed space when it has been sealed for some time.

2.5.4 The investigation team noted that there was no standard signage for enclosed spaces for use on ships, and while a standard is being developed by the IMO, there is merit for the Company to consider posting a graphic or infographic signage in conspicuous places on the ship. The signage should be in a manner that is understandable by all crew to provide a constant reminder of the risks of entering the cargo hold.

## 2.6 Incidental observations

EEBD being used as a rescue equipment

2.6.1 As highlighted under the IMO's Fire Safety Systems Code, the EEBD is meant for escaping from a compartment that has a hazardous atmosphere and should not be used for entering oxygen deficient voids or tanks on board ships. In the attempt to rescue the ASD1, the 3O used the EEBD to enter the cargo hold and subsequently had to leave the cargo hold due to difficulty in breathing, in addition to the hot environment.

2.6.3 The perception that EEBD is appropriate for rescue operation seemed to be a common understanding on board Nozomi. Besides the 3O, the Master, the ASD2 and the ASD3 also had the same understanding that using the EEBD for rescue operation in an enclosed space was permitted on board Nozomi., including the Master. Reasons for this perception could not be established. The crew also mentioned that the EEBD was one of the listed equipment used for enclosed space entry and rescue drills on board. It is pertinent for the Company to correct this misperception and to ensure that the correct type of rescue device is being used for enclosed space entry and rescue drills.

# 3 CONCLUSIONS

*From the information gathered, the following findings are made. These findings should not be read as apportioning blame or liability to any particular organisation or individual.*

3.1.1 The ASD1 had likely entered the No.5 cargo hold without the knowledge of the other crew members to retrieve a dog handle. The cargo hold had low concentrations of oxygen due to the cargo of coal. The ASD1 collapsed while climbing out of the cargo hold.

3.1.2 The maintenance of the booby hatch was an unplanned task and did not require entering of cargo hold. The dropping of parts into the cargo hold was not anticipated for this maintenance. The risks associated with working in the vicinity of a hazardous environment (cargo hold loaded with coal) had not been identified, a risk assessment was not carried out.

3.1.3 The hazards associated with the coal cargo had been overlooked when the maintenance of booby hatch was being carried out.

3.1.4 There was a misconception on board the ship that EEBD could be used for rescue operation and the crew used inappropriate equipment to rescue the ASD1. The crew also did not follow the assigned duties as per the muster list.

3.1.5  There were no signages to warn the crew to treat cargo hold as enclosed space when it has been sealed for some time.

# 4  SAFETY ACTIONS

*During the course of the investigation and through the discussions with the investigation team, the following safety actions were initiated by the relevant stakeholders.*

## 4.1  Actions taken by the Company

4.1.1  Immediately after the occurrence, the Company sent out an email broadcast to its fleet of bulk carriers, informing them of the loss of life accident, reminding the importance of safety of personnel on board ships and clear understanding with entry into enclosed space procedures established in its SMS. The Company also instructed Masters to discuss this occurrence with all the crew on board for lessons learnt.

4.1.2  The Company shared also an article with its fleet of bulk carriers the Loss Prevention Briefing[62] on the topic of enclosed spaces,

---

[62] Issued by the North of England P&I Association, edition of People/April 2012.

re-emphasising the IMO Resolution A.1050 (27) on the recommendations for entering enclosed spaces aboard ships.

4.1.3 After its internal investigation, the Company disseminated a safety bulletin to the fleet sharing additional details of the occurrence, learning points and measures for preventing similar occurrence:

- Raising safety awareness to all ship's crew on board, senior officers must take the lead to guide ship's crew accordingly on the safety to avoid incident/accident from happening;
- Duty officers on the bridge should be made aware of the deck work for the day;
- Improving relationships among all the crew on board, especially between senior officers and crew;
- Placing posters of job hazards and dangers associated when working at or near an enclosed space, at the common areas and crew living quarters for awareness; and
- Planning emergency drills with proper scenarios and practising it by ground deployment.

# 5   SAFETY RECOMMENDATIONS

*A safety recommendation is for the purpose of preventive action and shall in no case create a presumption of blame or liability.*

## 5.1 For the Company:

5.1.1 To ensure signages are placed in conspicuous places on board to warn ship's crew to treat cargo hold as enclosed space when it has been sealed for some time. **[TSIB-RM-2022-06]**

5.1.2 To ensure ship's crew perform rescue operation according to the muster list. [TSIB-RM-2022-07]

5.1.3 To ensure appropriate equipment are used for rescue operation in enclosed space and rescue drills on board its fleet of ships. **[TSIB-RM-2022-08]**

# Bibliography

Abate, V. (2015). *Le Verità Sommerse: Vittoriana Abate intervista il Comandante Francesco Schettino (Italian Edition)*. Graus Editore.

Almasy, S., & Khorram, Y. (2015, October 9). *El Faro had leaks, holes, other structural issues, former crew members say*. Retrieved from CNN: https://edition.cnn.com/2015/10/08/us/el-faro-missing-ship/

Anand, N. (2016). Light Bulbs, Red Lines And Rotten Onions. *Seaways: The International Journal of The Nautical Institute*, 7-9.

Anderson, P. (2003). *Cracking the Code: The Relevance of the ISM Code and its Impact on Shipping*. London: The Nautical Institute.

Armstrong, K. (2006). *A short history of myth*. Edinburgh: Canongate.

Ashhurst, C., Long, R., & Smith, G. (2016). *Risky Conversations: The Law, Social Psychology and Risk*. Scomata Press.

Barthes, R. (1957). *Mythologies*. Vintage Classics.

BBC News. (2015, January 4). *Hoegh Osaka cargo ship 'grounded deliberately' in Solent*. Retrieved from BBC News: https://www.bbc.co.uk/news/uk-england-hampshire-30673439

BBC News. (2017, May 12). *Costa Concordia captain's sentence upheld by Italy court*. Retrieved from BBC News: https://www.bbc.co.uk/news/world-europe-39903968

Becker, E. (2020). *The Denial of Death*. Souvenir Press.

Bergson, H. (1900). *Laughter: An Essay on the Meaning of the Comic*. London: MacMillan.

Boas, F. (1998). *Franz Boas Among the Inuit of Baffin Island 1883-1884*. University of Toronto Press.

Bohm, D. (1996). *On dialogue*. London: Routledge.

Bourdieu, P. (1972). *Outline of a Theory of Practice*. Cambridge: Cambridge University Press.

Bourdieu, P. (2023). *Habitus and Field: General Sociology, Volume 2*. Polity Press.

Brown, B. (2018). *The Gifts Of Imperfection: Let Go of Who You Think You're Supposed to Be and Embrace Who You Are*. Chicago: Hazelden FIRM.

Buber, M. (1937). *I and Thou (Scribner Classics)*. Edinburgh: T. & T. Clark.

Buber, M. (2002). *Between Man and Man*. Routledge.

Burgis, L. (2022). *Wanting: The Power of Mimetic Desire, and How to Want What You Need*. Swift Press .

Burrough, B., & Mckenna, J. (2012, April 12). *Another Night to Remember*. Retrieved from Vanity Fair: https://www.vanityfair.com/culture/2012/05/costa-concordia-sinking-scandal-italy

Campbell, J. (1995). *Myths to Live By: The Collected Works of Joseph Campbell.* Souvenir Press Ltd.

Catino, M. (2023). *Scapegoating: How Organizations Assign Blame.* New York: Cambridge University Press.

Clarke, L. (2001). *Mission Improbable: Using Fantasy Documents to Tame Disaster.* Chicago: University of Chicago.

Claxton, G. (1998). *Hare Brain, Tortoise Mind: Why Intelligence Increases When You Think Less.* Fourth Estate.

Claxton, G. (2016). *Intelligence in the Flesh: Why Your Mind Needs Your Body Much More Than it Thinks.* Yale University Press.

Claxton, G. (2018). *The Learning Power Approach: Teaching learners to teach themselves.* Crown House Publishing .

Cook, R. (2016, November 27). *Chesley Sullenberger: an old-fashioned kind of hero.* Retrieved from The Guardian: https://www.theguardian.com/film/2016/nov/27/chesley-sullenberger-sully-film-clint-eastwood-tom-hanks-miracle-hudson-river

Cook, R., & Woods, D. (1998). ATale of Two Stories: Contrasting Views ofPatient Safety. National Health Care Safety Council of the National Patient Safety Foundationat the AMA.

Cooling, R. (2011, November). Retrieved June 2023, from Apple Driving School: https://www.apple-driving.co.uk/reviews-nottingham.html

Court of Grosseto. (2012). *Captain's Interrogation Report*. 17/12/2012.

Csikszentmihalyi, M. (2002). *Flow: The Psychology of Happiness*. Rider.

Dahl, R. A. (1957). The concept of power. *Behavioral Science*, 2(3), 201-215.

Damasio, A. (2000). *The Feeling Of What Happens: Body, Emotion and the Making of Consciousness*. Vintage.

Damasio, A. (2003). *Looking for Spinoza: Joy, Sorrow, and the Feeling Brain*. Houghton Mifflin Harcourt.

Damasio, A. (2021). *The Strange Order Of Things: Life, Feeling and the Making of Cultures*. Robinson.

Di Lieto, A. (2015). *Bridge Resource Management: From the Costa Concordia to Navigation in the Digital Age*. Hydeas Pty Ltd.

Dinmore, G. (2012, March 2). *On the rocks*. Retrieved from Financial Times: https://www.ft.com/content/fd57f5ba-6462-11e1-b50e-00144feabdc0

Douglas, M. (1992). *Risk and Blame: Essays in Cultural Theory*. London: Routledge.

Egan, G. (2017). *The Skilled Helper*. Cengage Learning EMEA.

Elias, N. (1939). *The Civilizing Process*. Wiley-Blackwell.

Ellis, N., Bloor, M., & Sampson, H. (2010). Patterns of Seafarers Injuries. *Maritime Policy and Management*, 121-128.

Ellul, J. (1964). *The Technological Society*. Vintage Books.

# Bibliography

Evans-Pritchard, E. (1976). *Witchcraft, Oracles and Magic among the Azande.* Oxford: Oxford University Press.

Fairhurst, G. (2010). *The Power of Framing: Creating the Language of Leadership.* Jossey-Bass.

Frankl, V. (1962). *Man's Search For Meaning: an Introduction to Logotherapy.* Boston: Beacon Press.

Frazer, J. G. (2009). *The Golden Bough A Study in Magic and Religion.* OUP Oxford.

Freire, P. (1973). *Education for Critical Consciousness.* New York : Seabury Press.

Freud, S. (1905). *Jokes and Their Relation to the Unconscious .* New York: Penguin.

Gekara, V., & Sampson, H. (2021). *The World of the Seafarer: Qualitative Accounts of Working in the Global Shipping Industry.* Cham: Springer.

Girard, R. (1976). *Deceit, Desire, and the Novel: Self and Other in Literary Structure .* Johns Hopkins University Press .

Girard, R. (2013). *Violence and the Sacred.* Bloomsbury Academic;.

Gladwell, M. (2009). *Outliers: The Story of Success .* Penguin.

Higgins, E. T. (2011). *Beyond Pleasure and Pain: How Motivation Works.* Oxford: Oxford University Press.

Hilduberg, Ø. J. (2015). *THE DECISION TO EVACUATE A PASSENGER SHIP – AN ASSESSMENT OF THE NORMATIVE VIEW OF THE SHIPMASTER.* Lund: LUND UNIVERSITY SWEDEN.

Hooper, J. (2014, August 6). *Costa Concordia captain's seminar sparks row at Italy's biggest university*. Retrieved from The Guardian: https://www. theguardian.com/world/2014/aug/06/costa-concordia-captain-seminar-row-italy-biggest-university

Huffpost. (2017, May 9). *Pakistan International Airlines Pilot Allows Woman Into Cockpit, Puts Passengers' Lives At Risk*. Retrieved from Huffpost: https://www.huffpost.com/archive/in/entry/pakistan-international-airlines-pilot-allows-woman-into-cockpit_in_5c11f2fae4b0295df1fa42ee

Johnson. (2017). *Embodied Mind, Meaning, and Reason: How Our Bodies Give Rise to Understanding*. Chicago: University of Chicago Press.

Johnson, R. (1989). *Inner Work: Using Dreams & Active Imagination for Personal Growth: Using Dreams and Active Imagination for Personal Growth*. New York: Harper Collins.

Johnson, R. (1991). *Owning Your Own Shadow: Understanding the Dark Side of the Psyche*. New York: Harper Collins.

Jung, C. G. (1959). *The Archetypes and the Collective Unconscious*. Routledge.

Jung, C. G. (1968). *Man and His Symbols*. London: Random House.

Kay, J., & King, M. (2020). *Radical uncertainty: decision-making beyond the numbers*. New York NY: W. W. Norton & Company.

Kington, T. (2013, October 8). *Costa Concordia captain lapsed into indecision at crisis point, court hears*. Retrieved from The Guardian: https://

www.theguardian.com/world/2013/oct/08/costa-concordia-trial-captain-francesco-schettino

Klein, G. (1998). *Sources of power : how people make decisions.* Cambridge: MIT.

Kline, N. (1999). *Time to Think: Listening to Ignite the Human Mind.* New York: Hachette Book Group.

Kruglanski, A. W., & Gigerenzer, G. (2011). Intuitive and Deliberative Judgments are Based on Common Principles. *Psychological Review, 118*(1), 97-109.

Lacy, S. M. (2017). *Anthropology and the Study of Humanity: Course Guidebook (The Great Courses).* Chantilly: The Teaching Company.

Lakoff, G. (1998). *Philosophy in the Flesh: The Embodied Mind and Its Challenge to Western Thought.* Basic Books.

Lakoff, G. (2014). *Don't Think of an Elephant!: Know Your Values and Frame the Debate.* Chelsea Green Publishing.

Lakoff, G., & Johnson, M. (1980). *Metaphors We Live By.* Chicago: Chicago Press.

Le Coze, J.-C. (2020). *Post Normal Accident: Revisiting Perrow's Classic.* Boca Raton: CRC Press.

Levine, P. A. (1997). *Waking the Tiger: Healing Trauma: The Innate Capacity to Transform Overwhelming Experiences.* North Atlantic Books.

Levy, R. (1975). *Tahitians Mind and Experience in the Society Islands.* University of Chicago Press.

Libet, B., Gleason, C., & Wright, E. (1983). Time of Conscious Intention to Act in Relation to Onset of Cerebral Activity (Readiness-Potential): The Unconscious Initiation of a Freely Voluntary Act. *Brain*, 623-42.

Livingstone, C. (2023, March 15). *Bravo Captain Arma*. Retrieved from LinkedIn Post: https://www.linkedin.com/posts/alessio-torelli-7b6043185_leadership-japan-covid19-activity-7034933165320204288-8cSg/

Lloyd, M. (2019). *THE SINKING OF A SHIP : COSTA CONCORDIA REVISITED* . Independent.

Long, R. (2012). *For the Love of Zero*. Canberra: Scomata Press.

Long, R. (2012). *Risk Makes Sense*. Canberra: Scomota Press.

Long, R. (2018). *Fallibility and Risk: Living With Uncertainty*. Scotoma Press.

Los Angeles Times. (2012, January 16). *6th victim found in Italian cruise ship wreck*. Retrieved from Los Angeles Times: https://www.latimes.com/archives/blogs/world-now/story/2012-01-16/6th-victim-found-in-italian-cruise-ship-wreck

MAIB. (2016). *Report on the investigation into the listing, flooding and grounding of Hoegh Osaka Bramble Bank, The Solent, UK*. Southampton: Maritime Accident Investigation Board UK.

MAIB UK. (2001). *REVIEW OF LIFEBOAT AND LAUNCHING SYSTEMS' ACCIDENTS*. SAFETY STUDY.

Maiese, M. (2010). *Embodiment, emotion, and cognition*. New York, NY: Palgrave-Macmillan.

Malinowski, B. (2013). *Argonauts of the Western Pacific An Account of Native Enterprise and Adventure in the Archipelagoes of Melanesian New Guinea.* Waveland Press.

Maté, G. (2022). *The Myth of Normal: Trauma, Illness & Healing in a Toxic Culture.* New York: Avery.

Mercier, H., & Sperber, D. (2017). *The Enigma of Reason: A New Theory of Human Understanding .* London : Allen Lane.

Midgley, M. (2003). *The Myths We Live By.* Oxfor: Routledge.

MIT. (2013). *Cruise Ship COSTA CONCORDIA Marine casualty on January 13, 2012 Report on the safety technical investigation.* MINISTRY OF INFRASTRUCTURES AND TRANSPORTS.

Moskowitz, G. B., & Grant, H. (2009). *The psychology of goals.* New York : Guilford Press.

Muller, J. (2018). *The Tyranny of Metrics.* Princeton University Press.

Newberg, A., & Waldman, M. (2006). *Why We Believe What We Believe: Our Biological Need for Meaning, Spirituality, and Truth.* London: Free Press.

NTSB. (2009). *Loss of Thrust in Both Engines After Encountering a Flock of Birds and Subsequent Ditching on the Hudson River US Airways Flight 1549 Airbus A320-214, N106US.* Accident Report, National Transportation Safety Board, Washington.

NTSB. (2015). *Sinking of US Cargo Vessel SS El Faro Atlantic Ocean, Northeast of Acklins and Crooked Island, Bahamas.* National Transportation Safety Board, Washington.

Olshan, J. (2009, January 17). *Quiet Air Hero Is Captain America*. Retrieved from New York Post: https://nypost.com/2009/01/17/quiet-air-hero-is-captain-america/

Orsi, R. (2013, April 23). *The Quiet Collapse of the Italian Economy*. Retrieved from https://blogs.lse.ac.uk/eurocrisispress/2013/04/23/the-quiet-collapse-of-the-italian-economy/

Panama Maritime Authority. (2023, July). *Safety Investigation of the Grounding of M.V. Wakashio*. Retrieved from Panama Maritime Authority.

Parker, P. (1971). *To Know as We Are Known: Education as a Spiritual Journey*. New York: Harper Collins.

Perrow, C. (1984). *Normal Accidents: Living with High-Risk Technologies*. New Jersey: Princeton.

Polanyi, M. (1966). *The Tacit Dimension*. London: Routledge.

Postman, N. (2010). *Amusing Ourselves to Death*. New York: Penguin.

Power, M. (1996). *The Audit Explosion*. London: Demos.

Premack, R. (2019, March 12). *'You basically put a student pilot in there': The copilot of crashed Ethiopian Airlines Flight 302 had just 200 hours of flight experience*. Retrieved from Business Insider: https://www.businessinsider.com/ethiopian-airlines-flight-302-co-pilot-200-flight-hours-2019-3?r=US&IR=T

Ricoeur, P. (1986). *Fallible Man: Philosophy of the Will*. Fordham University Press.

Ricoeur, P. (2016). *Hermeneutics and the Human Sciences: Essays on Language, Action and Interpretation.* Cambridge: Cambridge University Press.

Robinson, K. (2006, February 01). *Do schools kill creativity?* Retrieved February 2023, from TED Talk: https://www.ted.com/talks/sir_ken_robinson_do_schools_kill_creativity?language=en

Seafarers International Research Centre . (2013). *Seafarers International Research Centre Symposium Proceedings.* Cardiff University, Cardiff.

Shore, B. (2023). *The Hidden Power of Rituals.* Cambridge: MIT Press.

Singh, K. (2015). *Hindu Rites and Rituals: Origins And Meanings.* India: Random House.

Slovic, P. (2010). *The Feeling of Risk New Perspectives on Risk Perception.* London: Routledge.

Smith, G. (2018). *Paper Safe: The triumph of bureaucracy in safety management.* Perth: Independently published.

Størkersen, K., Thorvaldsenb, T., Kongsvikc, T., & Dekker, S. (2020). How deregulation can become overregulation: An empirical study into the growth of internal bureaucracy when governments take a step back. *Safety Science*, 1-9.

Stanek, V. J. (2012, 01 17). *Cutting Close to Shore: A Nice Tradition, Normalissima.* Retrieved from Spiegel International: https://www.spiegel.de/international/europe/cutting-close-to-shore-a-nice-tradition-normalissima-a-809580.html

Stanley, A. (2022, March). *GLOBAL INEQUALITIES.* Retrieved from International Monetary Fund:

https://www.imf.org/en/Publications/fandd/is-sues/2022/03/Global-inequalities-Stanley

Tetlock, P. (2017). *Expert Political Judgment: How Good Is It? How Can We Know?* . Princeton: Princeton University Press.

Thorne, M., Long, & Robert. (2023). *SPoR and Semiotics: Methods to Tackle Risk*. Kamba: Scotoma Press.

TSIB. (2022). *Fatality of Crew Onboard Nozomi in Bangka Straits Indonesia*. Accident Report, Transport Safety Investigation Bureau, Singapore.

Tylor, E. B. (1871). *Primitive Culture: Researches into the Development of Mythology, Philosophy, Religion, Art, and Custom*. Cambridge: Cambridge University Press.

van der Kolk, M. B. (2014). *The Body Keeps the Score: Brain, Mind, and Body in the Healing of Trauma* . New York: Penguin.

Vaughan, D. (1997). *The Challenger Launch Decision Risky Technology, Culture, and Deviance at NASA*. Chicago: University of Chicago Press.

Veblen, T. (2006). *Conspicuous Consumption*. Penguin Group.

Walker, J. (2013, April 14). *Did Costa Cover-Up A Near Concordia-Like Disaster?* Retrieved from CRUISE LAW NEWS: Everything Cruise Lines Don't Want You to Know: https://www.cruiselawnews.com/2013/04/articles/collisions/did-cos-ta-coverup-a-near-concordialike-disaster/

Weathers, H. (2012, January 31). *Captain Coward had his eye on English dancer: After claims he was dis-*

*tracted by a woman on the bridge, passengers and crew reveal Casanova antics of crash skipper.* Retrieved from Mail Online: https://www.dailymail.co.uk/news/article-2089680/Costa-Concordia-Captain-Coward-Francesco-Schettino-eye-dancer-Domnica-Cemortan.html

Weick, K. (1995). *Sensemaking in Organizations.* SAGE Publications.

Weick, K., & Sutcliffe, K. (2001). *Managing the Unexpected: Assuring High Performance in an Age of Complexity.* Jossey Bass.

Winfield, N., & Sportelli, F. (2013, October 8). *Crew testifies about Concordia chaos, maneuver.* Retrieved from The Seattle Times: https://www.seattletimes.com/life/travel/crew-testifies-about-concordia-chaos-maneuver/

World Obesity Atlas. (2023, March 2). *Economic impact of overweight and obesity to surpass $4 trillion by 2035.* Retrieved from World Obesity Federation: https://www.worldobesity.org/news/economic-impact-of-overweight-and-obesity-to-surpass-4-trillion-by-2035

# About the Author

Nippin Anand specialises in the relevance of culture, belief, myth, and metaphors (language) in the areas of risk, safety and organisational learning.

Nippin is adept at telling stories that make people think and question their worldview. After being brought up in India and educated in the West, Nippin spends a lot of time travelling between the Eastern and the Western myths questioning the core ideas about why we believe what we believe and how people learn, unlearn, relearn and make decisions.

With his unique listening and observation skills and the ability to question the obvious, Nippin likes to be seen as a Critical Friend – someone who can hold a mirror to you and challenge your bedrock assumptions. All this can be uncomfortable but that is where learning and change begins.

Nippin is the Founder of Novellus. He holds a PhD in social sciences and anthropology, and a master's degree in economics and social psychology and a seagoing master mariner's (captain) license. He studies mythology, religion, anthropology, spirituality, neurosciences, depth psychology, linguistics, and semiotics (study of signs and symbols) to broaden his understanding of human 'being'.

Nippin can be contacted at:
LinkedIn: https://www.linkedin.com/in/nippin-anand/
Email: support[at]novellus[dot]solutions

www.ingramcontent.com/pod-product-compliance
Lightning Source LLC
Chambersburg PA
CBHW051708020426
42333CB00014B/887